BULLETPROOF

THE TRUTH ABOUT THE ASSASSINATION ATTEMPTS ON DONALD TRUMP

JACK POSOBIEC
JOSHUA LISEC

FOREWORD BY DONALD TRUMP, JR.

Skyhorse Publishing

Skyhorse Publishing books may be purchased in bulk at special discounts for
sales promotion, corporate gifts, fund-raising, or educational purposes. Special
editions can also be created to specifications. For details, contact the Special
Sales Department, Skyhorse Publishing, 307 West 36th Street, 11th Floor,
New York, NY 10018 or info@skyhorsepublishing.com.

Skyhorse® and Skyhorse Publishing® are registered trademarks of Skyhorse
Publishing, Inc.®, a Delaware corporation.

Skyhorse Publishing® is a registered trademark of Skyhorse Publishing, Inc.®,
a Delaware corporation.

Visit our website at www.skyhorsepublishing.com.

Please follow our publisher Tony Lyons on Instagram @tonylyonsisuncertain.

10 9 8 7 6 5 4 3 2 1

Library of Congress Cataloging-in-Publication Data is available on file.

Cover design by David Ter-Avanesyan

Hardcover ISBN: 978-1-5107-8336-2
eBook ISBN: 978-1-5107-8337-9

Printed in the United States of America

For Corey Comperatore

"Put on the whole armour of God, that ye may be able to
stand against the wiles of the devil."
—Ephesians 6:11

CONTENTS

FOREWORD BY
DONALD TRUMP, JR.

When you think about the life of Donald J. Trump, you might conjure up images of towering skyscrapers, reality TV, or the Oval Office. But there's a moment, a single heartbeat in time, that encapsulates the sheer audacity, the unyielding spirit, and the raw, unfiltered essence of who my father is. That moment was on a warm July afternoon in Butler, Pennsylvania, when the first attempt was made on my father's life.

As I write this, the memory of that day still makes my hair stand on end. Not out of fear, but because of the profound realization of what could have been. Here's a man who's been at the center of the storm, a lightning rod for attention of all kinds, yet when faced with death, his first instinct was to stand tall, fist in the air, not for himself, but for the nation he loves. That image, of my father, bloodied but unbowed, has become more than just a photograph; it's a symbol of resilience, of America's indomitable spirit.

Then, just two months later, my father survived another attempt on his life while golfing on a Sunday afternoon.

This book isn't just about the assassination attempts, it's about a testament to survival, to the will to fight back against those who would silence the voice of freedom. It's about the moments leading up to the shots, the chaos that ensued, and the aftermath that has left an indelible mark on our family, our movement, and our country.

I remember getting the call that day in July. The world slowed down, and for a moment, everything was silent. Then, the rush of emotions, the fear, the anger, but above all, the pride. Pride in a father who, even in the face of death, stood for something greater than himself.

Bulletproof isn't just my father's story, it's America's story. A story of a man who, despite all odds, continues to fight for what he believes in, for the America he envisions. The attempts on his life were not just attacks on what he stands for: freedom, strength, and the unwavering belief in the American Dream.

As you turn these pages, you'll walk through the events with a perspective that only those closest to the situation could provide. You'll understand the security failures, the human errors, but also the heroism, the resilience, and perhaps even the divine intervention that played into what happened this summer.

This book will delve into the investigation, inconvenient facts, the political fallout, and the personal impact on my father, those who attended the Butler rally, and on the nation. But more than that, it's a call to action. A reminder that the fight for America's soul is far from over.

I invite you to join us on this journey, not just as readers but as patriots, understanding that these attempts on my father's life were attempts to silence a voice that speaks for millions. This book is for those who believe in standing up, even when the odds are stacked against you, for those who believe in America, in its people, and in its future. Jack Posobiec and Joshua Lisec are doing just that by having written this book.

So in the spirit of my father, let's raise our fists to the sky, not in anger, but in solidarity, in defiance, and in the unbreakable will to see America great again.

Donald Trump, Jr.
September 16, 2024

THE SCENE

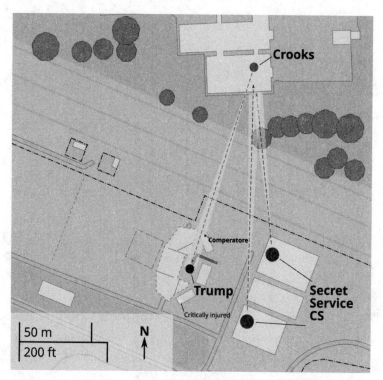

Approximate locations of shooter Thomas Matthew Crooks, Donald Trump, and the Secret Service Counter-Sniper Team (source: Cyrogigbyte / CC BY-SA-2.0).

Aerial photograph taken 10 minutes prior to an attempted assassination of Donald Trump (source: Designism / Creative Commons CC0 1.0).

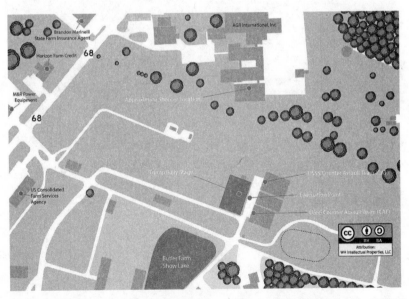

Trump Assassination Attempt Map (source: WH Intellectual Properties, LLC / Creative Commons Attribution-Share Alike 4.0 International license).

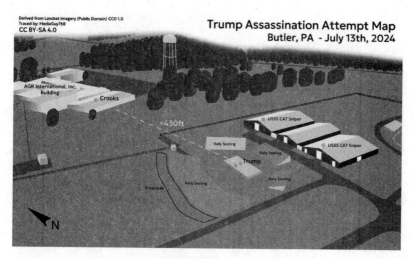

3D Trump Rally Map (MediaGuy768 / CC BY-SA 4.0).

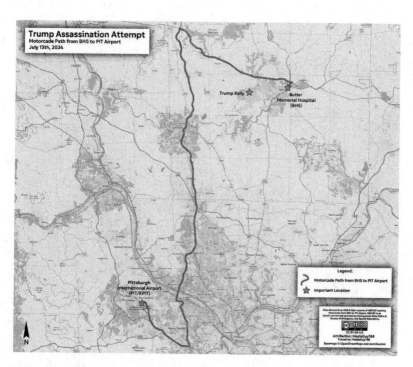

Motorcade Path (source: MediaGuy768 / Creative Commons Attribution-Share Alike 4.0 International license.

THE TIMELINE

Date	Trump & Activities	Crooks (Shooter)	Biden & Team Activities
2021		Donated $15 to ActBlue.	
Spring 2023		Began making weapons purchases.	
June	Denied additional Secret Service protection by Biden administration.		Local police offered drone security for the rally (later refused by Secret Service).
June 12			New poll shows Harris polling poorly amid concerns about Biden's age.
June 15	Speaks at The People's Convention in Detroit.		
June 22		Registered for intermediate handgun-pistol class at Keystone Shooting Center.	
June 27	Trump defeats Biden in debate, clips go viral.		Biden has poor performance in first presidential debate against Trump.
June 28			Biden calls Trump "a genuine threat to this nation."
June 29			

(Continued on next page)

Date	Trump & Activities	Crooks (Shooter)	Biden & Team Activities
July 2			Rep. Lloyd Doggett (D-Texas) becomes first sitting Democrat to call for Biden to drop out. Reports emerge of Michelle Obama discussing coalition of wealthy Black donors for Kamala Harris.
July 3	Trump campaign announces July 13 rally in Butler, PA. Leaked video of Trump in a golf cart predicting Biden will quit the race. "He just quit, you know. He's quitting the race," Trump said.		Biden speaks with Democratic leadership and governors to ease concerns.
July 5			Biden tells ABC News his debate performance was due to exhaustion. Biden posts on X: "I'm staying in the race."
July 6		Searches online for Trump event dates and Democratic National Convention date. Googled "how far away was Oswald from Kennedy" and "Where will Trump speak from at Butler Farm Show."	
July 7		Visits the site of the upcoming Trump rally.	
July 8			Biden says it's "time to put Trump in a bullseye" to donors. Biden dares other Democrats to challenge him at the convention.
July 11			Biden holds press conference at NATO Summit, makes naming errors.

Date	Trump & Activities	Crooks (Shooter)	Biden & Team Activities
July 12	Preparing for Butler, PA rally.	Practices at Clairton Sportsmen's Club rifle range.	Biden reaffirms he won't drop out at Michigan rally. FBI arrests Asif Merchant, a Pakistani man with ties to Iran, charged with plotting political assassinations including against Trump.
July 13	Arrives at rally venue around 6:02 p.m. 6:05 p.m.: Begins speaking. 6:11:34 p.m.: Raises hand to right ear after first shot. 6:11:35 p.m.: Drops behind the lectern for cover. 6:12:47 p.m.: Escorted off stage, mouths "Fight! Fight! Fight!" 6:14 p.m.: Taken to Butler Memorial Hospital. 8:42 p.m.: Posts statement on Truth Social. 11:21 p.m.: Leaves Pittsburgh International Airport.	Morning: Buys a five-foot ladder. Visited local shooting range to practice with AR-15-style rifle. 3:35 p.m.: Arrives at rally site with rifle and explosive device. 4:26 p.m.: Beaver County Emergency Service Unit counter-sniper texted colleague about suspicious person. 5:38 p.m.: Photos of Crooks shared in law enforcement group chat 6:08 p.m.: Seen jumping from roof to roof on video footage. 6:11:33 p.m.: Fires first shot. 6:11:37 p.m.: Fires last of eight shots. 6:11:49 p.m.: Fatally shot by Secret Service.	Biden campaign goes silent, pulls all ads and "outbound communications." Biden team issues memos to refrain from public comments.
July 14	7:36 a.m.: Posts on Truth Social about the attempt on his life.[1] Flew from Bedminster to Milwaukee with Lindsey Graham. Seen in public with bandage on ear.	Identified publicly as the shooter. Explosive devices found in Crooks's Hyundai Sonata. FBI accessed Crooks's email accounts. FBI says no clear motive or political ideology identified.	2:05 p.m.: Biden speaks about the incident in White House briefing room. 8:02 p.m.: Biden addresses the nation.

(Continued on next page)

Date	Trump & Activities	Crooks (Shooter)	Biden & Team Activities
July 15	Appears at Republican National Convention with bandaged ear alongside VP pick JD Vance.	FBI confirms Crooks's phone had saved photo of James Crumbley. Additional explosives found at Crooks's residence.	Biden interview with NBC's Lester Holt.
July 16	Continues at RNC. Personally reaches out to Helen Comperatore to express sympathy.	Crooks's parents hired Quinn Logue law firm.	Biden resumes campaigning in Las Vegas. Biden health scare in Las Vegas. Jack Black canceled Tenacious D world tour due to Kyle Gass's comments.
July 17			Biden considers dropping out of race. Obama., Pelosi, Schumer begin orchestrating "coup" to push out Biden. DHS Inspector General launches review of Secret Service protocols. Biden tests positive for COVID-19 while campaigning in Las Vegas. Biden returned to Delaware due to COVID-19.
July 18	Gives acceptance speech at Republican National Convention honoring victims of the assassination attempt. YouGov poll showed majority thought assassination attempt would increase Trump's chances.	FBI reviewing contents of Crooks's electronic devices.	More reports of Biden considering dropping out. Reports of Kamala Harris team discussing Biden stepping aside. Green Day concert incident with Trump mask.
July 19	Corey Comperatore's funeral held in Cabot, PA.		Ten more sitting Democrats call for Biden to drop out. Donors report fundraising has slowed.
July 20			Biden refuses to drop out of the race.

Date	Trump & Activities	Crooks (Shooter)	Biden & Team Activities
July 21	Posts commentary on Truth Social about Biden's exit.		Biden campaign co-chairman Cedric Richmond insists on *Face the Nation* that Biden will not step down. Biden announces he is dropping out of the race. Kamala Harris becomes presumptive nominee.
July 22			Secret Service Director Kimberly Cheatle testifies before Congress.
July 23		Crooks's body released for cremation.	Cheatle resigns as Secret Service Director.
July 24	David Dutch, a 57-year-old Marine Corps veteran wounded in the shooting, discharged from Allegheny General Hospital.		
July 26	Trump announced via a Truth Social post that he plans to return to Butler, PA for another rally. James Copenhaver, a 74-year-old rally attendee wounded in the shooting, discharged from hospital.		
July 29	Elon Musk posts about Google search issues regarding Trump.		Secret Service counter-sniper emailed entire Uniformed Division criticizing leadership.
July 30	Google acknowledges and begins fixing search issues related to Trump.		Acting Secret Service Director Ronald Rowe testified about security failures.
July 31			Democrats begin branding JD Vance as "weird" in coordinated messaging.
Late July/ Early August 2024			

(Continued on next page)

Date	Trump & Activities	Crooks (Shooter)	Biden & Team Activities
Aug 1	Senator Josh Hawley sends letter to Acting Director Rowe about security concerns.		Harris campaign focuses on "freedom" messaging.
Aug 2			Harris officially becomes the Democratic presidential nominee.
Aug 3	Jack Posobiec conducts site survey in Butler, PA.		
Aug 5			Media coverage of Harris becomes more positive.
Aug 8	Trump gives interview to Breitbart News about the assassination attempt.		
Aug 13	Trump provided more details about his planned return to Butler County during an interview on the social media platform X with Elon Musk.		Harris's team changes news headlines in Google ads, creating an illusion of media endorsement.
Aug 15	Rep. Ranna Paulina Luna posts previously unpublished photo of Crooks at rally.		
Aug 19			Biden speaks at Democratic National Convention.
Aug 21	Posts commentary on Truth Social about Biden's "demise" and the Democratic "coup."	Rep. Mike Waltz told reporters Crooks used encrypted messaging accounts on platforms located in Belgium, New Zealand, and Germany.	Biden expresses anger at being pushed out.
Aug 22			Harris gains popularity among younger voters, associated with "brat" meme.
Aug 23			Nancy Pelosi compares Trump to British threat during American Revolution.
Aug 25			Senator Cory Booker makes controversial statement about "killing" Trump's strain of Republican Party.

THE CHART

It's a hot day in Butler. Windy. They're packed in.

The president interrupts himself.

"I don't know if they could do it," he pulls away from the lectern, turning stage right, from our view. "Do you guys have access to that chart that I love so much?" he says to his staff off-camera.

The bill of his red *MAKE AMERICA GREAT AGAIN* hat hides his shaded gaze. His eyes twinkle already. We can feel it.

Return to stage center. To the cameras. He's going to do it.

"You don't mind if I go off-teleprompter, do you?"

There it is.

Grins. Whooping. Hollering. Fists. Waving. Signs with unmissable text. *Crooked Joe You're Fired.*

"Cause these teleprompters are so damn boring, I try and explain that—oh, it is! Wow!"

All eyes to the jumbotron screen to the right, following the President's.

ILLEGAL IMMIGRATION INTO THE U.S.

Quickly skimming, scanning. A big, beautiful bar graph. Everyone skims it at a glance. The older yellow bars are low; the newer yellow bars are high. That's not good. Squinting and reading. The subhead:

BIDEN WORLD RECORD ILLEGAL IMMIGRANTS, MANY FROM PRISONS AND MENTAL INSTITUTIONS.

Next line:

ALSO TERRORISTS

And then:

NOTHING LIKE THIS HAS EVER HAPPENED TO OUR COUNTRY BEFORE!

So true. There's more, but back to the president. He skips no beats.

"You guys are doing it," as he turns now to the left. "They're getting better with time, my guys. Take a look at that chart." Forefinger raised, reaching. That looks on-script. Just like God outstretching his hand in the *Creation of Adam*. Somebody must've said that. You know they did.

"Take a look at the arrow on the bottom. See the big red—red arrow, right?"

Oh yes. There at the bottom.

TRUMP LEAVES OFFICE
LOWEST ILLEGAL IMMIGRATION IN RECORDED HISTORY

"So that's when I left office."

And then came the flood.

"That was the lowest point, and that comes right from the government services, comes right out of Border Patrol. Take a look at that. So that arrow is the lowest amount of illegal immigration ever in recorded history into our country. And then—"

There's golf claps. Then whistles, cheers. Somebody hollers. Notice cell phones out and recording. This is historic. He's about to do it. The wind-up.

"And then the worst president in the history of our country took over," here he goes, "*AND LOOK WHAT HAPPENED TO OUR COUNTRY.*"

Boos, thumbs-down. The president leads, the people follow. It feels like a concert.

"Probably twenty million people." Boos, boos. Worst president.

"And, you know, that's a little bit old, that chart. That chart's a couple of months old, and if you, uh, want to really see something that's sad . . ." the president tilts away from the chart, to center-left.

"Take a look at what happened. . ." sharp tilt back.

To the chart.

A vowel escapes.

". . . o—"

over? over there, Mr. President?

Crack. POW.
Right hand whips up. Right ear.
Camera catches a blur. The president's fingers rub together. Red blur. Something between his—
Crack. POW.
He goes.
Crack. POW.

Crack. POW.
Crack. POW.
Crack. POW.
Crack. POW.
Crack. POW.
The suits rush up. United States Secret Service.
All down. Human dome. Over the president.
Screams.
POW.
A ninth.
There's no explanation. This isn't part of the speech.
The crowd goes down. The video camera shudders. Signs still seen. *You're fired . . . You're fired . . .* A blurry tee-shirt. *Mean Tweets, World Peace.*
POW.
Tenth.
There's no explanation. No answer. None asked, none given.
Deep in the chaos of silence rise voices—the Secret Service. The transcript reads:

> Get down! Get down! Get down! Get down!
> Hold! Hold! When you're ready! On you!
> Ready.
> Move!
> Up!
> Move! Go! We ready?
> He's down.
> Are we good?

Shooter's down.

Shooter's down?

Shooter's down.

Are we good to move?

Shooter's down. We're good to move.

Are we clear?

We're clear. We're clear.

Let's move. Let's move.

We're clear.

It's sixty seconds. Now we see him. He is risen, by the Secret Service. He's standing. He's moving. He pauses.

"Let me get my shoes."

And again.

"Let me get my shoes."

Blood streaks across his face.

"I got you, sir. I got you, there," Secret Service says.

Now a third.

"Let me get my shoes on."

"Hold that on your head. You're bloody."

"Sir, we've got to move."

"Let me get my shoes."

"Okay."

Agents speak over each other. Unintelligible. Silent. A female Secret Service member, far shorter than her male colleagues, finds herself stage center. Anonymous, back to the world, she shields the president. Up to the neck. We see him. They're trying to take him off. He won't go. He's trying to get back to the microphone. They're frozen. There's just enough room for—

Fist.

Three pumps. Three words. Shouting above it all.

Fight!

Fight!

Fight!

The president waves and fist-pumps more as the suits shuffle him off stage right. Now come the cheers, smiles, chants. Nobody on camera moves. Everyone holds. Nobody knows the shooter is down. No one knows if more shots are coming, if there are more shooters. Courage is contagious. Their president's faith is their own. If we do not hang together, we shall all hang separately. Next you hear them—the chants.

USA!
USA!
USA!

Nothing like this has ever happened to our country before.

THE SCENARIOS

When I (Jack) served in the US intelligence community, I was trained on how the intelligence community uses a method known as the Analysis of Competing Hypotheses (ACH) as a tool to navigate through the complexities of intelligence analysis, where multiple explanations for events or future scenarios are plausible. ACH was developed to counteract cognitive biases, particularly confirmation bias, where analysts might unconsciously favor evidence that supports their initial hypothesis. By listing all potential hypotheses related to an intelligence issue, analysts are encouraged to consider a broad spectrum of possibilities from the outset. This approach ensures that no stone is left unturned, promoting a more comprehensive analysis that might otherwise be narrowed by preconceived notions or groupthink.

I also learned that this is what the IC says it does, but not how it works in practice. In practice, the IC is told by the political appointees what they want to hear, and raw intelligence is then revised to fit those political goals. The only administration in recent history that did not operate this way was in office from 2017–2021. More on that later.

Here's how Analysis of Competing Hypotheses is supposed to work. In reality, ACH involves creating a matrix where each hypothesis is compared against all available evidence. This structured comparison isn't just about seeing which hypothesis has the most supporting evidence but critically evaluating how each piece of evidence aligns or conflicts with every hypothesis. This process, often described as "working across" the matrix, forces analysts to reassess their assumptions continuously. For instance, if new evidence emerges, it's not just added to support the leading hypothesis but is evaluated against all, potentially shifting the analysis's direction. This methodical approach helps in refining hypotheses, merging similar ones, or even generating new ones based on emerging patterns in the evidence.

Here are the steps of an Analysis of Competing Hypotheses:

1. **Identify Hypotheses:**
   List all possible hypotheses or explanations for the event or situation being analyzed. This should include both obvious and less obvious possibilities to ensure comprehensive coverage.

2. **List Significant Evidence:**
   Gather all relevant evidence, including facts, data, reports, and any other information pertinent to the issue. This step involves compiling both supporting and contradicting evidence for each hypothesis.

3. **Prepare a Matrix:**
   Create a matrix where hypotheses are listed across the top and pieces of evidence down the side. This visual tool helps in systematically comparing each piece of evidence against each hypothesis.

4. **Refine Hypotheses:**
   As evidence is analyzed, refine, merge, or split hypotheses if necessary. This step ensures that the hypotheses remain relevant and accurately reflect the complexity of the situation.

5. **Analyze/Diagnose:**
   Evaluate each piece of evidence for consistency with each hypothesis. Mark whether the evidence supports, contradicts, or is neutral for each hypothesis. This step involves critical thinking to avoid confirmation bias.

6. **Rate Hypotheses:**
   Rank or score how well each hypothesis explains the total body of evidence. This can be done through various scoring systems or qualitative assessments.

7. **Reconsider Rejected Hypotheses:**
   Reevaluate hypotheses that were initially rejected.
   New evidence or a different perspective might warrant
   reconsideration, ensuring no potentially valuable insights are
   discarded prematurely.

8. **Draw Tentative Conclusion:**
   Based on the analysis, identify which hypothesis best fits the
   available evidence. This conclusion is tentative, acknowledging
   the inherent uncertainties in intelligence work.

9. **Identify Indicators for Future Information:**
   Determine what additional information or events would either
   confirm or disprove each hypothesis. This sets the stage for
   ongoing intelligence collection and analysis.

10. **Sensitivity Analysis:**
    Conduct a sensitivity analysis to understand how changes in
    key pieces of evidence could alter the conclusions. This step
    tests the robustness of the analysis against different scenarios
    or new evidence.

Use of ACH extends beyond mere hypothesis testing; it's about foster-
ing rigorous, evidence-based analysis as standard operating procedure.
By encouraging analysts to double-check key evidence and reassess
the consistency of their arguments, ACH reduces the likelihood of
overlooking critical data or misinterpreting information due to bias.
Moreover, the process is designed to be transparent and traceable,
allowing for peer review and validation by other analysts or decision-
makers. This transparency not only enhances the credibility of the
analysis but also facilitates learning from past assessments, the idea
being to improve future intelligence operations. Through ACH, the
intelligence community aims to provide policymakers with the most
accurate, bias-reduced insights, crucial for informed decision-making
in national security contexts. Wouldn't it be great if that's how the IC
actually worked?

We have created an Analysis of Competing Hypotheses for the
Trump assassination attempt.

We present it to you now. At the end of the book, we will return to our ACH for reassessment.

- For guilt to be established, there must be motive, means, and opportunity.
  - *Motive*: The reason why someone would commit the crime. This could be anything from financial gain, revenge, or emotional disturbance.
  - *Means*: The ability to commit the crime. This could refer to access to the weapon used, physical capability, or knowledge needed to carry out the act.
  - *Opportunity*: The chance or occasion to commit the crime. This means the person was in a position where they could have committed the crime when it occurred.
- Regarding the attempted assassination of Donald J. Trump, there are three plausible scenarios that have surfaced as to why the hit on the former president was almost carried out.

Scenario 1: The Official Narrative

On July 13, 2024, former President Donald Trump was shot and wounded during a campaign rally in Butler, Pennsylvania. Three attendees were also shot, with one passing away. The shooter, identified as twenty-year-old Thomas Matthew Crooks, fired from an elevated position with an AR-15-style rifle. Trump was struck in the ear but survived the attack.

The official narrative is that Crooks acted alone, with unknown motivation for political violence. He was able to fire at President Trump due to a cascade of security failures that, while catastrophic, were the result of good-faith efforts. After firing eight rounds, Crooks was shot once by a local SWAT team officer, once by United States Secret Service counter-snipers, with the second hit—through the skull—proving immediately fatal. Following the incident, there were widespread calls for increased security for political candidates and a reduction in heated political rhetoric.

Motive, Means, Opportunity

The official narrative identifies Thomas Matthew Crooks as the shooter, but his specific *motive* remains unclear. The lack of a clear ideological or political leaning suggests the possibility of psychological reasons such as severe mental illness rather than a politically motivated attack. It is known Crooks searched online for information relating to mental disorders.

Crooks was a marksman who trained often, used a rifle he purchased from his father, flew a drone, made explosives, and he did so at a public open-air rally from the rooftop of a nearby building. *Means* established.

The question remains though . . . how would Crooks have known that would be the case? Luck? How would he know he had the perfect *opportunity*?

Scenario 2: The Iranian Plot

The argument for potential Iranian involvement, particularly by the Islamic Revolutionary Guard Corps (IRGC), in the plot to assassinate former President Donald Trump on July 13, 2024, stems from US intelligence reports indicating that Iran might seek to avenge the killing of General Qasem Soleimani, who was killed by a US drone strike ordered by Trump in 2020.

US intelligence reportedly received information from a human source suggesting that Iran had a plan to assassinate Trump. The Secret Service even discussed this.[1] This led to heightened security measures around Trump before the attack.

However, officials have stated that there is no direct evidence linking the July 13 shooter, Thomas Matthew Crooks, to the Iranian plot. The timing of the intelligence and the attack has fueled speculation, but US authorities have not confirmed a direct connection between Crooks and the IRGC or any Iranian operation.

Iran has officially denied any involvement, labeling the accusations as politically motivated. The Iranian government has reiterated its stance that Trump should be held accountable legally for Soleimani's assassination, rather than through acts of violence.[2, 3]

These developments have contributed to a complex narrative where the intelligence community remains vigilant about potential Iranian threats, even as specific links to the July 13 attack remain unproven

It was known that Crooks, the shooter, had used encrypted messaging apps and browsed the web using virtual private networks (VPNs) potentially more than a year prior to the Butler shooting. It *is* plausible that Crooks was engaging with Iranian intelligence or some form of assets, but there remains no publicly available evidence to support this assertion. It is not impossible by any stretch.

Motive, Means, Opportunity

The Iranian narrative suggests that the IRGC might have a motive to target Donald Trump as an act of revenge for the 2020 killing of General Qasem Soleimani, which was authorized and carried out by Trump. The assassination attempt could be seen as part of Iran's broader strategy to retaliate against US and US-proxy actions that have significantly impacted its leadership.

Iran's IRGC has the resources, training, and network to potentially carry out an assassination plot abroad, including access to operatives or proxies capable of executing such a mission. However, there is no direct evidence linking the shooter, Thomas Matthew Crooks, to the IRGC or any Iranian operation. As such, the *means* are more tenuous.

The heightened tension between the United States and Iran, along with intelligence reports of a possible Iranian plot, suggests that Iran might have been looking for an *opportunity* to strike. However, the narrative lacks concrete evidence that Iran specifically exploited the opportunity provided by Trump's rally on July 13, 2024—except for one:

The FBI arrested Asif Merchant, a Pakistani man with [ties] to Iran, one day before the Butler rally. Merchant was charged with a plot to carry out political assassinations on US soil, including against Trump. The arrest comes two years after US officials disrupted another Iranian scheme aimed at former Trump National Security Adviser John Bolton. Trump and his national security team have faced threats from Iran since Trump ordered the killing of Iranian General Qasam Soleimani in early January 2020.[4]

Scenario 3: The Inside Job

The argument for the "inside job" hypothesis surrounding the July 13, 2024, assassination attempt on former President Donald Trump primarily stems from several key points.

The numerous United States Secret Service security failures at the rally seem, to many Americans, too severe and too numerous to be merely coincidental. Secret Service agents and local police were seen in positions that seem to have allowed them to prevent the shooter from getting into position. In fact, Crooks's presence was known to law enforcement approximately ninety minutes before the shooting. Furthermore, failure to evacuate Trump from the stage due to a credible threat is beyond suspicious.

To be blunt, accusations of an "inside job" are driven by a deep-seated and hard-earned distrust of government agencies like the FBI and Secret Service. It is not implausible that these agencies might have been complicit or at least negligent in allowing the attack to occur. Despite the coincidences and suspicions, there is not yet publicly available confirmation that the assassination attempt against Donald Trump was an inside job. That said, we must consider . . .

Motive, Means, Opportunity

The inside job hypothesis posits that certain elements within the security or government apparatus may have had a motive to remove Trump, which we will expand on shortly. This hypothesis begins with deep distrust in government institutions—but does not end there.

It is indeed plausible that insiders would have the necessary resources and access to orchestrate an attack, including knowledge of security protocols and the ability to manipulate or override them. The fact that the shooter was able to position himself effectively and that security appeared to falter at critical moments supports this scenario. And the chaotic environment of a public, outdoor rally could have been exploited by insiders to create the perfect opportunity for an attack. The presence of security lapses and the rarity of their same lapses prior to this event give us pause.

ASSESSMENT: Of the three possible scenarios, a version of the inside job hypothesis is, in our view, the most compelling narrative. It is indeed possible for Crooks to have operated by himself but stepped into conditions set by political actors who wanted great suffering to come to Donald Trump—or at the very least did not take his security seriously so that someone like Crooks could do exactly what he did. Lone gunman Thomas Crooks had no known motive (according to the official narrative, that is). But we do know that the shadow elite, the oligarchical panopticon, that opaque collective networked institutional organism of the unelected managerial class of the military-intelligence-media industrial complex, all associated with the Democratic Party, they among all potential suspects have a uniquely known motive—to stop Trump. And they have been extolling it to the American people for a decade.

PART I
BEFORE THE SHOT
The Road to Butler

THE MOTIVE

Democrats and their allies, proxies, cut-outs, and saboteurs have done whatever they could to stop Donald Trump, eliminating democracy itself from America as the bitter ironic result. Over and over, we've seen extreme efforts from the regime—a word we'll use to refer to the oligarchical panopticon that possesses *de facto* control over the United States federal government, including but not limited to the military-industrial complex, the intelligence community, the political mega-donor class, corporate interests, and the tangled web weaving them all together beyond the public eye. They see us; we can't see them.

From the regime we've seen coordinated corruption such as Russiagate—the false claims and fake evidence purporting to show direct involvement in the 2016 US election by Russia's Vladimir Putin to help Trump win. Regime elites in media and government chased this wind for the entire first Trump term. Then there were the impeachments, the most notable of which came after President Trump exposed Biden family corruption in Ukraine via "the perfect phone call."[1] During and after the 2020 election, Trump and his closest allies suffered extreme lawfare, up to and including the taking of political prisoners by the elite. At the time of this writing, Trump himself has been found guilty of what we observe as trumped-up charges. We hope and pray justice prevails and all are reversed.

Notably, the anti-Trump stories of the last several years show the same cast of characters that lead the governing structure of the United States Secret Service, including Alejandro Mayorkas, Robert McCabe, and Peter Strzok. No surprise then that 45 percent of Republicans believe "there were multiple people involved in the assassination attempt on Trump," and one-third of all Americans believe that "the assassination attempt on Donald Trump was part of a broader plot or conspiracy."[2]

Why They Hate Trump

Alongside the direct and indirect political assaults and lawfare there is the matter of the culture war.

In the days after the assassination attempt, Democrat leaders and many liberal voices offered prayers and calls for unity with President Trump in a stand against political violence. This was peculiar, as they had done the exact opposite for years prior to J13. The paradox of left-wing rhetoric surrounding President Trump was not lost on those with eyes to see and ears to hear. Three days after the failed assassination, Mike Solana summed up this paradox with a piece entitled "Thoughts and Prayers for 'Literally Hitler.'"[3] We need say no more. But we will anyway.

Since Trump descended the golden escalator into American politics in 2015, announcing his candidacy for president, establishment media and Democrat-aligned voices have stained the previously spotless Trump reputation with comparisons to fascist leaders of world history such as Adolf Hitler and imperials such as Julius Caesar—both of whom died violently, one a direct assassination, (Caesar stabbed by the Senate, Hitler by suicide due to the Soviet Union's Red Army capture of Berlin, Germany). Edited photos published and pushed by major press gave Trump a Hitlerian mustache and a Caesarian laurel crown.[4, 5] Left-wing commentator Andrea Junker posted on X on March 3, 2024, "Have you ever wondered why Germans didn't do anything about Hitler? Well, the rest of the world is wondering exactly that about Americans and Trump."[6] She is not alone in this rhetoric; there are currently 41,300,000 search results on Google alone for the longtail keyword "Trump Hitler." At the time of this writing, PBS, *Politico*, Reuters, and *Vanity Fair* are among the top culprits for equating the two figures—and this particular Google search result set came only one and a half months after the shooting in Butler.[7, 8, 9, 10] They just don't let up.

The natural conclusion then, is that left-wing news and their allies intended to create legitimacy in the public consciousness for a Trump assassination. As we state repeatedly in our previous work covering far-left atrocities, *Unhumans*, "this is what they do." For years, media together with elected and unelected Democratic Party elite have also accused President Trump, without evidence, of promoting "the Big Lie" on one issue or another.[11] This term is found in the history books in sections on Nazi propaganda, further revealing intent to legitimize violence towards the president.[12] This is what they do. It is no surprise then that Trump suffered (and survived) two previous assassination attempts, one in Las Vegas, Nevada, and the other in Dayton, Ohio, both in 2016.

The seeming intent to activate a radical to "punch a Nazi," as again the media have advised during the Trump era, became impossible to ignore in the days leading up to July 13, 2024.[13] Then-president Joe Biden had just said it was "time to put Trump in a bullseye," and the left-wing billionaire and Jeffrey Epstein island enthusiast Reid Hoffman said worse.[14, 15]

> [Peter] Thiel, who was in the audience at the panel, spoke up and sarcastically thanked Hoffman for putting money behind lawsuits against Trump, saying the legal action had turned the 45th president into a "martyr."
>
> "Yeah, I wish I had made him an actual martyr," Hoffman reportedly replied.[16]

Following the failed assassination attempt, Biden and Hoffman both attempted to reframe their comments, with Biden notably and hilariously noting he said "bullseye"; he didn't say "crosshairs."[17]

(Perhaps Biden was too aware of his party's own past when it comes to the subject of "crosshairs." When Democratic Congresswoman Gabby Giffords was shot by a psycho obsessive Jared Lee Loughner, the Democrats immediately blamed Sarah Palin (campaigning against Obamacare at the time) for "targeting" Giffords with "crosshairs." Basically, accusing Palin of calling for Giffords's assassination. This attack—a precursor to the confession-by-projection charge of "sto-chastic terrorism" before such a fancy term was being pushed to try to squash former anonymous users on X who happened to like reposting crazy lefties being crazy on TikTok—ended up floundering.[18] (Mostly because, as everyone pointed out, the Democrats did the exact same thing at the time.[19])

The subject came up on *Dr. Phil*, of all places, where the host asked Trump about Biden and Harris's rhetoric towards him, following the attempt in Butler, PA.

> "The TV doctor . . . asked Trump if he thought Kamala Harris and Joe Biden were "OK" with him being shot.
>
> "I'm not saying that they wanted you to get shot, but do you think it was OK with them if you did?" he asked.
>
> Trump responded by saying "I don't know" twice before adding, "There's a lot of hatred. I don't know why." He went on to boast about his presidency's achievements, claiming those successes created a hatred among Democrats that meant some wanted to see him assassinated."[20]

Trump later directly referenced some of the words that Biden had used:

> "They're saying I'm a threat to democracy," Trump said. "They would say that, that was standard line, just keep saying it, and you know that can get assassins or potential assassins going. That's a terrible thing. . . . Maybe that bullet is because of their rhetoric."[21]

Thoughts and prayers for literally Hitler.

Because of course they never meant any of this. Or did they? What about known left-wing celebrities? When Robert DeNiro, Johnny Depp, and Madonna wished death upon President Trump, did they mean it? What about George Lopez, Mickey Rourke, and Marilyn Manson? Did they? Note that public figures called for peaceful protests and toned-down rhetoric only *after* the shooting failed. (This is what they do.)[22, 23, 24, 25, 26, 27]

In 2017, New York City's Public Theater staged a production of Shakespeare's *Julius Caesar* as part of its annual "Shakespeare in the Park" series, where Julius Caesar was portrayed as Donald Trump and his wife as Melania Trump. The play drew attention for this, with Caesar dressed in a business suit and a long red tie, resembling Donald Trump. The play sparked intense debate and controversy, particularly for its depiction of Caesar's assassination, which seemed a clear political statement. Notably, Delta Airlines and the Bank of America dropped their sponsorship of the play once the brutal and bloody content was revealed to directly target the sitting president of the United States.

To make matters worse, the opening of the play coincided with an act of extreme political violence in Washington, DC that has been nearly memory-holed by the mainstream media. On June 14, 2017, during a practice for the annual Congressional Baseball Game for Charity, a crazed Russiagate believer opened fire on Republican members of Congress, seriously injuring House Majority Whip Steve Scalise and several others. The shooter was an ardent fan of MSNBC, and was convinced that Republicans were Russian agents, as his news outlet had informed him. He thought killing Republicans was saving his country. It's what his news outlet had told him.

And yet, the performances of Julius Caesar continued. This did not sit well with many Americans, including this book's coauthor Jack Posobiec. I (Jack) traveled to Central Park one night and watched the play. The blood coming off of the Trumpian character was worse than something from a Quentin Tarantino film. And yet the crowd laughed and clapped, as the stand-in for Donald Trump was butchered before their eyes night after night after night. And on the night that I arrived, I set to work with Laura Loomer in tandem, her storming the stage while I filmed and called out to the audience, denouncing their normalization of political violence. The story quickly became national news. Some voices in the conservative sphere loudly criticized me and Laura for our tactics, saying that we had infringed on the free speech rights of the actors. I (Jack) quickly replied to them, "I didn't infringe on free speech. I simply added my speech to their speech."

The actor who played Brutus, Corey Stoll of *House of Cards*, later wrote that he ran backstage sobbing. The real danger, however, was missed in the new controversy. One side of the political spectrum was becoming comfortable with depictions of political violence, even in the wake of an assassination attempt.

Then, not two months after the Trump assassination attempt, Nancy Pelosi, speaking on the final night of the Democratic National Convention, turned the violent rhetoric back up to eleven.

> Pelosi appeared on [MSNBC] to talk about the party's mission to beat Trump in November, whom she suggested is as much of a threat to democracy as the British government was during the American Revolution.
>
> "The times have found us," Pelosi declared to network anchor Andrea Mitchell, noting that liberals are facing the same stakes that were present in 1776 and then the Civil War.
>
> "We have to defeat a person who is a threat to our democracy of the kind that we have not seen—At the beginning of our country, Thomas Paine said that times have found us. Declare war, establish a new nation."
>
> Rep. Nancy Pelosi, D-Calif., compared the threat of former President Trump to the threat that the British posed to the American colonists during an MSNBC segment on Thursday.
>
> She continued, comparing it to another fraught time in American history.
>
> "Abraham Lincoln took up that charge to keep our country together years later—decades later, and now the times have found us to save our democracy," she said, adding, "That is what we are here to do."[28]

Literal calls for *literal* war against Donald Trump. *Literal* death wishes. *Literal* fantasies of his murder. On August 25, Senator Cory Booker said to Jake Tapper on CNN that he hoped the 2024 election would "finally kill that strain of the Republican Party," referring to Trump and his supporters.[29] *Strain* as in a virus, which one must *kill?* And the left accuses *us* of dehumanizing tactics. Projection. This is what they do.

So, what's really going on here? What's the motive for wishing death upon a presidential candidate, devoting your platform to inciting violence towards him and his supporters, and then shirking all accountability and responsibility for involvement only *after* Trump tilts his head at the absolute last split-second? In a word, what's the *motive?*

Because Donald Trump committed the unpardonable sin of the elite—he became a class traitor. His America-first, working class values-based message from 2015 onwards has put enmity between him and the establishment news media and political institutions infiltrated by literal communists (see *Unhumans*). Ironically, while Trump was firmly seated among that upper class for most of his adult life, he was praised and adored. Trump received an award from the National Association for the Advancement of Colored People (NAACP), funded Democratic US presidential campaigns, and is honored with a Hollywood Walk of Fame. Activism, politics, and entertainment— Trump was on the right side of their history for years. You can easily find a thousand and one more examples of Trump's lifelong celebration by such institutions. Only when his public personal brand shifted from New York City and Los Angeles to swing states and the Rust Belt and all the Middle American suffering therein did he fall out of favor.

Perhaps even more alarming to the regime was that during his presidency, Donald Trump made it a point to avoid entangling the United States in new military conflicts, a stance that sharply contrasted with the hawkish tendencies of his predecessors. Despite immense pressure from both political allies and adversaries, as well as the entrenched interests of the military-industrial complex, Trump remained steadfast in his commitment to peace and diplomacy. He sought to de-escalate tensions with adversaries like North Korea and reduce the American military presence in conflict zones such as Afghanistan and Syria. This approach, while garnering support from those who favored

a less interventionist foreign policy, angered powerful defense contractors and Pentagon officials who thrived on the profits and influence
generated by perpetual warfare. Trump's refusal to initiate new wars
or expand existing ones became a defining feature of his presidency,
highlighting a deep divide between his administration and the military-industrial establishment. In effect, this all amounted to Trump
being the only president since perhaps John F. Kennedy to betray the
military-industry complex in addition to defying the elite class from
which Trump hails.

In addition, Trump's anti-globalization policies pose a significant
threat to the powerful elites who have long benefited from the inter-
connected global economy. By imposing tariffs and renegotiating
trade deals, these policies challenge the status quo that has allowed
multi-national companies to maximize profits through cheap labor
and global supply chains. As a result, these corporations stand to lose
billions, disrupting the wealth and influence of the elites who control
them. However, for Middle America, these same policies offer a life-
line. By incentivizing the return of manufacturing jobs to the United
States, they promise to revive struggling communities, restore lost
industries, and provide stable employment to millions of American
workers who have been left behind in the global economy. This shift
represents a direct challenge to the established order, redistributing
economic power away from the global elite and back to the American
heartland.

We're reminded of how the Gospels depict the hatred of the
Pharisees and the Sadducees for Jesus Christ, who was in effect a class
traitor by associating himself, a rabbi, with known sinners, thieves,
and the poor and lame, who many at that time believed were simply
experiencing the karmic consequences of sin in their family. Those
cast out of elite religious society, Jesus made his fellowship.

What we have witnessed with Donald Trump is more than historical, it's biblical. We ought not be surprised. As with Jesus Christ,
Trump puts the elite to shame by fulfilling *their* responsibility. In
Unhumans, we wrote of *noblesse oblige*, the ancient, transcendent calling for the rich and powerful to help raise the poor and suffering out

of their conditions, if at all possible. Modern-day elites have instead embraced Cultural Marxism, we've argued, and so disdain the immiserated American underclass simply because the vast majority are straight white Christians. The elites are put to shame.

And that is the very secret to the motive—the shame. According to the Map of Consciousness, documented by pioneering consciousness researcher David R. Hawkins, shame is the lowest a human being can be and feel.[30] It is associated with the emotional state of humiliation and a miserable outlook on life. Shame drives those who succumb to it to, in a word, "elimination."

Now you see it. **Trump must be eliminated, for he puts them to shame**. His rhetoric and policies demonstrated sympathy and support for "the least of these" in the globalist elite worldview, as Jesus might say. And this is the fundamentally human reason why they want Trump dead. It's not the fascist accusations; that's all simply incitement. Because of course a conscience-challenged radical who is handy with a firearm and is also an opportunist will take that shame-driven rhetoric seriously. The accusers don't believe it, of course. That is their bluff, and the assassination attempt called it.

Thoughts and prayers indeed.

This is what they do.

THE RACE

On August 20, 2023, Donald Trump made the following announcement on Truth Social:

> New CBS POLL, just out, has me leading the field by "legendary" numbers. TRUMP 62%, 46 Points above DeSanctimonious (who is crashing like an ailing bird!), Ramaswamy 7%, Pence 5%, Scott 3%, Haley 2%, Sloppy Chris Christie 2%, "Aida" Hutchinson 1%. The public knows who I am & what a successful Presidency I had, with Energy Independence, Strong Borders & Military, Biggest EVER Tax & Regulation Cuts, No Inflation, Strongest Economy in History, & much more. I WILL THEREFORE NOT BE DOING THE DEBATES!

First of all, that's Trump being Trump. Second of all, Trump's commanding-in-chief lead over all other contenders for the 2024 Republican Party presidential nomination meant the debates—and the primary itself—was a consolation prize race for clout (and possibly book deals)—or possibly a race for vice president. Really, the race for Republican nomination became America-first versus globalist neoconservatism.

Perhaps no story captured the imagination and then the bewilderment of political observers quite like that of Florida Governor Ron DeSantis. Initially, DeSantis entered the race with a robust profile, buoyed by a significant legislative record that appealed to conservative voters, especially on issues like education, abortion, and economic freedom. His governance during the COVID-19 pandemic, where he prioritized economic recovery over stringent lockdowns, had earned him a reputation as a bold, decisive leader. However, many Trump supporters were confused why he would be running against Trump, after Trump had taken him from a back-bench Congressman to his endorsed candidate for Florida governor. DeSantis owed his political rise to Trump, and in turn, stabbed him in the back for it and ran against him. This did not bode well with Trump supporters. The establishment loved it, as it gave them a chance to knock Trumpist population away forever, and so they spent tens of millions on DeSantis and DeSantis online influencers.

The fall of DeSantis was as dramatic as his rise. Several factors contributed to this rapid decline. Firstly, his campaign rollout was marred by technical difficulties, setting a tone of unpreparedness that contrasted sharply with his image as a competent administrator. Moreover, DeSantis's attempt to navigate the fine line between appealing to Trump's base while differentiating himself proved perilous. His positions on issues like Ukraine and his responses to Trump's legal woes were seen as either too cautious or misaligned with the party's base, alienating both Trump supporters and those looking for a clear alternative.

National scrutiny played a significant role too. As DeSantis moved from being a state governor to a national figure, the lens through which he was viewed saw every misstep, and there were many. His interactions, which seemed genuine in Florida's political arena, appeared stiff or inauthentic on the national stage. He lacked any basic charisma. This perception was compounded by a campaign strategy that seemed to shift too frequently, from focusing on policy to personal attacks on Trump supporters, which neither endeared him to new voters nor solidified his base.

In retrospect, DeSantis's campaign for the presidency in 2024 serves as a case study in ego, self-delusion, and political realities. DeSantis was taken in by the establishment money thrown at him and thought he could betray Trump and defeat him. Instead, he was humiliated. The case highlights the challenges of transitioning from state to national politics, the importance of personal charisma in an age of media saturation, and the enduring influence of Trumpism within the GOP. DeSantis's story is not just one of political ambition but of the harsh realities of electoral politics where perception can often overshadow policy, and where timing, messaging, and the political landscape can dictate the fate of even the most promising candidates. Ultimately, his disloyalty led to his downfall.

Truth in a Time of Lies

Another interesting candidate was a former classmate of JD Vance, Vivek Ramaswamy, who came from biomedical sciences to politics with an energy storm unlike any we've ever seen (with, uh, a notable exception). The first millennial-generation Republican to reach national prominence, Vivek—whose slogan in the primary race was, without irony and not as a joke, "truth"—immediately assumed the role of Trump surrogate on stage during the debates, in viral social media clips, and in long-form interviews. He defended the first Trump administration record, debunked infamous left-wing hoaxes about Trump, and famously predicted that President Joe Biden would *not* be the eventual nominee due.

Unfortunately, Vivek's greatest hurdle was the same that the warhawk establishment media erected for Democrat-turned-independent candidate-turned Trump supporter Robert F. Kennedy Jr. in 2024, pro-peace Democrat presidential candidate-turned (also) Trump supporter Tulsi Gabbard in 2020, and independent Republican Ron Paul in 2008: invisibility. Vivek repeatedly noted that Republican primary polls and reports on the various candidates featured in national news media suspiciously left him out. Ultimately, he would finish fourth in the Iowa Republican caucus, drop out of the race, and pledge full support to the Trump campaign.

All other contenders quickly dropped out as well, as Donald Trump rolled up the 2024 Republican nomination with unprecedented ease. From the end of the primary to the very first debate between Trump and Democratic nomination winner—the incumbent Joe Biden—it was obvious to many that Trump would likely have a commanding lead over Biden, who had suffered from allegations of mental decline and ailing physical health since 2020.

Kamala 2020

Many public figures in Trumpworld famously predicted that the Biden-Harris ticket would ultimately become just Kamala. Turns out they were just one election early! For example, *Dilbert* creator and bestselling author of the national bestseller *Win Bigly*, Scott Adams, had predicted repeatedly that Biden's vice president, Kamala Harris, would replace him on the ticket, with these predictions going back to 2020.[1] Five days after the Biden inauguration, on January 25 2020, Adams suggested that establishment news media "don't expect [Harris] to stay 'vice' for long."[2] Months later, Adams described the situation:

> We've seen what happens when the president has a plan but the situation on the ground deteriorates faster than the plan anticipated.
> I'm talking about Biden's dementia and Harris as the replacement. None of the intel showed him declining this rapidly.[3]

Two years later, on August 1, 2023, Scott updated us:

> Biden won't be serving a second term. That question has been answered.
> But watch the faces of the Democrats defending Biden today. It's hilarious and educational.[4]

What exactly did Scott see that 14 million Democrats who voted for Biden in the 2024 party primary failed to, or simply weren't shown? Why these allegations of dementia, together with an intentional Democratic Party cover-up?

Well, it turns out that that is exactly what it looked like. Both of us, the coauthors of this book, have had elderly family members succumb to accelerating then rapid mental and physical decline, in some cases due to dementia and other neurological diseases. It's awful. And those with access to real news, such as uncensored, unedited clips published on the X platform (formerly Twitter) witnessed exact parallels as far back as the 2020 US presidential campaign. Physician Kelly Victory, MD had been tweeting updates and analysis on Biden's obvious decline for as long. Dr. Victory characterized Biden's candid moments as such:

> Biden's obvious signs of Parkinsonian dementia:
> 1. Shuffling gait
> 2. Stiff "tin soldier" arms
> 3. Difficulty initiating forward gait
> 4. Difficulty changing direction once gait is initiated
> 5. Lack of facial expression ("flat facies")
> 6. Difficulty with word finding
> 7. Difficulty tracking (i.e. on a teleprompter)
> 8. Difficulty with enunciation/slurred speech
> 9. Angry, inappropriate outbursts ("frontal lobe behavior")
> 10. Worsening cognitive changes as the day progresses ("sun downing")
> 11. Frequent confusion and/or loss of direction[5]

All this was known by less than half of the voting public in America—until June 27, 2024. Prior to the debate, it was simply "known" in left-wing circles that Biden was "sharp as a tack" and suffered no obvious mental or physical ailments or decline. He was literally the best man for the job of leader of the free world. All else was to suggest conspiracy theory, from those bad people on the far right.

To reframe it, that simply means "right so far."

The Shade War

Coauthor Jack Posobiec, no stranger to uncovering political intrigue, was one of the first to shine a spotlight on what became known as the "Shade War" within the White House. This conflict, simmering beneath the polished surface of political decorum, involved none other than Vice President Kamala Harris and First Lady Jill Biden. My (Jack) initial reports citing a White House insider, which began circulating in 2021, detailed an escalating tension that was more than mere political rivalry; it was a battle for influence and legacy within the Biden administration. My insights, often shared through my platform on X (formerly Twitter), provided a rare glimpse into the internal dynamics of the White House, revealing how personal and political ambitions could clash in the highest echelons of power.

As the Shade War unfolded, my reporting became a chronicle of the subtle and not-so-subtle jabs exchanged between Kamala Harris and Jill Biden. I covered moments like Jill Biden's increased public appearances, which some interpreted as a strategic move to bolster her husband's image amidst his declining health, directly challenging Kamala's visibility. My sources within the White House, often unnamed (of course) but described as "officials" or "advisors," fed me tidbits of information that painted a picture of a White House divided. These reports not only captured the public's imagination but also provided a narrative framework for understanding the undercurrents of power struggles within the administration. And sometimes, things really are exactly how they look.

Now, the culmination of my coverage on the Shade War came with my reporting on direct confrontations between advisors of Kamala Harris and those of Joe Biden, marking a shift from covert to overt conflict. I called out how Kamala's team was openly discussing the need for Biden to step aside as president, using phrases like "time to pass the buck." This escalation, first reported by me on July 18, 2024, underscored the depth of the rift and the stakes involved. I was able to document a significant and unprecedented chapter in modern White House history and also provide a roadmap to navigate and reveal the complexities of political power plays. When was the last time the public got to witness a show like this? Ever?

I also called out the fact that traditional media outlets either missed or chose to ignore *all* of this. The Shade War was not just a political drama; it's a reflection of the broader tensions within the Democratic Party regarding leadership, policy direction, and the future of progressive politics in America.

And ultimately, the Shade War brought us to this realization: Kamala Harris worked with Nancy Pelosi and the Obamas to push Biden out of the 2024 race.

More on that later.

THE DEBATE

"Geriatrics experts say . . . claim that Joe Biden is 'senile' is wrong."[1]
   "Biden is 'fit for duty' after annual physical . . . doctor says."[2]
   "Biden Deemed 'Healthy, Active, Robust'."[3]
   "'I'm in good shape': Joe Biden defends his health."[4]
   "'No New Concerns' for Biden's Health After Annual Physical."[5]
   "Biden's detractors saying 79 years old is too old to be riding a bicycle: Come on, man."[6]
   "[Biden is as] sharp as a tack."[7]

Joe Biden was not pulled from the presidency because he has dementia. He was pulled from the presidency because the American people found out.

The regime didn't care that Biden had dementia. They liked it. This made him all the more pliable for their many agendas. At least, until they couldn't cover it up anymore.

You've heard of misinformation and disinformation, but you may not know the difference. *Misinformation* is inaccurate information spread *without* the intent to deceive. It occurs when people share incorrect information believing it to be true. It is what it is. But *disinformation* is known false information spread *with* the intent to mislead. And there's a third—*malinformation*. Malinformation refers to facts based on reality that are used to inflict harm, such as mass deception. Unlike misinformation (and again, that's false info spread without intent to deceive) and disinformation (again, false information spread with intent to deceive), malinformation is true information that is weaponized to mislead.

The narrative surrounding President Joe Biden manufactured by the media prior to his contested 2020 election victory and during his presidency is a working example of all three. No, Biden's detractors do not say seventy-nine years old is too old to ride a bicycle; the public simply expressed concern over high-profile accidents Biden became known for in viral videos (misinformation).[8, 9] Definitely not sharp as a tack either; it's not reasonable to observe Biden firsthand and conclude as much (disinformation).[10] But yes, it *is* true it was reported that there were "'no new concerns" relating to Biden's health. Take this literal. *No new concerns.* Implying what? *There are concerns, but they are old. Just no new ones.* Interesting. True information, intent to deceive.

In fact, the Biden White House went so far as to create a new term for these incidents: *cheap fakes.* We were told that whenever a video of Biden went viral appearing frail and confused, that it was a cheap fake. And that seeming intent to deceive the world as to the Biden health crisis was indecent-exposed in the starkest possible context: the first (and last) 2024 US presidential debate between Joe Biden and Donald Trump. Trump, of course, had been speaking and posting at length for many months as to the absurdly obvious nature of Biden's decline. Memes were made; laughs were had. Some of us felt a little ashamed, because we have octogenarian family members enduring the same age-related decline, but with a bit more dignity. The allegation facing the White House—and the entire Biden family—is that they were keenly aware of all this and had been for years and lied anyway. Power corrupts.

At The People's Convention in Detroit, Michigan, where your humble coauthors launched our previous book *Unhumans,* Trump keynoted the weekend's activities. This was Saturday, June 15, 2024. With less than two weeks left till the debate, Trump bragged that his acceptance of the debate was a persuasion masterstroke, hinting (as we perceived his remarks live and in person) that this would metaphorically take Biden out of the race:

> Is anybody going to be watching the debate in this room? They gave me an offer that I couldn't accept. They said it's Fake [Jake]

Tapper is the moderator. They said it's a sit-down. It's a virtual room. Nobody in, nobody allowed in. Nobody allowed, not even your family . . . there'll be no audience whatsoever. And they turn off your mics when you finish speaking. They're trying to make this very exciting. They turn off your mics so that you can't talk while the other man is talking.[11]

Shortly thereafter:

[I]t's like the mob. They gave me an offer I couldn't accept. I said, "I accept." Because we want to get them to debate because here's what happened. They made an offer that was so ridiculous and they knew I was going to say no. And then they could go and they say Biden wanted to debate, but Trump refused to debate. But Trump refused to debate. He wouldn't do it. But I said yes. And now they don't know what the hell they're doing.

But remember this, all of their persecution of me and others is only happening because I'm running for president and leading very big in the polls.[12]

Big if true (it was).

With a staggering viewership of over 51 million, this event was a testament to the enduring significance of political debates in an era dominated by social media echo chambers. This debate, more than any other, became a focal point for the entire political spectrum, illustrating how debates have evolved into critical battlegrounds where candidates are forced to confront each other directly, away from the curated content of their respective social media bubbles.

In an age where information is consumed in bite-sized, often biased snippets, the full-length debate offered a rare opportunity for the public to see both candidates unfiltered. Social media, with its capacity for instant reaction and viral content, turned the debate into a real-time spectacle. However, unlike the tailored posts and tweets that dominate political discourse, the debate required viewers to engage with the candidates' unscripted responses, gaffes, and moments of clarity. This format, while often criticized for its theatrical elements, became essential because it was one of the few instances where supporters of both parties, along with the undecided, tuned in simultaneously, providing a shared experience in an otherwise fragmented media landscape.

It is clear that without the aid of his professional team of staffers, Biden was clearly suffering from mental decline. There was no way to hide it, and at a debate watched by everyone, there was no way to cover it up anymore. His team had lost it. The country, and the world, saw that the President Had No Clothes. The debate will go down in history as the event that started the stone rolling downhill that eventually ended the Biden presidency.

Sharp, Focused, Confused, Forgetful

Biden's performance at the presidential debate with Trump was so appalling, the entire news establishment suffered a cognitive dissonance seizure concurrently, exemplified by the Associated Press headline post-debate:

> Biden at 81: Often sharp and focused but sometimes confused and forgetful.[13]

We the people were assured that Biden's mishaps and gaffes these last few years had been mere coincidences and no worse than Trump's. But behind closed doors and with no recording devices present, this is no one you would want negotiating with Vladimir Putin, Hamas, the Taliban, or North Korea. This is why the White House blocked release of an audio recording in which Biden was interviewed by special counsel as to his mishandling of classified information, we assess.

The debate itself covered the topics you'd expect, with the usual set of memorized zingers from both sides. But the linguistic kill shot came from Trump, after this wandering about moment from Biden:

What I've done—since I've changed the law, what's happened? I've changed it in a way that now you're in a situation where there are 40 percent fewer people coming across the border illegally. It's better than when [Trump] left office. And I'm

going to continue to move until we get the total ban on the—
the total initiative relative to what we're going to do with more
Border Patrol and more asylum officers.[14]

Moderator Jake Tapper offered Trump to reply, who then said, "I really
don't know what he said at the end of that sentence. I don't think he
knows what he said either."[15]

And we're done. Biden's catastrophic performance proved the so-
called far right-wing conspiracy theory correct. And so, following the
cognitive dissonance display trying to make sense of the mis-dis-mal-
information marathon of the entire Biden administration run to cover
up his complete and total health decline, establishment media and
their Democrat-aligned voices retreated to a personal attack, summed
up as "actually, Trump is worse." No surprise there. As Scott Adams
commented:

> After the debate debacle, Democrats changed their messaging
> from "Biden is fine" to "He's better than a liar."
>
> Biden is literally the most dangerous liar in American his-
> tory. The Fine People Hoax divided the country like nothing
> before.[16]

You might recall the sole reason Biden gave (and continued to give)
for his 2020 presidential run was in fact the Fine People Hoax—the
oft-repeated, ever-debunked false claim that Donald Trump referred
to literal neo-Nazis as "fine people." Nothing like that happened. In
fact, quite the opposite.

> [Y]ou had people—and I'm not talking about the neo-Nazis
> and the white nationalists, because they should be condemned
> totally—but you had many people in that group other than
> neo-Nazis and white nationalists, okay? And the press has
> treated them absolutely unfairly. Now, in the other group also,
> you had some fine people, but you also had troublemakers and
> you see them come with the black outfits and with the helmets

and with the baseball bats—you had a lot of bad people in the other group too.[17]

There it is, Trump condemning the actual pro-hate groups on both the fringe-right and fringe-left (in the latter case, so-called "antifa"). And yet Biden built the very foundation of his administration, policy, and legacy on the worst lie in American history.[18] What continues to fascinate but not surprise is that the Democrat media machine, most notably the network MSNBC, continues to push the hoax seven years later.[19]

The anti-Trump response to the debate was initially a complete set of narcissistic personality disorder (NPD) traits. That set is better known by the acronym *DARVO*, which stands for *deny, attack,* and *reverse* the *victim* and the *offender*. First Biden's obvious decline was denied, then his opponent Trump was attacked, under the guise of defending Biden, whose entire administration and family were in fact culpable for what we dare to call . . . the Big Lie.

And so all eyes were on those closest to Joe Biden the man, in the very long days after his catastrophic debate performance, particularly on his wife Jill Biden, often seen guiding, pulling, or otherwise tugging her husband around in public as he shuffled about looking dazed and confused. Then of course there is the vice president, Kamala Harris, who stood to gain the most from a Biden exit. And of them and the entire administration's staff, together with the pro-Biden news media establishment, we ask the question that started the Shade War:

What did they know, and when did they know it?
After the debate, a leaked video depicting Trump in a golf cart beside son Barron foretold the future.

"How did I do at the debate the other night?" Trump asked, handing a crisp $100 bill to someone off-camera. He then referred to Biden as an "old broken-down pile of crap," as one does.

"He just quit, you know. He's quitting the race," Trump immediately added. "And that means we have Kamala. I think she's going to be better." On went the golf glove. "She's so bad. She's pathetic. She's so f—ing bad." Back to Biden. "Can you imagine that guy dealing with Putin and the president of China, who's a fierce person?" Then after a few reinforcing remarks about Joe versus the world, "They just announced he's—he's probably quitting."[20]

The leaked video was published on July 3, 2024. At that time, no such announcement had been made.

But much was yet to occur.

PART II
THE SHOT
Nine Days in July

DAY ONE, JULY 13, 2024:
THE SHOT

The air was thick with humidity as the western Pennsylvania heat pressed down on them like a heavy blanket. Rally-goers wiped their foreheads, already damp with sweat, and looked around at the bustling rally grounds. Colorful banners flapped lazily in the stifling breeze, and the murmur of voices rose and fell like waves crashing against a shore.

The crowd was a sea of faces, animated with excitement and energy despite the oppressive weather. Eager attendees pushed their way through, clothes clinging uncomfortably to their skin, searching for familiar faces. They had come to meet friends, all eager to support a cause they believed in deeply. The atmosphere was charged, a palpable sense of camaraderie and purpose in the air.

This day, **July 13, 2024**, Donald Trump would be arriving in the small town of Butler, Pennsylvania, about 40 miles north or so of the city of Pittsburgh. That same evening, Jill Biden, the First Lady of the United States, would be holding a dinner event in Pittsburgh, for the Italian Sons and Daughters of America. Trump, however, was hosting a political rally. The Republican National Convention would be taking place in two days, after all, and he wanted to make a good show, as well as hit the key state of Pennsylvania every chance he could.

Both Jill Biden and Donald Trump were at events within the same Secret Service field office area. A lot of the Secret Service was also in Milwaukee, preparing for the RNC. At this point, Secret Service is totally stretched thin, so they said. This wasn't a normal situation, and because of the lack of resources, the security posture was much lower. Susan Crabtree and Erik Prince have both reported that Jill Biden was awarded twelve Secret Service postholders for her evening event, while President Trump was awarded only three USSS postholders for his outdoor rally in broad daylight.

The normal crowd of people who would be around President Trump aren't there. His "A-Team" (including former Marine Chris LaCivita and political consultant Susie Wiles) aren't necessarily with him as much. Running a national campaign takes work, and it takes boots on the ground.

This wasn't just a random run-of-the-mill campaign stop. There was a strong theory that President Trump would bring his vice-presidential pick to that rally. He was holding a rally right on the border of Ohio that day, and we now know that he had also had a meeting at Mar-a-Lago with Senator JD Vance, who would go on to become the nominee.

We had heard that this was one of several plans under discussion. The vice-presidential nominee must be named on the first day of the convention. The idea for introducing him here was, "Well, why not just bring him to a rally and do it there?"

Ultimately, it was just a political question. "When are we going to get more bang for our buck for the announcement?" Now, the VP pick was not made until Monday, so Vance didn't end up traveling, but this was one of several plans under discussion. People watching this had every reason to believe Trump *and* his VP pick would be there.

The rally was set up like most other rallies are. In this case, there's a set of bleachers behind the podium—you always see these from the media cameras. But there's also bleachers off to the side, to the back left and back right, and above those was a JumboTron.

Like so many rallies, it was a mix of electric excitement and noise, in the summer heat. "It was beautiful outside," David Mosura, a witness to the shooting, said. "It was hot but it was beautiful."[1] People were enthusiastic. Something about this rally was different, and people could tell before it even started. Sean Parnell, Army Ranger combat veteran and author, was up on the stage opening for Trump, and he could tell that this rally wasn't like the others:

> I've been on the stage with President Trump five times, and from the moment that I walked into that rally, something just felt different. Like it was surreal, there was something in the air, couldn't quite put my finger on it.
>
> I spoke on stage, the flag got twisted up but ended up looking like an angel, or Jesus on the Cross, or an eagle . . . it was crazy, crazy enough that for the last 48 hours, people had been sending me different vantage points of it happening. And I didn't see it at the time, but I'm seeing it now, and piecing it all together after the fact.[2]

And then the music started. Lee Greenwood, "And I'm proud to be an American," rings out in the humid air as the crowd raises their smartphones to film Trump's arrival.

One attendee, Ben Shrader, was a special guest at the rally, and had the opportunity to meet Trump and take a photo a few minutes before the former president was heading out to speak. While others were in the bleachers, Shrader was in the VIP section with the mayor and a few other special guests, located to the left of the stage.[3]

Parnell, meanwhile, after speaking with the president, also sat down in the front row. "If you watched the rally on television, I was directly to the president's left, like maybe twenty feet away from where the podium was."[4]

At 6:03 p.m., Donald Trump walks to the podium. The crowd is cheering, chanting "USA! USA! USA!"

BBC News caught an interview with some attendees who attempted to walk into the rally after:

> So we walked up and probably five to seven minutes of Trump speaking—I'm estimating here, I have no idea—but we noticed a guy crawling . . . like bear crawling up the roof of the building beside us. Fifty feet away from us. So we're standing there and

we're pointing at the guy crawling up the roof . . . he had a rifle,
you can clearly see him with a rifle. Absolutely. We're pointing at
them, the police are down there running around on the ground.
And we're like, "Hey man, there's a guy on the roof with a rifle!"

And the police are like "Oh what!" like they didn't know
what was going on. We're like, "Hey, right here on the roof! You
can see him from right here! He's crawling."

And next thing you know, I'm thinking to myself, "Why is
Trump still speaking? Why have they not pulled him off the
stage?" I'm standing there pointing at him for two to three minutes, Secret Service is looking at us from the top of the barn.
I'm pointing at that roof, just standing there like this, and next
thing you know, five shots rang out.[5]

One of the attendees, who goes by the name @BrickSuit, later identified as Blake Marnell, described it to coauthor Jack in an interview.[6, 7]

And I'm a dead front, dead center in the front looking right at
the podium. I may be ten yards away from where the president
is gonna give his remarks. And he comes out, the entry music
plays, everything is going well. We're a few minutes into the
speech.

So President Trump brought up a slide where he's talking
about the rapid and incredible increase in illegal aliens crossing
our border from his administration compared to Joe Biden it's
administration.

And I was looking off to my left at that slide, so I was not
looking at the president when the first set of noises came out.

At 6:11 p.m., as Trump is looking at a chart displaying figures for
the rise in illegal immigration, his hand darts to his ear. @BrickSuit
continues:

I happened to be looking at the one on the left which was the
one that he was looking at as well, which would have been his

right, reversed. So I'm looking at that. I hear the first set of noises, very sharp cracks. I did not recognize them as being gunshots at first. I thought maybe it was a prank, you know, a really sick joke . . .

So I turned further to my left, looking in the crowd around me to see if maybe I could see something that would indicate, you know, what exactly what was going on. Maybe there was some firecrackers, you know, up. . . . A group of people reacting in a small bunch that would say, "Hey, this is where this is coming from." I didn't hear that.[8]

Parnell described seeing the shots himself.

. . . And he turns again, just like this, and it was at that moment that five or six shots rang out. I watched the whole thing. I heard the shots, I saw President Trump grab his ear, do something like this, and just went prone. Which by the way, was the exact right, from a tactical standpoint, exactly what he was supposed to do. But then the Secret Service was on him. And before I knew what was happening, because I knew instantly it was sniper fire, I had my wife, who was right next to me on the ground. We could hear the bullets crack over our head like a whip.[9]

David Mosura described what he saw, as close as he was to the president.

So the first round went off, and where I was sitting, I was so close I actually seen [sic] the hair under his hat flip up. There was a . . . I've been describing it as a misty debris. There was a misty debris that flew off the back, off his head. And looking back on it, that was probably tissue mixed with hair from him getting hit.[10]

Shrader, meanwhile, described what it was like from his vantage point in the VIP section:

> So we're sitting there. We get maybe just a few moments of him speaking. It's about thirty minutes after I got my photo with him, we get a few moments of him speaking and I hear *pop pop pop pop pop* and like . . . darts. I immediately know what a guns sounds like, and I'm thinking, "Somebody pulled out a handgun or something!" This is the first thought that's come to mind. So I duck, and I turn around as I do, and I look behind me. And I just see a lower body and legs and a *ton* of blood.
>
> And this is ten feet and right behind me. If it had been any different, we might not be talking right now. . . . I'd never seen anybody get shot before. It's not something glamorous like the movies. It's a terrible thing. I couldn't tell, man, woman, all I could see is a lot of blood. All over the bleachers.[11]

@BrickSuit thought it was fireworks. He wasn't the only one. One attendee, Michael, thought the same. "Some people thought it was fireworks. *I* thought it was fireworks!"[12] What @BrickSuit thought was a firecracker, some kind of joke, was actually a bullet.

Shrader, meanwhile, saw the crowd do the *opposite* of what he did, while laboring under the impression that the popping sounds were fireworks. They didn't go down.

> A lot of people, when the shooting started, they stood up and they looked around and they were like, "Oh, somebody snuck fireworks in!" I heard that multiple times.[13]

Parnell described the same behavior.

> And everybody else around us is kinda standing around . . . by the way, I don't mean that in a negative way. People were saying, "Oh, it's fireworks!" I'm like, "It's not fireworks, it's a sniper, everybody get down on the ground!"

When you're in a moment like that . . . it kinda kaleido-scopes around you. So lots of things happen at once. So first five shots rang out, Trump grabs his ear, goes prone. Secret Service is on him. And then I hear the *thump thump* a few seconds later, two, three, four seconds later, of the counter-sniper engaging with a heavier-caliber rifle. And at the exact same moment there was a few more shots. And so I think they were engaging at the same time. And that's when I think the people sitting right behind us were tragically hit, one in the stomach and one in the head.[14]

Another eyewitness, Todd Gerhart, a vendor at the site, saw the aftermath of the shot.

There was some liquid flying out of one of the cranes, and the bullets had hit the hydraulic lines, and there . . . and there's big, black speakers that these cranes hold up, and down comes the speakers. It didn't hit anybody.[15]

Immediately, Trump dropped, diving under the podium as people screamed. More cracks echoed, and black-suited Secret Service agents dove down on top of him. @BrickSuit recounted it himself.

So I turned from my left back to look at the president straight ahead, and he was no longer there. And I could see the Secret Service agents coming onto the stage and basically jumping on top of him . . .

And I should tell you, too, that this is only like five minutes into the rally. Everybody's standing up at this time. Nobody's sitting down. It was a hot day, but enthusiasm to see President Trump was high. Energy was high and everybody was still standing up.

But at this time, you know, I heard people saying, "Get down, get down." And I, I kinda kneeled down for a little bit.[16]

Screams still filled the air, shouts and cries at the sight of Trump dropping to the ground. Was he okay? Had they just witnessed history?
The start of a civil war?

Had they just witnessed the assassination of a presidential candidate?
For a moment, nobody knew.

Mosura recounted seeing Trump on the ground:

I'm looking around and I see Trump's feet. It's all you can see.
They had everything else covered up. He was missing his shoe,
and his feet were not moving. And I thought, "Man, they did
this right in front of us!"[17]

Then it went quiet. As Todd Gerhart noted, "It's despair. You . . . I
mean, you don't know what's going on."[18] @BrickSuit continued on
with his own account of the events.

And then when the shots stopped and I thought it was safe, I
stood up again and I was just focusing on the well-being of the
president.

There was no screaming in the crowd, not . . . There was, but
not that you couldn't hear anything. There was no panic.

I was able to focus on what was going on in front of me, and
I could hear what the Secret Service agents were saying. And
something I took comfort in at that time was they didn't seem
overly panicked. They weren't calling for medical. They weren't,
you know, they weren't saying anything that indicated to me
that there was a really grave injury there, until they said, "Let's
get ready to move him." And that may be the parlance that they
use when they, when they move a protectee from one place to
another, they say, "Let's get ready to move him."

But I interpreted it as how are they gonna move him? Are
they, are they carrying him out? Is he incapacitated? Is it worst-
case scenario?

And before I could get all the way to the end of that thought
process, we saw him stand up. [19]

Tom Natoli, the Man in the Green Hat who stood directly behind Trump, in an exclusive interview for this book, described it like this:

> When I saw him go down, I thought he was he was gone. And it was like I felt a huge punch to my gut.
>
> You know? It was like somebody hit me in my gut, and it was like, I just don't believe this. The only reason I wasn't, you know, fearful was I just had this surge of anger come over me. You know, I just had this intense feeling of anger came over me. And I kept saying to myself, how dare they do this to the president? How dare they? How dare they do this for my president? You know what I mean? [20]

Mosura described what happened the moment leading up to the now famous photo.

> It was surreal. Like you said at the beginning, this is Butler! Who expects this? What are the odds that it happens at all? What are the odds that it happens in Butler, Pennsylvania? What are the odds that it happens and I'm standing right there? Especially when everybody prior to this, everybody was happy, everybody was laughing and enjoying everything he was saying, and enjoying the atmosphere!
>
> . . . Like I said, when they had him on the ground, and I could just see his feet, I honestly thought to myself, "They killed him, he's dead." And at that point, I looked up and I was still looking around for who was shooting, and at that point I see the person in the bleachers that was hit. So when I'm making my way down, at that point I made the decision, I'mma make my way down to those bleachers and try to get to that person.
>
> At some point they stood him up. And I remember hearing it, but I'd never seen it. I never seen them stand him up, until I heard the crowd. When I heard the crowd roar when he stood up. I looked up and seen him standing there for a split second. [21]

What came next would end up plastered on T-shirts, billboards, and across every computer monitor and television screen in America. After a moment where the Secret Service, huddled around Trump, managed to get him on his feet, he broke through their human shield-wall with an upraised fist.

Fight!
Fight!
Fight!

The crowd erupted into cheers. As @BrickSuit recounted:

> . . . then I saw his face. And I saw his eyes. And I saw the fire in his expression. And he raised his fist, and he made that gesture. And I could tell he was saying something. I didn't know what he was saying at the time. But I knew then, and I felt then that he was, he was gonna be alright.[22]

Jack's friend Raheem Kassam, observed what everyone who saw that moment realized:

> I think all of you can probably agree with me here is that the extraordinary nature to take a bullet, to be in front of crowd, but your first thought . . . your first thought is probably like, you know, "Am I dead?" The second thought is, "These people are counting on me to get up and inspire them." And when you think about President Trump's entire career, his entire trajectory, that has been it. And that moment was a microcosm of just who he is as a human being. Knock him down, get back up, knock him down, get back up, every single time.[23]

Trump was then rushed off stage, fist in the air, bloodied face held high.

The aftermath was chaos. One attendee even recounts that he had gotten into a fistfight with someone.[24] Confusion, but not panic, as the crowd did not start scrambling.[25] "But what was amazing is the whole crowd sat there under control. It was unbelievable," another witness described.[26] Shrader recounts it himself.

From there . . . there was a lot of confusion. No one had cell service, that's something that really has to be taken into account, because so many people were on their phones. So throughout the crowd there are rumors spreading. "Was Trump seriously injured?" When I looked up there, I didn't think he'd been hit at all. When I looked up there, he looked strong as ever!

. . . A tactical team moved up into the bleachers—guys in body armor, helmets, rifles—where the person had been shot. I yelled "Shooter, shooter!" and I hit the deck at this point, make myself the smallest target, what else is there to do?

There was a lot of confusion. People were not sure about what was going on. Some people got up on *chairs,* and were looking around, just because a lot of people thought, "It's just fireworks" or it was just something else. But once people saw [the injured] . . . what happened next, sort of, was, as people realized somebody had been hit—and, funny enough, screams were a well documented thing. I don't remember the screams. For me, that was just blotted out . . .

. . . And as people saw the person who had been shot . . . there was a lot of blood, it was not a small amount. And basically, they were looking, and then fear, I wouldn't say fear, but concern, started spreading out from the VIP section. Because where the person got hit was in the bleacher, I believe it was the union section . . . Ten feet, not far at all . . . people tried giving him CPR, and from what I saw, from popping up and looking, there was no response.

. . . Who expects this? I didn't expect this in the least . . . I thought overall the security was good. There were a lot of them, there were tons! And when we'd gone backstage, they had tons of guys in military gear, rifles, ready to go. And I was shocked, I didn't see this coming, and I will admit, y'know, I'll walk over

broken glass to vote for the former president, especially after
something like this.

   But I don't think I will go to another rally for years, for any
political candidate. Just because, to hear the whizzing of the
bullet and to . . . to literally have somebody where you could
walk over to them in moments, just get hit. And then to see
that and the aftermath of that is not something that you want
to see.[27]

Mosura told his family afterwards that it would sink in. That the enor-
mity of what they witnessed would hit them.

   When we [Mosura and his niece] were in the car ride home, and
   I even told my sister, I said, "You don't realize it right now, what
   happened. But tonight or tomorrow, you'll be laying in bed,
   and you'll just be sitting there thinking, and then it's gonna
   click in your head. And it might bother you, but eventually
   you're gonna realize the magnitude of what happened."

      My niece asked me, she goes, "When's the last time anything
   like this happened?" And I said, "I think Ronald Reagan in
   1980." This doesn't happen! . . . I never ever ever ever dreamed—
   or had nightmares—that this would ever happen. Ever.[28]

Later, at the RNC, Trump recounted the assassination attempt from
his own perspective.

   As you already know, the assassin's bullet came within a quarter
   of an inch of taking my life. So many people have asked me
   what happened. "Tell us what happened, please." And therefore, I will tell you exactly what happened, and you'll never
   hear it from me a second time, because it's actually too painful
   to tell.

      It was a warm, beautiful day in the early evening in Butler
   Township in the great Commonwealth of Pennsylvania. Music
   was loudly playing, and the campaign was doing really well. I

went to the stage and the crowd was cheering wildly. Everybody was happy. I began speaking very strongly, powerfully and happily. Because I was discussing the great job my administration did on immigration at the southern border. We were very proud of it.

Behind me, and to the right, was a large screen that was displaying a chart of border crossings under my leadership. The numbers were absolutely amazing. In order to see the chart, I started to, like this, turn to my right, and was ready to begin a little bit further turn, which I'm very lucky I didn't do, when I heard a loud whizzing sound and felt something hit me really, really hard. On my right ear. I said to myself, "Wow, what was that? It can only be a bullet."

And moved my right hand to my ear, brought it down. My hand was covered with blood. Just absolutely blood all over the place. I immediately knew it was very serious. That we were under attack. And in one movement proceeded to drop to the ground. Bullets were continuing to fly as very brave Secret Service agents rushed to the stage. And they really did. They rushed to the stage.

These are great people at great risk, I will tell you, and pounced on top of me so that I would be protected. There was blood pouring everywhere, and yet in a certain way I felt very safe because I had God on my side. I felt that.

The amazing thing is that prior to the shot, if I had not moved my head at that very last instant, the assassin's bullet would have perfectly hit its mark and I would not be here tonight. We would not be together. The most incredible aspect of what took place on that terrible evening, in the fading sun, was actually seen later. In almost all cases, as you probably know. And when even a single bullet is fired, just a single bullet, and we had many bullets that were being fired, crowds run for the exits or stampede. But not in this case. It was very unusual.

This massive crowd of tens of thousands of people stood by and didn't move an inch. In fact, many of them bravely but automatically stood up, looking for where the sniper would be. They knew immediately that it was a sniper. And then began pointing at him. You can see that if you look at the group behind me. That was just a small group compared to what was in front.

Nobody ran and, by not stampeding, many lives were saved. But that isn't the reason that they didn't move. The reason is that they knew I was in very serious trouble. They saw it. They saw me go down. They saw the blood, and thought, actually most did, that I was dead.

They knew it was a shot to the head. They saw the blood. And there's an interesting statistic. The ears are the bloodiest part. If something happens with the ears they bleed more than any other part of the body. For whatever reason the doctors told me that.

And I said, "Why is there so much blood?"

He said, "It's the ears, they bleed more."

So we learned something. But they just—

They just, this beautiful crowd, they didn't want to leave me. They knew I was in trouble. They didn't want to leave me. And you can see that love written all over their faces. True.

Incredible people. They're incredible people. Bullets were flying over us, yet I felt serene. But now the Secret Service agents were putting themselves in peril. They were in very dangerous territory.

Bullets were flying right over them, missing them by a very small amount of inches. And then it all stopped. Our Secret Service sniper, from a much greater distance and with only one bullet used, took the assassin's life. Took him out.

I'm not supposed to be here tonight. Not supposed to be here.

[Crowd chants "Yes, you are."]

Thank you. But I'm not. And I'll tell you. I stand before you in this arena only by the grace of almighty God.

And watching the reports over the last few days, many people say it was a providential moment. Probably was. When I rose, surrounded by Secret Service, the crowd was confused because they thought I was dead. And there was great, great sorrow. I could see that on their faces as I looked out. They didn't know I was looking out; they thought it was over.

But I could see it and I wanted to do something to let them know I was OK. I raised my right arm, looked at the thousands and thousands of people that were breathlessly waiting and started shouting, "Fight, fight, fight."

Thank you.

Once my clenched fist went up, and it was high into the air, you've all seen that, the crowd realized I was OK and roared with pride for our country like no crowd I have ever heard before. Never heard anything like it.

For the rest of my life, I will be grateful for the love shown by that giant audience of patriots that stood bravely on that fateful evening in Pennsylvania.[29]

Later on, in an interview with Breitbart, Trump described just how *lucky* he was.

"So what are the odds that I'm looking to the right?" Trump said. "The poster is never used early, and it's never on the right it's always on the left. If you take the odds of this whole thing it's like 10 million to one and you only have an eighth of a second."

As Trump said this, he started moving his head to various angles and pointing out he'd be dead in all but one angle in which he's alive which he thankfully is today.

"I'm turning, and I'm dead here, I'm dead here, I'm dead here, dead, dead, alive, dead," Trump said. "So, think, you only have this exact spot right here. This is an amazing phenomena. It's millions to nothing. There's about an eighth of a second where I'm good. The rest of the time you're dead."[30]

He further explained that he doesn't use the graphic that saved his life until the end of the speech, and that the odds that it would have been different this time was astronomical. For one, Trump doesn't typically look at the immigration poster. It's usually on the opposite side from where it was that day at Butler. He doesn't usually look at it. And if he does use it *and* look at it, it's towards the end of the "show," as Trump put it.

Trump detailed the second he was shot as he continued explaining the angles that saved his life.

"So when I'm looking at the audience, I'm like this—he's got me right here," Trump said. "Then I go look like this when he's ready to shoot because I have the immigration sign. So I'm going like that. I said 'you take a look at how well we did,' and boom. Then remember I took my hand and I looked my hand has blood all over my hand. All over—and I went down. If I didn't go down I would have been hit. That I don't consider as lucky because that's going down. The amazing thing is if my head is even turned like this I get hit. If it's turned like this I get hit. The only thing I could have been is flat. I'm like this, and he was exactly there 90 degrees—dead parallel."[31]

In the Bible, the Holy Spirit is consistently referred to as a gust of wind. In fact, the term Holy Ghost and the word "gust" have the same root in Old English. For those who believe, as we do, God Himself intervened to protect the former president that day.

Ephesians 6:11 is "Put on the full armor of God, so that you will be able to stand firm against the schemes of the devil."

Donald Trump was shot at 6:11 p.m.

Unfortunately, the shooter wasn't the only casualty. Two people—David Dutch and James Copenhaver—were wounded, and tragically, one man—Corey Comperatore—lost his life.

David Dutch, a fifty-seven-year-old Marine Corps vet who served in Desert Storm, had been struck twice—once in the stomach, and once in the liver.[32] He was hospitalized, and put in a medically induced coma. On Wednesday, July 24, he was discharged from Allegheny General.[33]

James Copenhaver, seventy-four years old, had been standing on Trump's left side when he was shot in his arm and abdomen. As his lawyer explained:

> He had almost heard or even seen something kind of whizz past them, which we're assuming is a bullet. And he . . . looked down at his arm and . . . felt pain initially, but he didn't even realize that he had been shot a second time at that point. . . . He had mentioned that he was in quite a bit of shock at that time. There was a lot of pandemonium. People were screaming. No one really quite knew what was going on right away.[34]

His lawyer followed up that account with an assurance that Copenhaver "is unafraid to voice his support for Trump, and he will not allow those who disagree with his views to silence him or prevent him from exercising his rights."[35] He was discharged from the hospital on Friday, July 26.[36]

Unfortunately, not every casualty was so lucky.

Fire Chief Corey Comperatore was in the crowd when the shots rang out. And while others screamed and panicked, Comperatore threw himself over his wife and daughters, shielding them with his own body.[37] One of the bullets fired claimed his life, but his wife and two daughters survived the shooting because Corey yelled at them to "get down!" He took a bullet that may have been headed in their way, killing him instantly. He gave his life to protect those most important to him.

His daughter Allyson recounted what had happened:

> I was the one that my dad threw down. As he was throwing me down, that was when he was shot and he ended up falling onto me.
>
> I don't remember hearing any other shots. I don't remember feeling any other shots. In that moment, I was trying to take care of him.

I was really confused when he was on me. I had turned around, and I went, "Dad," and when I turned is when he fell down, and that's when I started screaming and instantly I was trying to keep him from bleeding.[38]

Meanwhile, his other daughter Kaylee said:

I started screaming, but in my head, I kept saying, "Wake up," like this is a dream.

And then you realize it's not a dream, and you feel like your whole world is just over.[39]

Helen, devastated by the loss, said she remembers Corey not as a victim, but as a hero—a man who lived his life with courage, love, and selflessness.

He was just a wonderful man, and I want everybody to try not to remember him as the man that was shot at the rally. Just try to remember Corey as, he was a great man that was a great father. He was a great husband.[40]

And at the Republican National Convention, Trump took the stage accompanied by Comperatore's firefighter jacket and helmet.[41]

But how did the Trumpworld react to this?

Honestly, with a "We told you so."

Major movers and shakers in these dissident spaces were *predicting* that someone would go after Trump. That with all the escalating rhetoric, with all the hyperbolic announcements during Trump's presidency that *any day now* he would snap and plunge America into a dictatorial nightmare, with all the horrified mock-terror at his actions on social media after Biden took office . . . this was bound to happen. What had we been saying the whole time?

"We warned you!"

And we had! Alex Jones, Tucker Carlson, Steve Bannon, Scott Adams, Roger Stone . . . and coauthor Jack Posobiec had sounded the alarm loudly that someone would go after Trump. They would *need* to, if the media was to be believed. Trump was a "threat to our democracy" and "needs to be stopped."[42, 43] Or, consider the words of President Joe Biden, delivered June 28, a mere *two weeks* before the assassination attempt:

> I've got a lot more to say, but I'm not going to take a lot of your time. Let me close with this. Donald Trump is a genuine threat to this nation. That is not hyperbole. He's a threat to our freedom. He's a threat to our democracy. He is literally a threat to the America that we stand for.[44]

Literally a threat to the America that we stand for.

America, land of the free and the home of the brave, under threat from this wannabe dictator. And somehow, he's hoodwinked most of the electorate into giving "Literally Hitler"—as the meme goes—a fair chance at the ballot box. Someone needed to stop him, *by any means necessary.*

At least, according to the media coverage of Trump.

You had to be blind—willfully or otherwise—not to see it. We weren't. We had seen this coming *years* before it happened.

Steve Bannon predicted that an assassination attempt was not off the table, pinning the blame—according to his suspicions—on the Deep State as *far back as August 2022,*[45] almost *two years* before Trump would come within a half-inch of death. "I do not think it's beyond this administrative state and the Deep State apparatus, to actually try to work on the assassination of President Trump. I think everything is on the table."[46]

Tucker Carlson, speaking on the *Adam Carolla Show* in *August 2023,* described how Democratic escalation left them no other choice. The trajectory was clear.

> If you begin with criticism, then you go to protest, then you go to impeachment, now you go to indictment and none of them work. . . . What's next? Graph it out, man! We are speeding towards assassination obviously, and no one will say that, but I don't know how you *can't* reach that conclusion. They have

decided—Permanent Washington, both parties—have decided that there's something about Trump that's so threatening to them, they just can't have it.[47]

Scott Adams, meanwhile, tweeted on September 12, 2023:

> Half of the so-called "news" this week looks like a coordinated op to jail or kill Trump and Musk.
> How crazy that idea would sound a few years ago.
> Democrats will pretend to not understand this post and attack me personally. I feel sorry for them.[48]

What was the news? That Trump was "a criminal and he's crazy and he's stupid."[49] That while Biden may be old, the opposing choice was "depravity."[50] That all his followers—half the country—are in a cult, and that abducting them to "deprogram" them is rejected only because it's logistically infeasible.[51] That he's a threat to witnesses at federal trial, a "danger to the community" and "should be detained pending trial"[52] and that the threat of Trump needed to be "neutralized."[53] So much of a threat, mind you, that lawsuits were filed to remove Trump from the ballot in Colorado.[54] So much of a threat to democracy, it seems, that the subjects (sorry, citizens) of Colorado need to be legally barred from democratically electing him.

Alex Jones, speaking at Turning Point Action in Detroit on 6/16/2024 (where we were launching our book *Unhumans* at the time). "They are going to try to assassinate President Trump, make no mistake about that. They are going to try to pull out all the stops!"[55]

But it wasn't just political pundits who were growing vocal. Several heads in Silicon Valley were turning to see Trump's courage under fire. First came a name we're all very familiar with. Elon Musk pledged millions of dollars to the Trump campaign.[56] He was quickly followed by Marc Andreessen and Ben Horowitz, then venture capitalist David Sacks (who had previously supported Hillary Clinton), cofounder of Palantir Joe Lonsdale, and venture capitalist Doug Leone.[57] They were later joined by Jacob Helberg, an advisor for Palantir, and Sequoia Capital partner Shaun Maguire.[58, 59]

Where was the media in all this?

While the video evidence of the assassination attempt was going viral on Twitter/X, the media rushed to publish headlines like . . . "Secret Service Rushes Trump Off Stage After He Falls at Rally," courtesy of CNN,[60] making it sound like Trump wandered around the stage and took a tumble, and either a) he's overreacting to a scraped knee and getting Secret Service involved, or b) he's as old and infirm and this fall posed a major risk to Trump's frail life (no doubt to distract from Biden's incoherent rambling and sunsetting behavior).

Or take this doozy of a headline, from *USA Today*. "Trump removed from stage by Secret Service after loud noises startles former president, crowd."[61] If you search for that, they've changed it to "Trump wounded at rally in assassination attempt; gunman killed."[62] Maybe the first headline—which insinuated that Trump got spooked by some unspecified loud sound and panicked and called the Secret Service to take him away—was a bit too much of a liability to leave up.

Or this one, courtesy of the Associated Press immediately after the shooting. "BREAKING: Donald Trump has been escorted off the stage by Secret Service during a rally after loud noises ring out in the crowd."[63] Maybe less egregious than the others mentioned above, but it sounds more like a paranoid reaction, rather than *a presidential candidate being shot*. (Note that that article's headline has since changed.)

But all of these headlines are true. *Technically* true.

Rather than covering the shooting as an unfolding event, the mainstream media was busy spreading *malinformation*. They didn't directly lie, nor did they promote unproven claims (such as one man claiming the cameraman was the intended assassin, and had been killed by local law enforcement and whose death was being covered up).[64] No, instead, they told the truth. Just not the whole truth.

Every headline was *technically* accurate (true information) but made to imply an inaccurate turn of events (true information weaponized to harm). Note that those headlines did anything they could to avoid calling it an assassination attempt. And when called out for that, mainstream media outlets release copium excuse pieces trying to justify not calling a spade a spade by saying that calling gunshots anything other than "loud pops" would be "irresponsible."[65]

FBI Director Chris Wray got in on this too in a public hearing, as our coauthor Joshua noted.

Notice that in the hearing yesterday, Wray gave equal plausibility to bullet OR "shrapnel."

This assigns EQUAL CLOUT to the known fact that Trump was SHOT . . . and to the Far-Left Conspiracy Theory that he was NOT.

. . . Wray further cast aside the credibility of the known, objective fact that Trump was shot by strategically offering a non-answer to the question of the eight bullets fired.

Wray just hypnotized half the country into "knowing" Trump was not shot, which gives Kamala the mass media persuasion & energy & sympathy advantage.[66]

And how did Joe Biden, who said that they needed to put Trump in a bull's-eye, react? Thoughts and prayers, the usual, and nothing about their own inciting rhetoric.

And what of the shooter? Did he act alone? More on that coming up next.

DAY TWO, JULY 14, 2024: THE SHOOTER

On June 22, 2024, US Air Force veteran Bill Jenkins registered for an intermediate handgun-pistol class at Keystone Shooting Center in Cranberry, Pennsylvania. There was only one other student. In Jenkins's words:

> He was quite young. Very quiet. Seemed friendly. Nice kid.
>
> So we went into the range and each took our booths. We were right next to each other, and he had already . . . loaded and was firing before I had gotten my gun even loaded . . . [s]o I figured he was experienced. And he ended up doing better than me because on the further distances, he had shot one area so many times that it blew out a hole in the target.
>
> Towards the end of the classroom discussion . . . [e]ventually I got into politics. He wasn't saying anything. He remained quiet. So I was kind of, you know, waiting to see what this guy would do because he was getting a little tense there. And he never said a word. He just sat there, kind of smiled, looked, and didn't say anything.
>
> So I was surprised at that, not knowing what was going to happen in the future. But even then, I was kind of like, "How come this guy isn't saying anything? Yay or nay?"[1]

That quiet young man was identified on **July 14, 2024**, publicly as Thomas Matthew Crooks—the man who shot President Donald J. Trump and three of his supporters.

Before Butler

From the outset, Crooks's life seemed unremarkable to the casual observer. He attended Bethel Park High School, where he graduated in 2022, appearing in school videos as just another student, albeit one who would later be scrutinized for every action and expression.[2] And while some students said he was bullied (for wearing hunting/camo outfits to school and also for wearing COVID masks), both the school and other students denied or downplayed it.[3, 4, 5] However, conspiracy theorists argue that his presence in a BlackRock advertisement, albeit brief and unpaid, was no coincidence but rather a deliberate marker, a breadcrumb for those who would later connect the dots to financial giants and their alleged control over global events.[6]

Crooks was born in a modest home to a family described as "politically mixed" by the *New York Times*.[7] He excelled academically, and even won a "Star Award" from the National Math and Science Initiative.[8] He was a bit of a loner, interested in computers, and worked at a nursing home where he assisted in the kitchen.[9] While doing that, he had earned an associate degree in engineering science from his local community college and intended to attend Robert Morris University.[10, 11]

The narrative thickens with Crooks's political affiliations. A registered Republican who also donated to a progressive PAC, this dichotomy fuels theories of manipulation, suggesting he was being groomed or influenced by forces with an agenda beyond the political spectrum.[12] His research into past assassinations, encrypted communications, and interest in both Trump and Biden as targets, paints a picture of a young man not driven by ideology but by a form of accelerationism, a desire to hasten systemic collapse or change through extreme acts. Among the myriad of searches, terms like "major depressive disorder" stood out, suggesting Crooks might also have been grappling with his own mental health, possibly undiagnosed or untreated.[13] This revelation came not from a direct admission but from the digital breadcrumbs he left behind, indicating a self-awareness or at least a curiosity about his own psychological state.

His searches weren't confined to personal introspection; they ventured into the realm of public figures and political events. Crooks had researched not only Trump but also other high-profile individuals like President Joe Biden, Attorney General Merrick Garland, and even members of the British Royal Family.[14] This broad spectrum of interest in powerful figures suggested not a political motive in the traditional sense but perhaps an obsession with power, fame, or the act of disruption itself. His queries into past assassinations, including that of John F. Kennedy, alongside logistical searches like "how far was Oswald from Kennedy," indicated a mind that was not only planning but also learning from historical acts of violence.[15]

The juxtaposition of these searches with more ordinary inquiries, like his last known search for pornography just before the attack, adds layers to his psychological profile.[16] This mix of the profound with the trivial in his search history underscores a life where the line between normalcy and extreme behavior was blurred. While investigators found no direct evidence of mental health issues in his physical interactions or social media presence, the depth of his online inquiries—from historical assassinations to the mechanics of his planned attack—suggests a mind that was possibly wrestling with deep-seated issues, perhaps exacerbated by isolation or a quest for significance.

This paints a picture of a young man whose actions might have been driven by a mix of personal turmoil, a quest for notoriety, and a fascination with violence, rather than a coherent ideological stance. The FBI's deep dive into his devices aimed to uncover any co-conspirators or deeper motives but found a portrait of a troubled individual whose actions were likely the culmination of his internal struggles rather than external influences.

What was Crooks doing on the gun range that day in June? We know. Why had he googled "how far away was Oswald from Kennedy" on July 6, then "Where will Trump speak from at Butler Farm Show"?[17, 18] We know. Why had Crooks visited a local shooting range on July 13 to practice with his father's AR-15-style DPMS DR-15 rifle?[19] We know.

And why were there remote-detonatable bombs found in Crooks's Hyundai Sonata? That we don't know. Crooks had used a fake name to purchase six "chemical precursors" together with twenty-five separate purchases from online gun stores. "Crooks took great pains to conceal his online activities, which shows he was engaged in meticulous planning even well ahead of the campaign rally. . . . It was not immediately known if any of the purchases were actual firearms, though federal law requires background and ID checks before buying a gun in most cases," reported the *New York Post*.[20]

About those bombs, we first heard they were rudimentary pipe bombs. That does not seem to be the case. The bombs were in ammo cans, a source in the federal explosive ordinance community tells us exclusively, which was later confirmed.[21, 22] I (Jack) actually predicted as much earlier.[23] The source saw photographs of the improvised explosive divides. As of this writing, we don't know if they were metal or plastic, but the containers looked plastic-like and contained some sort of tannerite or fuel oil–type mixture. Electric matches from fireworks were to be used as detonators. We don't think that would've worked other than starting a fire or perhaps mechanically exploding the cans. It doesn't seem to us that Crooks knew enough to be effective, but he was certainly in the right direction.[24]

Although Crooks did score higher than 1500 on his SAT and could name every US president correctly and in order, we are not convinced that this is the sort of device a random twenty-year-old would come up with on his own.[25, 26, 27] In fact, if he knew how to conceal his internet activity, why would he bother trying to design his own IEDs and instead not use the dark side of the web to look up how to do it, or even contact someone who knew how? Is that why we haven't seen any pictures of the explosives? At least we've seen pictures of the detonator (found beside Crooks's body), provided by local police, not federal law enforcement.[28] Investigators suggested that Crooks's plan was to detonate the vehicle during the shooting as a distraction, or perhaps after.[29] The more questions go unanswered, the more questions surface.

Why was Crooks using encrypted messaging accounts on various platforms located in Belgium, New Zealand, and Germany? Why does "a health care aid need encrypted platforms not even based in the United States, but based abroad—where most terrorist organizations know it is harder for our law enforcement to get into?"[30] Why? Was he in communication with someone(s) through those accounts, perhaps on the matter of how to build explosives? We don't know. We the public need to see the sophistication of these bombs. And not just these, but that of the pipe bombs from January 6, 2021.

Recall that an alleged pipe bomb was discovered directly outside the Democratic National Committee headquarters. United States Secret Service, DC Metro PD officials, and Capitol Police officers, after having been informed of the presence of the alleged bomb, did nothing. Vice President–elect Kamala Harris was right inside. Passersby were allowed to walk around and in front of the alleged bomb. It's all on video.[31] Yet it was never acknowledged by law enforcement or in the news media that there *was* a bomb threat to her life. Why was there no "Kamala Harris sworn in as vice president after surviving an assassination attempt on her life on January 6" outcry at the outset of the Biden-Harris administration? And why is there video of what looks to be a police officer carrying a bag to the location where the alleged pipe bomb was found fifteen minutes later?[32]

Are you thinking what we're thinking? (You are.)

Back to Crooks now, we've also learned that additional explosives were found at his place of residence. What kid is like that? Our sons are not (yet) twenty years old, but if we learned our kids were literally making homemade bombs, we're going to find out. Are we going to show them a better way to run that circuit? Say, "Are you winnin', son"? No. We are going to shut that down as fast as humanly possible while extolling the virtues of keeping yourself off watch lists.

Speaking of the Crooks home, why was the entire house cleaned like a hospital room, and why was silverware missing?[33] A candid photo of Crooks's father, to put it crass, seemed to reveal a sloppy family you'd expect to be hoarders, at least in our opinion.[34] And some reports stated so as well. If indeed the explosives were built in the Crooks house, why are the shooter's parents "unlikely to face criminal charges," at the time of this writing?[35] Especially after school shooter

Ethan Crumbley's parents were both sentenced to ten years in prison because the gun in their home, used in the crime, had not been secured properly. But there's more, from CNN:

> On his primary cellphone, investigators found an image of the arrest photo of Ethan Crumbley—the student who shot and killed four classmates at a Michigan high school in 2021— along with information about Crumbley and his parents, who were both found guilty of involuntary manslaughter, the first time parents of a school shooter have been prosecuted.[36]

Perhaps this open loop is why Crooks's parents hired Quinn Logue, a Pittsburgh-based law firm specializing in both criminal defense and civil suits including wrongful death and personal injury?[37] What did they know and when did they know it? Were they in on it? It is also reported that Crooks looked up info on Ethan Crumbley and his parents, perhaps worried the same would happen to his mother and father. In an interview with Monica Crowley two-and-a-half months after the shooting, President Trump would describe the situation as "suspicious." To the question, "Does it look increasingly to you like this was a suspicious, maybe even inside job?" Trump replied:

> Well, it's strange. The father hired the most expensive lawyer. He lives in the area, supposedly, not very much money. He hired the most expensive lawyer. Think of this. Who's paying for this lawyer in Pennsylvania. High end, very, very expensive lawyer, top of the line, right? You know, where does he get the money to hire a lawyer that costs hundreds of thousands of dollars? Is the lawyer doing it for free? I doubt it. Are the Democrats paying for his legal fees? . . . Maybe they are. Maybe they're not, but who's paying for this lawyer? . . . There's so many things going on here, that you do have to wonder. I wasn't thinking this way 3 weeks ago. But the more you see it, the more you say there could be something else. And that's really dangerous for the country."[38]

At the very least, his father, Matthew Crooks, contacted local police to alert them his son and a rifle had gone missing; this was shortly after Trump was hit.[39] Police were then dispatched to the Crooks home. However, US Representative and former Navy SEAL Eli Crane says he has received information that the Crooks home was indeed hospital-like scrubbed (including of that silverware) **prior** to local investigative units arriving.[40] A user on X (formerly Twitter), @RPEnheim connected the dots for us:

> Basically the insinuation would be that assets scrubbed all DNA evidence that may connect someone outside the family to the home.
>
> This would tie into public info claims that several phones' data are tired to that location.
>
> Pointing to someone was in Crooks' home helping him.[41]

That's right; we can't forget about the phones. The Heritage Foundation's Oversight Project "found the assassin's connections through . . . in-depth analysis of mobile ad data to track movements of Crooks and his associates. To do this, [the Project] tracked devices that regularly visited both Crooks's home and place of work and followed them."[42] A follow-up post in that thread read, "Someone who regularly visited Crooks home and work also visited a building in Washington, DC located in Gallery Place. This is in the same vicinity of an FBI office on June 26, 2023. Who's [sic] device is this?"[43]

Whose device indeed. Note that it was Spring 2023 that Crooks had begun making his weapons purchases, so the assassination preparation had likely already begun.[44] Left-wing media dismissed this information as, as one outlet put it, "catnip for MAGA conspiracy theorists," instead of attempting to corroborate or invalidate the information.[45] Why so little curiosity? We might know. You might, too.

Chatter online the day after the shooting failed to surface Thomas Crooks's personal social media accounts. It's as if he was a total ghost. This defies plausibility. What twenty-year-old in the United States is a ghost on social media? We know he used those encrypted accounts, and he also knew how to use virtual private networks (VPN) to conceal his online activity. He also used Tor, the anonymous internet browser. It's obvious he masked his identity online just long enough. How did he know to do that? The FBI claims they accessed Crooks's email accounts and "found no indications that anyone else was involved in the attack" and that his activities online "largely related to weapons and ammunition purchases,"[46] details which the agency reportedly related to President Trump in a private meeting, the standard victim interview. The adverb *largely* is heavy-lifting. The FBI initially claimed that the ninth and tenth shots fired in Butler were from Secret Service counter-snipers, when only the tenth was. Why lie?

We're reminded of the Gell-Mann Amnesia effect, which is "the phenomenon of a person trusting newspapers for topics which that person is not knowledgeable about, despite recognizing the newspaper as being extremely inaccurate on certain topics which that person is knowledgeable about."[47] We know we have Gell-Mann Amnesia as to FBI claims surrounding the attempted assassination of Donald Trump and the shooter.

> Three days after the Trump campaign announced the rally in Butler, a western Pennsylvania town about an hour from Crook's [sic] home, Crooks made numerous searches online for well-known political figures and political events. He searched for the date and location of the Democratic National Convention, which takes place in August in Chicago, and for the location of the Trump rally. He also searched for information on Trump, Biden and other major political figures.
>
> On the day of the rally, Crooks made several internet searches, including for photos of the location of Trump's speech and for a local gun store not far from his home, where he purchased bullets that day.
>
> Investigators have found data showing that Crooks had visited the location of the rally a week before it was to be held.[48]

So, how did he know that the Butler, Pennsylvania, rally was to be an unusually low-security event (more on this in the *Review* chapter)? For that matter, why was the Butler rally the first Trump rally since 2020 that CNN livestreamed? But we digress—back to Crooks.

Did Crooks know that the Secret Service would be split between multiple events—the Trump rally, the Jill Biden event (also in Pennsylvania), and security preparations for the Republican National Committee convention the following week?[49] As far as we know, the web-browsing, news-consuming public was not made aware of this logistical security compromise. And above (almost) all, why would a kid die for a shot to kill Donald Trump? Despite Crooks's reported intelligence, he had a community college degree and worked at a nursing home. He'd asked his boss for July 13 off work because he had "something to do."[50] We know so little about this kid beyond the basics that describe many millions of young people around the country.

With questions come only more questions. There has been a news vacuum around the most dramatic event that has happened in the United States—and its instigator—since September 11, 2001. Consider how left-wing media would have (and have, actually) treated anyone associated with the January 6, 2021 Trump supporter entrapment event at the US Capitol building. What would they do? They would go after them. Knock on doors. Everything on camera. Talk to siblings, cousins, coworkers, classmates. Anyone publicly identifiable as having ever met the January 6 protestor. Journalists would find the name of their grocer. They would find out every single medication and recreational drug he was on. With Crooks, we've got a couple of interviews, like the one opening this chapter. There's no publicly identified motive beyond what's been reported as to his phone's contents—photographs of Trump, photographs of Biden, internet searches about the RNC and DNC, the British royal family, known mass shooters, and pornography.[51, 52] Yes, the last internet search of his life was for porn. We know so much about Crooks yet so little.

Now, let's rewind to July 13, morning of, and observe Crooks's actions. At 9:27 a.m., Crooks entered a Home Depot located in Bethel

Park, Pennsylvania. CCTV footage showed him entering alone. A couple minutes later, he purchased a five-foot aluminum dual platform ladder. That's the only time we saw the ladder. At 9:42, Crooks left the store. The ladder is in place by 10:30 a.m. This is important because at that same time, two local law enforcement snipers were in position on the second floor inside the American Glass Research (AGR) building, the eventual site of the shooting. But they didn't scope out the roof of this building personally; they went in there, looked out the windows, but apparently never stepped foot on the roof or at around back where Crooks would find his way up.

Around 3:00 p.m., Crooks flew a drone above the rally site. Now, Jack knows from living in Washington, DC, that nobody can just operate drones around law enforcement, or around federal VIPs. Donald Trump Jr., recently said that he wanted to bring one of his drones up outside a party at Mar-a-Lago, the Trump residence in Florida, but the software wouldn't allow the drone to even take off because a Secret Service detail was in the vicinity.[53] And recently, Jack's cousin was getting married in southern Pennsylvania pretty close to Wilmington. She wanted to have a drone up at her wedding, but because Biden happened to be in Wilmington at that point, and she was within a protected thirty-mile radius, she was prohibited from drone use.

With that drone, his firearm and detonator, and other supplies, Crooks brought a rangefinder. The distance, having gone there myself, is a short 140 yards. That's a bootcamp shoot; he didn't even use a scope but iron sights, which likely would have better concealed his presence than a large, easily visible scope atop the rifle. Speaking of rifle, on August 15, 2024, Florida congresswoman Ranna Paulina Luna posted on the X platform a grainy yet make-outable (and previously unpublished) photo of Crooks with that same rifle in plain-as-day view of the rally. Representative Luna's caption read:

I have just obtained a photo that was taken by individual at rally in PA of Crooks with the gun used to shoot at President Trump walking around building prior to assassination attempt.

This photo was submitted to LEO in PA. To my knowledge this photo has not been released until now.[54]

Jack was shocked by how close the AGR building is—and therefore how close Crooks was—to the Trump rally site. It was unmissable to rallygoers and to law enforcement, or ought to have been. In fact, my first thought upon witnessing the building's close proximity there in person three weeks after the shooting was, *How in the heck did Crooks think this was a good idea?* Because Secret Service and other local law enforcement would have to have been *all over* that place—or at least that's what any reasonable person would have assessed. Anyone in a normal situation that close to a former US president carrying a firearm should have assumed they would be quickly unarmed if not unalived, no questions asked.

That did not happen. Louisiana congressman Mike Kelly, chairman of the House Bi-Partisan Task Force on the Attempted Assassination of Former President Donald Trump, wrote in the committee's preliminary investigative report:

8 shots were fired by Crooks from his firing (and dying) position on the AGR rooftop. The position provided excellent concealment for Crooks from the northern counter-sniper team due to the foliage/branches of two trees. Crooks' firing position did NOT offer excellent concealment from the southern counter-sniper team. However, it should be noted that **the would-be assassin perfectly positioned himself to minimize the threat of counter-fire from the ground or the USSS counter-sniper teams. Crooks' firing position was also several feet back from the actual peak of the AGR rooftop. By choosing this position, Crooks effectively minimized the sky-lined profile of his head and upper body.**[55]

Emphasis ours. Because how could Crooks have known that "USSS had never, prior to J13, assigned a counter-sniper team to a former POTUS, including Trump" and that the Butler rally would be different? Or didn't he? Did he?[56]

At 4:26 p.m., a Beaver County Emergency Service Unit counter-sniper texted a colleague, "Someone followed our lead and snuck in and parked by our cars just so you know."[57] Of the suspicious person, who turned out to be the shooter, he also wrote, "I'm just letting you know because you see me go out with my rifle and put it in my car so he knows you guys are up there sitting to the direct right on a picnic table about 50 yards from the exit."[58]

Catch that? They saw Crooks. Crooks saw them. They knew Crooks knew. And yet . . . nothing. The kid didn't fight, flee, or freeze. Why wasn't he worried?

And at that very same minute—at 4:26 p.m.—Crooks was spotted by Trump supporters selling merchandise walking around the rally, near other vendors.[59] A short while later, he accessed the AGR building roof by climbing up HVAC equipment and piping—not the ladder.[60]

Then around 5:10 p.m. on July 13, law enforcement took the first known photographs of Crooks in position, just below the counter-snipers inside the AGR building. Those images, much less the presence of an unknown individual with a rangefinder (you can't even bring an e-cig with you anywhere near these events), were not relayed to Trump's direct body detail; they were all sent out on stage at the rally totally and completely clueless. In fact, it wasn't until 5:38 p.m. that the photos of Crooks were shared in a law enforcement group chat.

"Kid learning around the building we are in. AGR I believe it is," the text read. "I did see him with a range finder looking towards stage. FYI. If you wanna notify SS snipers to look out. I lost sight of him."[61]

"Call it in to command and have a uniform check it out," another officer texted.[62] According to *The New York Times*, the photos eventually made their way to the Secret Service through a series of steps at the command center.[63] Trump's Secret Service detail would lodge complaints that they had not been informed that local police were tracking a suspicious person, however.[64]

Then at about 6:00 p.m., another group text message showed an officer guessing that Crooks moved toward the back of the AGR building "away from the event." No, he was on the roof and would open fire eleven minutes later at 6:11 p.m. But not before a Butler County Deputy Sheriff possibly interrupted him. According to the *New York Post*:

> The local cop, hoisted up by a fellow officer, was hanging off the edge of the roof when he was spotted by Crooks, who pointed his AR-style semi-automatic assault rifle at him.
>
> "Right now, (the shooter is) training on the president. These guys breach the roof," [Butler County Sheriff Michael Slupe] said of the two cops. "So he turns around and potentially eliminates that threat.
>
> "The officer is like 'I'm dead or I drop. I drop.' He turns back around," he said of the shooter.
>
> The cop ducked his head, lost his grip and fell eight feet to the ground, Butler Township Manager Tom Knights told NBC News Tuesday.[65]
>
> . . . "Now timing is everything . . . He turns around and at this point in the speech, obviously as we all know, the president is looking way back to his right and he gets hit on the ear . . . If I'm interrupted and I move my gun, you are going to have to reassess that whole situation at this point, so yes, you can make a case that those two officers saved the president's life," Slupe argued.[66]

Did a local cop falling off a roof do what the most powerful organization of professional bodyguards in the world could not? Or would not? Ultimately, more than ninety minutes passed from the time law enforcement knew of a suspicious person until he was able to fire eight rounds.

So many opportunities were missed, which we'll expose further in the *Review* chapter, with yet another being revealed by newly released (at the time of this writing) bodycam footage. Crooks was seen at 6:08 p.m. jumping from roof to roof, apparently to get into position.[67] This was witnessed, yet nothing was done to halt his advance.

At 6:11 p.m. on July 13, Thomas Matthew Crooks fired eight rounds at the Butler, Pennsylvania rally, wounding President Donald J. Trump together with two supporters, and killing a third attendee—Corey Comperatore.

It defies belief that a twenty-year-old who changes bedpans for a living was able to pull this off. It defies belief to such an extent that it becomes reasonable to presume he had help. Otherwise, the luck involved is extraordinary. Perhaps too extraordinary.

Now it gets weird. It came out that Thomas Crooks had used the same shooting range that known federal employees used in his hometown: Clairton Sportsmen's Club. Consider the profile of Crooks on paper, a young white male without many prospects and no friends, a quiet loner with some technical aptitude and skill with firearms. We're reminded of the discontents that the Federal Bureau of Investigation entrapped as part of the fake Governor Gretchen Whitmer kidnapping plot. "The four men charged with planning to kidnap Michigan Gov. Gretchen Whitmer were swayed by informants and federal agents who targeted them for their anti-government views," reported the Associated Press.[68] That all began with group chats, too, and escalatory rhetoric.[69] Note that the "foiled plot" narrative likely helped Gov. Whitmer win reelection in 2022. Was that why it happened in the first place?

The similarities align. Speculation abounds, albeit educated speculation. Journalist Julie Kelly went so far as to say of Crooks, "There is no way to convince me Crooks acted alone. I have zero doubt he was in communication with an FBI or DHS asset before July 13."[70] The way we see it, we either entertain all possibilities or we drop the story; the information will get less and less, so we can't drop the story. We must proceed.

The most damning question of all, which we will explore in full on the Day Five chapter, is *why was the shooter on law enforcement radar for ninety minutes without a response?*

On a completely and totally unrelated note, let's now ask, *Who was The Man in the Gray Suit?*

Senator Ron Johnson and Maria Bartiromo on FOX News made the nation aware of this mystery man:

> A guy in a gray suit walks up the ladder and goes up to the roof, and this guy in the gray suit didn't appear to have credentials . . .

. . . Everybody assumed he was the Secret Service. So he tells one of the local law enforcement send those pictures [of Crooks' body] to this cell phone and he gives him a number to, and everybody assumes, oh, that must be Secret Service. It turns out it wasn't Secret Service.[71]

The Man in the Gray Suit was later identified as someone from the Bureau of Alcohol, Tobacco, Firearms and Explosives (ATF) Philadelphia office. The ATF simply requested the photos of Crooks for facial recognition purposes. That's more an FBI thing, but OK. In subsequent attempts to establish further talks with the individual at that number, Senator Johnson's staff received a boilerplate email directing all questions to their main office and spokesman. The Man in the Gray Suit has gone dark. But there's a loose thread, and we're going to pull it.

This individual was probably an augment from the ATF office who was sent to Butler at the same time that apparently no additional Secret Service were available. They couldn't get anyone from all the other offices? OK, so we're relying on local police to secure what is obviously the most opportune building for an assassination shot at President Trump. It was completely unguarded from the roof, with nobody on it, and nobody thought to put anybody on it. Or didn't they?

We've been told there were counter-sniper teams, local law enforcement, county sheriff employees, and so on in support of Trump security on July 13. But now we're told that there was an ATF agent who showed up in a gray suit with no credentials. He wore no uniform; he wasn't wearing the blue jacket with the yellow lettering we've all seen that says *ATF*. Does that mean he was plainclothes? Does that mean he was in fact . . . undercover? And if The Man in the Gray Suit was there plainclothes as federal law enforcement, how many more did they have in the crowd that day at Butler? How many?

"The feds have yet to share a motive for the attack," wrote the *New York Post*.[72] The keyword here is "*share*."

One more time.

How many?

While we ponder that, let's escalate the uncertainty with these sobering bullet points from the Task Force's preliminary investigative report. It gets a little graphic.

- All 8 casings were recovered and are allegedly in proper possession of the FBI. Thomas Matthew Crooks' rifle is also allegedly in the proper possession of the FBI. I will need to examine all of the physical evidence that has been harvested by law enforcement and is in the possession of the FBI. All of it.
- The 9th shot fired on J13 was from a Butler SWAT operator from the ground about 100 yards away from the AGR building. Shot 9 hit Crooks' rifle stock and fragged his face/neck/right shoulder area from the stock breaking up. The SWAT operator who took this shot was a total bad*ss; when he had sighted the shooter Crooks as a mostly obscured by foliage moving target on the AGR rooftop, he immediately left his assigned post and ran towards the threat, running to a clear shot position directly into the line of fire while Crooks was firing 8 rounds. On his own, this ESU SWAT operator took a very hard shot, one shot. He stopped Crooks and importantly, I believe the shot damaged the buffer tube on Crooks' AR. I won't be certain of this until I can examine Crooks' rifle, but I'm 99% sure, based upon reliable eye-witness ESU tactical officers who observed Crooks' rifle before the FBI harvested it as evidence. This means that if his AR buffer tube was damaged, Crooks' rifle wouldn't fire after his 8th shot.
- Crooks "went down" from his firing position when shot 9 was fired, and the SWAT officer was certain of his hit. According to the ESU SWAT operator, Crooks recovered after just a few seconds, and "popped back up."
- The 10th (and, I believe, final) shot was fired from the southern counter-sniper team. I will not be 100% certain of this until further investigation. However, I am quite sure that the USSS southern counter-sniper team fired the

killing shot, which, according to my investigation, entered somewhere around the left mouth area and exited the right ear area. Instant over. This entry-exit aligns with USSS southern counter-sniper team position.

- The FBI released the crime scene after just 3 days, much to everyone's surprise. I interviewed several First Responders who expressed everything from surprise to dismay to suspicion regarding the fact that the FBI released the crime scene so early after J13. It should be noted that the FBI was fully aware of the fact that Congress would be investigating J13. The FBI does not exist in a vacuum. They had to know that releasing the J13 crime scene would injure the immediate observations of any following investigation.

- The FBI cleaned up biological evidence from the crime scene, which is unheard of. Cops don't do that, ever.

- My effort to examine Crooks' body on Monday, August 5, caused quite a stir and revealed a disturbing fact . . . the FBI released the body for cremation 10 days after J13. On J23, Crooks was gone. Nobody knew this until Monday, August 5, including the County Coroner, law enforcement, Sheriff, etc. Yes, Butler County Coroner technically had legal authority over the body, but I spoke with the Coroner, and he would have never released Crooks' body to the family for cremation or burial without specific permission from the FBI.

- The coroner's report and autopsy report are both "late." As of Monday, August 5, they were a week late. The problem with me not being able to examine the actual body is that I won't know 100% if the coroner's report and the autopsy report are accurate. We will actually never know . . . Again, similar to releasing the crime scene and scrubbing crime scene biological evidence . . . this action by the FBI can only be described by any reasonable man as an obstruction to any following investigative effort.

- There are videos on the internet showing a dark figure or a shadow on the water tower on J13 . . . However, I do not

believe it was possible for a "2nd shooter" sniper to be on
top of that water tower on J13, nor have I seen any evidence
that supports the theory of a 2nd shooter. I'm not saying
conclusively that there was no other shooter somewhere or
that no other conspirators were involved in J13, but I'm saying
that based on my investigation thus far, there were 10 shots
fired on J13, and all shots are accounted for, and all shots align
with their source. Crooks' 8 shots (3 plus 5), ESU SWAT 1
shot, USSS southern sniper team 1 shot. Over.[73]

The feds have yet to share a motive for the attack. In fact, their
conclusion (as of this writing) is that Crooks was driven by a "mixture of ideologies" including potentially anti-Semitism, he "acted
alone," he had no "foreign involvement," and had "no definitive
ideology associated with our subject, either left leaning or right
leaning," despite having donated $15 to Democratic fundraising
powerhouse ActBlue in 2021 and being a registered Republican.[74]
That is just . . . weird.

One of the reasons we don't have access to a lot of the documentation we might use to determine a motive is even *more* suspicious.
When one of my (Jack) reporters tried to get records from the community college Crooks attended, we were denied. Why?

Because those records were part of an *ongoing criminal investigation.*

The letter, from the Community College of Allegheny County
in response to attorney Wally Zimolong, denies the request for
records on Crooks pertaining to his student files, records, docu-
ments, communication, disciplinary records, or other data con-
taining his name.

"Please be advised that your request is denied on the basis
that it requests records that relate to an ongoing criminal investigation, which are exempt from disclosure," the letter reads.

"Specifically," the letter continues, "the records that you have
requested are within the scope of a grand jury subpoena issued
to CCAC by the United States District Court for the Western

District of Pennsylvania, and which the U.S. Attorney's Office has confirmed relate to an ongoing criminal investigation."

The purpose of a federal grand jury is [to] consider criminal charges against a target or range of targets. This is the first indication that a grand jury has been empaneled in the district to investigate the attempted assassination.[75, 76]

There's one thing. Crooks is dead. Who are they trying to indict? There is a possibility it might be Crooks's parents.[77] But we'll have to wait to see how that pans out.

Is there more? There is. President Trump said to Breitbart News on August 8, 2024:

> I think [Thomas Matthew Crooks] was very liberal. He was very smart—a good student and all of that. But very mixed up.
> . . . I think [Crooks' motive] might have had something to do with the left . . . Certainly, the way they [talk] about "threat to democracy" all the time—I think that's a terrible statement to make. They don't believe any of it. A lot of people think it's their rhetoric that caused this. Their rhetoric is terrible. All I want to do is make America great again.[78]

Thomas Matthew Crooks—very liberal, very smart, very mixed up.
Mixed up by what, Mr. President? Mixed up by whom?
By whom?

DAY THREE, JULY 15, 2024: THE PICK

On June 28, 2024, fifteen days before the shot, independent journalist Mike Cernovich put in words the anxieties of millions of Trump supporters with this concise warning, both to the public and to the man himself:

> Trumps VP choice is more important than ever, after last night, [the debate with Joe Biden]. He must choose his vice president with one issue in mind.
> ASSASSINATION INSURANCE.
> The regime loves Tim Scott. Can you imagine? He is so compromised. He'll do what he's told.
> Trumps VP choice must keep him alive.[1]

"The regime," of course, refers to that oligarchical panopticon we wrote of in the *Motive* chapter. And South Carolina senator Tim Scott is indeed *not* known for being one of those Trump supporters (he ran against Trump in the 2024 Republican presidential primary).

So, why "assassination insurance"? It's simple; Cernovich's unspoken assertion that we happen to agree with is that Trump's choice for vice president must be **more hated** than Trump himself. In other words, those who would wish Trump real bodily harm, when learning of Trump's VP pick, must be made to think, *Wow, Trump's not nearly as bad as this guy.* We use "bad" in the sense that a bad review from a bad person is a good review, as our coauthor Joshua is known to say.

In another light, Trump's VP choice would be a bandage to help the Trump ticket heal from high assassination risk. Just as a literal bandage is applied immediately after a wounding, so, too, is the metaphorical one. And so on **July 15, 2024**, at 2:04 p.m., Ohio Senator JD Vance was announced as the VP choice.[2]

JD Vance isn't your average Senator. He wasn't from any particularly wealthy political dynasties, wasn't born to wealthy parents. In other words, he wasn't a creature of the Swamp. Instead, he was like a lot of us, born in flyover country in Middletown, Ohio, to a hardscrabble life. Raised by his grandmother, Vance learned the value of a good work ethic and the importance of faith, and he took those lessons through the Marine Corps and into the world of venture capital.[3]

Coauthor Joshua knows the area well. These are the places full of "deplorables" who "cling to their guns and religion," as a former presidential candidate and a former president had said. It's the same part of the USA where Trump flags fly in every yard. It's the place forgotten by the managerial elite. But not by the American people, who, by and large, resonated with Vance's story. They were the reason his book, *Hillbilly Elegy,* had become a #1 *New York Times* bestseller,[4] and had even been made into a film for Netflix directed by Ron Howard, starring Amy Adams and Glenn Close.[5]

Ironically enough, Vance opened *Hillbilly Elegy* with the following quote, in an attempt to say why "the existence of the book you hold in your hands is somewhat absurd."[6]

> The coolest thing I've done, at least on paper, is graduate from Yale Law School, something thirteen-year-old J.D. Vance would have considered ludicrous. But about two hundred people do the same thing every year, and trust me, you don't want to read about most of their lives. **I am not a senator,** a governor, or a former cabinet secretary. I haven't started a billion dollar company or world-changing nonprofit.[7]

Vance is from a place sold out by the elites, left with nothing but the rotting shells of factories gone long out of business. But that place—Flyover Country, Hicksville, whatever other name coastal elites might want to call it—was not forgotten by President Trump in his inaugural address January 20th, 2017:

> January 20th, 2017, will be remembered as the day the people became the rulers of this nation again.
>
> The forgotten men and women of our country will be forgotten no longer.
>
> Everyone is listening to you now.
>
> You came by the tens of millions to become part of a historic movement the likes of which the world has never seen before.
>
> At the center of this movement is a crucial conviction: that a nation exists to serve its citizens.
>
> Americans want great schools for their children, safe neighborhoods for their families, and good jobs for themselves.
>
> These are the just and reasonable demands of a righteous public.
>
> But for too many of our citizens, a different reality exists: Mothers and children trapped in poverty in our inner cities; rusted-out factories scattered like tombstones across the landscape of our nation; an education system, flush with cash, but which leaves our young and beautiful students deprived of knowledge; and the crime and gangs and drugs that have stolen too many lives and robbed our country of so much unrealized potential.
>
> This American carnage stops right here and stops right now.
>
> We are one nation—and their pain is our pain. Their dreams are our dreams; and their success will be our success. We share one heart, one home, and one glorious destiny.[8]

Vance's own book was such a breakout hit that even the *New York Times* was recommending it in 2016 for those shocked liberals who saw their whole world crumble around them when Donald Trump won the presidency.[9]

And boy, is JD Vance the Left's worst nightmare for a VP pick.

For one thing, Vance is even *more* pro-life than Trump. Currently, JD Vance holds an A+ Score from the Susan B. Anthony Pro-Life America group, while Trump faced flak from them for saying that the *Dobbs* decision moved the pro-life ball back into the court of the states.[10, 11] Vance had said that, "There is something sociopathic about a political movement that tells young women (and men) that it is liberating to murder their own children."[12] He compared the institution to slavery, stating, "There's something comparable between abortion and slavery, and that while the people who obviously suffer the most are those subjected to it, I think it has this morally distorting effect on the entire society."[13]

Trump may have run on the slogan "Build the Wall!" but Vance has shown himself to be just as hardline on immigration. He stated that, should the GOP take over Congress in the 2022 midterms, they should make funding the border wall part and parcel to funding other parts of the government.[14] Effectively, holding the government hostage unless it pays the ransom of one big, beautiful wall. He's also called for deporting illegal immigrants, stating that, "You start with the most violent people, the people who have criminal records." [15]

While Trump focused on a catch-all populist message, he never really leaned into his faith that much. JD Vance, on the other hand, has been quite public about his Catholicism,[16] enough so that his faith has been dubbed "radical"[17] by all the fashionable atheists who write for *The New Yorker*. They can accept a Catholic like Joe Biden, who doesn't let the Roman Catholic Church's actual position on abortion (considering it a heinous sin)[18] affect his voting record, but JD Vance? Someone who *actually believes* in all this silly, supernatural stuff? And tries to follow the commands and beliefs of his faith? The horror! (Never mind that most religious folk *actually believe* the faith they confess.)

JD Vance is also a bit of a crypto bro. While Biden has been trying to force crypto firms to "collaborate" with the government,[19] and has vetoed bills allowing for financial firms to engage in crypto and Bitcoin trading,[20] JD Vance isn't just cryptocurrency-friendly, he actually holds a lot of Bitcoin (at least according to his 2022 financial filings).[21] This may also explain why several Silicon Valley investors, which we mentioned before, have been throwing in with Trump, like Musk and Andreessen.[22]

Vance has also been fairly bullish on Second Amendment rights. Praised by the NRA, they go on to describe Vance as a " a patriot with deep ties to Heartland America and to the values and struggles of its resilient, self-reliant people."[23] He's also hated by all the right people, like Everytown for Gun Safety and Moms Demand Action, two hardline gun control groups.[24] And a bad review from a bad person (or in this case, two bad groups) is a good review, as Joshua likes to say.

And more to the point, he's said he wants to abolish the ATF![25]

While all of this may seem like a Republican Party hardliner's dream, when it comes to economics, Vance breaks hard with your average Republican. He supports more government intervention, not to crush small businesses in favor of large multinational conglomerates of the kind favored by the Davos crowd, but to protect American workers and American jobs,[26] to see those "tombstones" of factories open up again. It's about facing the "failure of what he'll call the 'market fundamentalism' of the GOP"[27]—in other words, not buying into RINO "The free market will solve all our problems!" nonsense.

JD Vance also says what we all saw, and what the mainstream will punish you for daring to express; the 2020 election was a sham. While RINOs, sighing with relief that Orange Man was out of office, bought the party line that "They were not rigging the election; they were fortifying it,"[28] Vance said what, in his words, the "average Trump-fan Republican voter" in his hometown would say. "That is an illegitimate election."[29]

Vance also shows his America First bona fides when it comes to financing overseas wars, namely the war in the Ukraine. In fact, he wrote a *New York Times* op-ed about how the real problem is not Republican stonewalling, but math; he's not willing to dig our country into debt to ramp up weapon production to fail overseas again.[30] "The notion that we should prolong a bloody and gruesome war because it's been good for American business is grotesque. We can and should rebuild our industrial base without shipping its products to a foreign conflict."[31]

And unlike so many RINOs who cower before the media in fear of being called a bigot for objecting to the grooming and sterilization of children in the name of transgender madness, JD Vance says what we all know; that "gender-affirming care" is a moral monstrosity. He introduced a bill into the House, the *Protect Children's Innocence Act*, that "would ban the genital mutilation, chemical castration, and sterilization of innocent children by classifying the performance of so-called "gender-affirming care" on a minor as a Class C felony."[32] He also pointed out the obvious, that "American children are being targeted and indoctrinated with gender ideologies on social media platforms—children also face pressures from radical teachers, mental health counselors, and healthcare providers, often without receiving proper warning of associated risks."[33]

The above reasons should give you a good idea why not just hardcore leftists, but also Neocons and the Vote Blue No Matter Who liberals *hate* JD Vance, and they *hate* that he was picked as the VP. Lefties especially attacked him for his normal opinions. "We're effectively run in this country, via the Democrats, via our corporate oligarchs, by a bunch of childless cat ladies who are miserable at their own lives and the choices that they made, and so they want to make the rest of the country miserable too."[34] And of course, said childless cat ladies miserably protested that they were *not* miserable at their own lives, and threw enough of a hissy fit that they ended up making his point.

It also helped that Vance endorsed our last book, *Unhumans*. An endorsement which, by the way, we placed first on the back cover, three months prior to his announcement. An endorsement which reads as follows:

In the past, communists marched in the streets waving red flags. Today, they march through HR, college campuses, and courtrooms to wage lawfare against good, honest people. In *Unhumans*, Jack Posobiec and Joshua Lisec reveal their plans and show us what to do to fight back.

Meanwhile, neocons like Bill Kristol are hand-wringing that JD Vance is the face of a new and different Republican Party, and not the neocon platform he once knew and loved. "This isn't just different from [the past] but really repudiates so much of the Bush, McCain, Romney Republican Party."[35] (That he thinks describing the GOP as the "Bush, McCain, Romney Republican Party" is a *good* thing shows how bad it's gotten).

But fortunately for us, the neocons were not calling the shots.

With JD Vance as Trump's running mate, other people argued that the party had appeared more firmly rooted in Trump's ideology, making it increasingly difficult to distance from his legacy once he's no longer at the forefront.

> The Associated Press: Donald Trump selected Ohio Sen. JD Vance as his vice presidential pick. He announced the decision on his Truth Social Network on Monday. Trump and Vance were officially nominated to the GOP ticket on the first day of the RNC in Milwaukee.[36]

People do not quite realize what was going on behind the scenes, but a tweet raised concerns about the forces working to block JD Vance, and pointed to the intense opposition he faced. Those familiar with the situation described it as a concerted push by some of the most controversial figures in Washington, who were fixated on blocking Vance in favor of other candidates. Tucker Carlson stated:

> Lindsey Graham is a liar. No one lobbied harder against JD Vance than he did, and in the sleaziest, most vicious way. He was doing it this morning. This is why everyone hates Washington, because people like Lindsey Graham are happy to lie right to your face, smiling as they plot your destruction. It's disgusting.[37]

Coauthor Jack Posobiec reported in real time while guest-hosting for *War Room* (while Steve Bannon had been thrown in prison by the regime) that Vance was likely to be the pick but was being strongly opposed by neocons such as Karl Rove, Rupert Murdoch, and Kellyanne Conway—interestingly, this segment was on the morning of July 13th, hours before the shooting of President Trump would dominate the headlines. I (Jack) accurately reported that an entire neocon coalition was attempting to sway Trump away from picking a populist VP like Vance. Later it was learned that at the same time, President Trump was meeting with Vance at Mar-a-Lago. Lindsey Graham himself flew with President Trump from Bedminster to Milwaukee the day after the shooting and reportedly spent almost the entire time attempting to convince President Trump not to make the Vance pick. Trump rejected Graham's advice.

It's been pointed out to us that one can often judge individuals by their allies and opponents, much like judging a tree by its fruit. In JD Vance's case, some of the most notorious figures responsible for the country's woes over the last fifteen years were strongly opposed to him. Their efforts were described as desperate, marked by last-minute manipulations and corruption, reflecting the high stakes they perceived. This faction, it was argued, should be purged from the Republican Party and aligned with individuals like David Frum and Bill Kristol. The lingering question remains: Why are these people still within the party's ranks?

We can find another island of misfits somewhere, and they can go right next to the first one and they can hang out.

A notion was raised that individuals like Rove, Frum, Kristol, and Bolton, who advocate for violence and murdering people in faraway countries, might be more at home within the Democratic Party. These figures, often dealing with personal difficulties, seem to feel empowered by endorsing conflicts like the one in Ukraine. This raises the question of why they remain connected to the Republican Party when their values appear to align more closely with a different political ideology.

For the neocons, this is actually where they came from originally. Their migration from the Democratic Party is well-documented, especially during the Vietnam War era. Figures like Irving and others couldn't align themselves with the anti-war sentiment that was gaining traction within the Democratic Party. They needed the war, the killing, the destruction—the very things that can only be described as demonic in nature to want that level of death. We've been to many of the places affected like China, Vietnam, Russia, but Poland—that's been affected by this is where Jack's family comes from—countries deeply scarred by such atrocities. It's horrific. It's an actual atrocity.

And it was also on **July 15, 2024**, that the former president was seen in public wearing a literal bandage on his ear. It was a large pad of gauze, dressed by Dr. Ronny Jackson, Representative from Texas, and Trump's former White House doctor. "The bullet took a little bit off the top of his ear in an area that, just by nature, bleeds like crazy," which meant that, "The dressing's bulked up a bit because you need a bit of absorbent. You don't want to be walking around with bloody gauze on his ear."[38]

It was bulky, it was obvious, and it became the latest fashion sensation at the RNC,[39] which coincidentally had also begun on July 15, 2024. It was a statement of solidarity; we were all Trump, as attendees began wearing bandages on their ears, too. The bullet may have only hit Trump, but it was aimed at all of us. "We need a symbol about political violence not being acceptable in America," stated Jackson Carpenter, a Texas delegate.[40] Another delegate, Joe Neglia from Arizona, described it as "a new sign of unity within the party."[41]

It turned the convention itself into a real-world time to heal. Everyone adopting bandages as an act of solidarity made the whole event a communal bandage for Republicans, conservatives, and Trump supporters.

It was also an event where, by the way, there were hundreds of protesters denouncing Trump and *refusing* to denounce his assassination attempt. It should have been easy. "I hate the guy, but nobody should try to kill the dude." And somehow this was too much for most of the protesters.

When Jack did a little poll outside the convention with the leftist protesters, this is what happened:

We asked over 100 leftists yesterday if they would condemn the Trump shooting

Not one would

You have to understand, leftist revolutionaries don't see Trump and Trump supporters as innocent, they see them as obstacles in their way[42]

There's a reason our last book was called *Unhumans*. When one protester, identified with a group of socialists, was asked whether he denounced or opposed the assassination of President Trump, he kept insisting that he was here to "denounce the Republican agenda."[43]

Another protester, in an interview with one of my (Jack) reporters on the ground at the RNC, stated that "No human being should be killed," to which my reporter announced, "We got one that agrees President Trump shouldn't be killed!" To which the protester quickly corrected him. "I didn't say that."[44]

DAY FOUR, JULY 16, 2024:
THE BACKLASH

"I was blindsided by what was said at the show on Sunday," the statement published on Instagram on **July 16, 2024**, reads. "I would never condone hate speech or encourage political violence in any form."

And yet . . .

This is what they do.

On this day, actor, comedian, and musician Jack Black announced the cancellation of the current Tenacious D world tour following a comment that his bandmate Kyle Gass made on stage in Sydney, Australia, about the Trump assassination attempt.[1] From *The Hollywood Reporter:*

> At the performance in Sydney on Sunday, Black and a "robot" presented Gass with a birthday cake. In the clips, Black is heard saying, "Make a wish," to Gass, who before blowing out the candles says, "Don't miss Trump next time," to laughter and applause from the Sydney crowd.
>
> "The line I improvised onstage Sunday night in Sydney was highly inappropriate, dangerous and a terrible mistake," Gass said in a statement posted to Instagram following the news that the tour has been canceled. "I don't condone violence of any kind, in any form, against anyone."[2]

Five days later, the Gass apology was deleted.[3] This is what they do.

Two weeks later, alt-rock band Green Day held a concert in Washington, DC, which I (Jack) actually attended with my family. The Posobiecs were there for Smashing Pumpkins, but we stayed for some of the Green Day show. We left before the . . . incident. During one particular tune, lead singer and guitarist Billie Joe Armstrong, from stage, raised up a rubbery Trump mask as if it were a severed head, mimicking the infamous Kathy Griffin photo depicting the same.[4] Must we say it again? We must.

This is what they do.

And that doesn't surprise us. One-third of Democrats polled in a survey on July 18 agreed with the statement, "I wish Trump's assassin hadn't missed."[5] Fortunately, this is what *we* do—we hold the blood-thirsty accountable. The Iron Law of Exact Reciprocity we wrote of in *Unhumans* has returned. The law called for responding in kind. The cancelers become canceled.

For Tenacious D, the results were swift. Kyle Gass lost his agent from Greene Talent;[6] not because of a simple salary negotiation or other normal business practice, but because he said something that left him more radioactive than Chernobyl. Jack Black, the other half of Tenacious D, also informed that the rest of the tour was canceled,[7] with Frontier Touring stating that all purchased tickets for those shows would be refunded.[8] Tenacious D had also been scheduled to perform several concerts for Rock the Vote in October, and at this point it appears that plan has been scuttled.[9]

It might seem like the Right—the New Right at least—is finally applying the same rules the Left has been trying to enforce on all of us; only rather than punishing public figures for not embracing their insane politics, we're insisting that *calling for someone's death* is bad. Except the Left doesn't limit itself to public figures. If you're some random dude working in some retail job who has opinions on Twitter/X that crazy coastal elites can't stand, you're fair game.

But now that's changing. And that's a good thing. We didn't make this bed, but if we have to lie in it, so should they.

A worker at restaurant chain Tupelo Honey—a cafe featuring "a revival of Southern food and traditions rooted in the Carolina mountains we call home"[10]—is, according to the company, "no longer employed"[11] after said worker was found to have replied to a news article with the caption "so close."[12] This was highlighted by the one and only infamous Libs of TikTok, a.k.a. Chaya Raichik.[13]

But of course, Tupelo Honey wasn't the *only* place to have foaming-at-the-mouth leftists ready to dehumanize and fantasize about the death of a president. No, of course, this is just the kind of thing that ought to be in our public schools.

An elementary school teacher, Jennifer Ripper, went viral after she replied "my thoughts exactly" to someone lamenting that the shooter missed.[14] An elementary school teacher. And yes, she also identified herself as a teacher.[15, 16] The school district did not detail if the teacher was disciplined, but instead sent an email to parents informing them of their social media policy.[17]

A Sioux Falls School District behavior specialist (someone who would ostensibly be working with special needs students) Cassandra Oleson decided to post to Facebook, "Shoot ‑ If only he would've had his scope sighted in correctly" in reference to the shooting.[18, 19] And unlike the last school board, this one took action; the Sioux Falls School District stated that "The individual is no longer employed" by them.[20]

Or take teacher Alison Scott, of Ardmore City Schools, located in Oklahoma, who had said "Same!! Wish they had a better scope" in response to someone praising the shooter on Facebook.[21] The school superintendent stated that the school district would be investigating, before later stating, "I have investigated it enough. I will be taking her teaching certificate. She will no longer be teaching in Oklahoma."[22, 23]

Bellarmine University professor John James of Kentucky had decided it would be a good idea to post "If you're gonna shoot, man, don't miss." over an article about the assassination.[24] At first, the person was "placed on immediate unpaid leave."[25] That got followed up with the news that that person was no longer employed.[26]

Then there's the case of former Fire Chief James Simmonds. On Facebook, someone screenshotted his comment, "A little to the right next time please," which he followed up with the delightful ". . . he's not the only one in my life I wished death on" in response to someone calling him out for his dehumanizing, insane rhetoric.[27] The Prospect Park Fire Company informed the public that he resigned after the board met July 14th. [28, 29]

Or take the infamous Home Depot Lady. When she was found to have said on Facebook, "To [sic] bad they weren't a better shooter!!!!!!"[30] The Home Depot acted quickly. "Hi, this individual's comments don't reflect The Home Depot or our values. We can confirm she no longer works at The Home Depot."[31]

This is a marked change to the Right's strategy from years past. Before, if anyone so much as complained, the neocon experts who claimed they knew better were quick to condemn and disavow. Now? People are reacting, and they're not going to take it anymore.

Take this account, Reddit Lies (@reddit_lies) on X/Twitter, an anonymous account devoted to exposing the insanity (and often degenerate and criminal behavior) of Reddit users.[32]

This is why Trump was almost assassinated.
Because "MAGA would do it to us."[33]

What followed was a screenshot of a meme explaining that "a MAGA" would "shoot you and everyone you care about" if they had a chance.[34] They also found a screenshot full of people saying that Trump was "a child raper" and that innocent lives lost were "a sacrifice Trump is willing to make."[35]

Another tweet called out famous streamer Destiny for the "tremendously bad take" that Comperatore, by the mere fact that he attended a Trump rally, deserved to die.[36] The tweeter summed it up with "This country is doomed with such a childish mindset."[37] Destiny, whose real name is Steven Bonnell, made several controversial comments regarding Corey Comperatore, the man who died shielding his family during an attempted assassination of Donald Trump. Destiny mocked Comperatore, calling him a "f*cking retard" for MAGA talking points. Destiny suggested that if any conservative fans had been killed at an event, he would make fun of them the next day on Twitter. Despite backlash, Destiny remained defiant, stating he would never apologize for how he treats conservatives. This stance led to his temporary suspension from the streaming platform Kick for "hate speech." When he appeared on Piers Morgan's show, Destiny refused to condemn the assassination attempt on Trump, as Trump was an insurrectionist, as were Trump supporters. He argued that while nobody deserves to die, he wouldn't "get on his knees" to beg for sympathy over the incident. Following his comments, Destiny's X account was demonetized by Elon Musk for content deemed inappropriate for advertisers.

Sunlight, as the saying goes, is the best disinfectant, and it's a good thing the New Right isn't going to just take the fact that we're living in a country where a sizable piece of it thinks we're unhumans, and deserve to die. And this time, we're not having a neocon wagging his finger and shaking his head and mutter something about civility. This time, we've learned to fight back.

DAY FIVE, JULY 17, 2024:
THE REVIEW

The Department of Homeland Security's Inspector General announced the official launch of a comprehensive review of the Secret Service's protocols for securing Trump's campaign event on July 13, 2024, including the agency's counter-sniper preparedness and operations:

> On Wednesday, **July 17, 2024**, DHS OIG initiated a review of USSS Counter Sniper Team preparedness and operations. Our objective is to determine the extent to which the Secret Service Counter Sniper Team is prepared for, and responds to, threats at events attended by designated protectees.[1]

Emphasis ours. At the time of this writing, it is not yet known what the Inspector General's review uncovered. In absence of such, this chapter stands in its place.

Almost one month to the day later, journalist Collin Rugg published on X newly released bodycam footage from Butler, Pennsylvania, law enforcement. We direct your attention to these excerpts from the transcript, which begins only nine minutes after the shooting occurred:

> "I f—ing told them they needed to post the guys f—ing over here . . . the Secret Service . . . I told them to post f—ing guys over here . . .
>
> What the f—? I wasn't even concerned about it because I thought someone was on the roof . . .

Why were we not on the roof?"[2]

"Never ascribe to malice that which is adequately explained by incompetence," Hanlon's razor tells us. In the case of the United States Secret Service that day, we wonder, *Why not both?*

Former Secret Service agent-turned-author and host Dan Bongino has expressed on numerous occasions concerns as to the state of the agency. Bongino wrote in his 2017 memoir *Protecting the President*:

> The president of the United States is in genuine danger if the Secret Service doesn't change course soon and evolve with the rapidly changing threat environment.
>
> The threats to the White House and the president are swiftly evolving in this new era of weaponized drones, micro-sized video surveillance technology, vehicle attacks on civilians, small arms tactical assaults, and technologically advanced and difficult-to-detect explosives. And if the decision makers in the Secret Introduction Service refuse to evolve with this series of threats, then, tragically, we may suffer the first loss of a president since John F. Kennedy.[3]

Bongino was almost a prophet, as July 13 unfolded with a determined gunman breaching top-level protection protocols with ease so astonishing it looks close to intentional. Quoting from *The Gateway Pundit*, we consider that Thomas Matthew Crooks was able to complete the following tasks under the literal and digital noses of the Secret Service:

> Thomas Crooks was able to do the following on July 13:
> 1. Flew a drone over the Pennsylvania fairgrounds and got aerial footage of the rally layout on the day of the event—including 2 hours before Trump took the stage.
> 2. Got a range finder through security.
> 3. Evaded law enforcement officers from several different state, local, and federal agencies.

4. Somehow "climbed" up on a roof with his rifle, 450 feet away from Trump, bear crawled to the perfect vantage point as bystanders alerted police, and was still able to take 8 shots at Trump.
5. Parked a vehicle full of explosives near the Trump rally.
6. Crooks was able to walk around the premises after snipers took a photo of him looking suspicious.
7. A sniper located in the second-story window was only 40 feet away from Crooks and didn't neutralize him.
8. Trump was still able to take the stage after Crooks was pegged as suspicious by the Secret Service.[4]

How?

How?!

Or perhaps, **how not**? For more than *two years* prior to the Butler rally, the Biden administration had denied Trump additional Secret Service protection. Specifically, his team perceived a need for "magnetometers and more agents to screen attendees at sporting events and other large public gatherings that Trump attended" and "had also requested more snipers and specialty teams at other outdoor events."[5]

In fact, both of your humble coauthors, Jack and Joshua, were subject to a Secret Service security breach at a Trump event just a few weeks before the shooting. In mid-June 2024 at the Turning Point Action People's Convention in Detroit, we were launching our previous book *Unhumans*, and had an in-person interview with Steve Bannon before he was hauled off to federal prison. Our appearance was only supposed to last a few minutes, but in the middle of the show inside the venue, we were suddenly surrounded by Secret Service agents. This included Jack's wife and children. We were told we couldn't leave the *War Room* set. We asked what was going on, and were informed the Secret Service had accidentally left a door open and that unchecked people were walking in from the street into the venue, circumventing the magnetometers. Trump was due to speak in a few hours. We were then stuck there for over an hour as the room was evacuated and the venue re-checked by bomb dogs and electronic equipment. Each of us, including Jack's kids, needed to be wanded again. We couldn't understand how such a thing could have happened. When we were finally allowed to leave the set, we made our way up to tape an episode of the Charlie Kirk show. Charlie himself mentioned he'd been having trouble with Secret Service at multiple events. Little did we know what would occur just one month later.

After the Butler rally debacle, a whistleblower notified Senator Josh Hawley that the Secret Service told agents working the Butler rally *not* to request additional manpower resources for the rally, further warning that any such requests would be *denied*. Note, that this contradicts acting Secret Service Rowe's testimony, who said no resources were ever denied.[6] The Secret Service also refused drone security that local law enforcement had offered to provide.[7] In response to these details, Mike Cernovich wrote, "It was an assassination plot by the deep state."[8]

Now, we must consider that former U.S. Secret Service director Kimberly Cheatle, who resigned in disgrace, claimed in sworn testimony on July 15 that "additional security enhancements [were] provided [to] former President Trump's detail in June [2024]."[9]

The point of a system is what it does.

In 2022, Cheatle was made director of the Secret Service by none other than President Joe Biden. Her previous role was as a security guard executive at PepsiCo, literally guarding soda pop. Is inability to discharge duties a bug, or a feature? Regardless, watch what they do; disregard what they say.

On the morning of July 13, the Secret Service didn't even show up to the security briefing provided to local special weapons and tactics (SWAT) and sniper teams. Typically, events of this magnitude— an outdoor rally of a presidential candidate to be attended by many thousands—need to staff up with extra bodies. Think local police, state troopers, yes, the Secret Service, and of course augments such as Department of Homeland Security temp employees, who would be standing in for the Secret Service in some instances.[10] Because since November 1963, outdoor events have always been and will always be the most potentially fatal event a politician can attend. Law enforcement know that for one of these outdoor events, the first thing to worry about is all the tall buildings. This is why the Butler rally was held in a field rather than in a suburban or urban area; cities have more vantage points, as alleged Kennedy assassin Lee Harvey Oswald seemed to demonstrate.

When it comes to securing an outdoor rally for a former president like Donald Trump—who is about to become the nominee for president of the United States—the stakes couldn't be higher, yet initial security plans seemed alarmingly lax for someone like Donald Trump, who has faced multiple credible threats to his life for the last decade or so. They weren't even going to provide counter-sniper teams initially for this outdoor rally, which is one of the most dangerous positions a politician can be in. Now, we the public have been told that the counter-sniper team showed up just the day before to do some casing, not a week prior. Jack has been involved with and even accompanied presidential visits and overseas trips and has stated that advance security teams are out there weeks before or more, checking the motorcade route, inspecting bridges, doing essential security preparation.

None of the usual was done here. Eight days before the rally, local police were informed. Five days before, they met with the Secret Service and learned the rally would be held at the Butler Farm Grounds. There was an initial request from the campaign to hold the event at a local airplane hangar, but that was already in use that day. Three days before, the Secret Service conducted a site visit. No counter-sniper teams were present. On the day of the rally, at 9:00 a.m., they held a briefing with a forty-six-page slide deck from the local Butler ESU. Local SWAT and sniper units were present, but the staging locations were laid out. According to attendees, the Secret Service didn't attend the briefing. No federal law enforcement was present. Initially, the Secret Service didn't plan to provide sniper units but changed course for unclear reasons. The briefing included an outline of the security perimeter for the event in areas of responsibility, or AORs.

Now, every single presidential event is controlled by the Secret Service. Kimberly Cheatle, the former director who resigned in disgrace, claimed that Butler rally security was assigned to the local police. That's not correct, hence *resigned* and *disgrace*. Now, they may have been in areas considered outside the perimeter, but the Secret Service has command of every single hierarchy for a presidential visit, period. Full stop. Anyone brought into this is working through their operational plan. The concept of operations (the "con-op") would be devised by the Secret Service and then disseminated to all other protective teams. But at the basic sync-up meeting that morning, again, the Secret Service wasn't there. Such meetings typically cover radio frequencies, communication plans, the basic workflows of the day, threat detection and response, and worst-case scenarios. And they couldn't be bothered to show up. Nor could the Secret Service counter-snipers use radios at the rally itself, when time was of the essence. X user @ amuse matches our shock and dismay:

> I don't know what shocked me more, finding out that the Secret Service had never provided Trump counter sniper protection until the Butler rally or that they didn't provide the Secret Service snipers radios but told them to use their personal cell phones to text each other.[11]

Moreover, leaked personal text messages revealed that those counter-snipers were aware of Crooks up to ninety minutes before the incident. And yet they had no direct communication with the SWAT team's snipers who were stationed in the very same building where Crooks took the shots. Local law enforcement did not have Secret Service cell phone numbers nor did they have radio access; local police in Butler had radios available for the Secret Service, but nobody bothered to pick them up.[12] CNN of all outlets explains the ramifications:

> The next day, three minutes before shots were fired toward Trump, local police radioed that a man was on a nearby roof. That warning never made it to the Secret Service, whose snipers didn't know the would-be assassin was on the roof until shots rang out. In the 15 seconds it took for snipers to lock onto and kill the shooter, he was able to fire off eight shots.

Standing over the gunman's dead body minutes later, a local police officer who responded to the initial warning expressed frustration that his own radio calls about a man on the roof seemed to go unheeded by the other officers.

"That's what I was f**king calling out bro, f**king 'On top of the roof,'" the officer said, according to body camera footage.[13] "We're not—we on the same frequency?"[14]

Next up, both Christopher Paris, the Commissioner of the Pennsylvania State Police, and Richard Goldinger, the Butler County District Attorney, provided insights into the actions of local police officers before the shooting. Their statements, given during congressional hearings and subsequent clarifications, offer other strange circumstances around the shooting.

Christopher Paris's testimony painted a picture of significant security lapses. He confirmed that two officers from the Butler County Emergency Services Unit (ESU) actually left their assigned overwatch posts in the building with a vantage point over the area where Thomas Matthew Crooks, the shooter, eventually fired the shots. Paris explained that these officers left to search for Crooks after he was spotted acting suspiciously.

This decision led to a direct confrontation with Crooks, where one officer attempted to climb onto the roof where Crooks was positioned, only to be deterred when Crooks aimed a weapon at him. Paris's account highlighted not just the physical movement of officers but also the broader communication and coordination failures between local law enforcement and the Secret Service, which contributed to the security breach.

Richard Goldinger, however, provided a different perspective in his response to Paris's testimony. He disputed the narrative that the post was entirely abandoned, clarifying that only one of the ESU officers left the building briefly to search for Crooks. Goldinger emphasized that this officer returned to the post after not finding Crooks, and there was always another officer present, suggesting that the post was never completely unmanned. He also pointed out the visual limitations from their location, indicating that even if they had stayed, they might not have seen Crooks climbing onto the opposite side of the building.

None of this makes sense.

To be entirely accidental defies belief.

So, police teams outside the Secret Service text chats had to communicate through an intermediary during the event. They set up a tactical operation center, or a communication center, called the Butler Communication Center or the "TOC." Communication had to go through the TOC, then to its liaison, then to the Secret Service, through their liaison, back to the TOC, and then to the police. This was instead of being on the same frequency and simply saying, "Hey, there's a guy crawling on the building." Which, by the way, would contradict the acting Secret Service director, Ronald Rowe, Cheatle's replacement, who claimed on July 30 that the shooter was prone. No. Crooks was visible *from the ground* at the rally moving about, as caught on camera while President Trump was speaking.[15]

Speculation continues over how a twenty-year-old kid, whose day job involved changing bedpans at a nursing home, could have possibly known the location of the unprotected area. Despite his ordinary background, he managed to find the one spot with a height advantage—a building that was left unguarded. The circumstances seem almost too fortunate to be coincidental.

We were also told that, at one point, the Butler police sent a couple of units to check out the roof because they suspected someone might be up there. It's unclear why the sniper team inside the building didn't simply look down from inside and check the roof themselves. On the ground, one officer hoisted another on his shoulders to get a better look, but they couldn't see any ladder. They went up there, and one officer saw Crooks, who then turned and aimed his rifle directly at the officer. The officer ducked down, and according to the officer's report, Crooks then swung the rifle back around and began firing at Trump. This wasn't a situation where he was lying in wait, totally unintercepted. The shots rang out within seconds of him switching his sight picture from the officer back to Trump.

Being able to switch the sight picture that far at that range, maintain your composure, and still get off a shot, which has a little bit of connection to the ear, is still a skilled shot. But not skilled enough. A little detail Jack will add is that, in the US military, even with basic training, you're not trained to go for headshots; you're told to aim center mass. Why? Because the head turns. The head moves around, making it a smaller target. Center mass includes vital areas like the central nervous system, the brainstem, spinal column, lungs, and heart. There are many important areas there. So as long as you're aiming along that parallel axis, you're likely to hit something important. A shooter's center mass also has a larger target area. It's a target-rich environment if aiming for center mass. We can't help but wonder if Crooks, by aiming for Trump's head, was attempting to recreate the Zapruder film—the black-and-white close-up film that recorded the assassination of President Kennedy, gory details and all. Because as far as we are aware, Trump was *not* wearing a bulletproof vest on July 13. So we can only speculate that this was someone who wanted to put on a sick and evil show for those who bloodlusted for one. See *Motive* chapter.

And it further seems that the Secret Service countersnipers were to give Crooks the benefit of the doubt. No, really. The shooter was indeed spotted and spotted with a rifle. Why was he allowed to fire multiple rounds? And why did the Secret Service counter-sniper wait until after a local SWAT operator returned fire and struck Crooks, to fire?[16] And why did the FBI lie about that? Perhaps you can tell us. Here's how it went down:

When the SWAT officer saw Crooks as a moving target on the rooftop, he quickly left his post and sprinted towards the man, "running to a clear shot position directly into the line of fire while Crooks was firing," Higgins said.

"He stopped Crooks and importantly, I believe the shot damaged the buffer tube on Crooks' AR," Higgins added later, citing eyewitness testimony.

If the shot damaged the buffer tube on the rifle Crooks was using, it would have left Crooks unable to fire more shots.

Crooks went down from his firing position but popped back up several seconds later, the SWAT officer said.

That's when a shot from a U.S. Secret Service counter-sniper struck Crooks, killing him, according to Higgins.[17]

Why wait? Not just for Crooks but for a local as well, Secret Service? From video footage, it's evident that the Secret Service counter-sniper was lying prone, with Crooks clearly in his sight. He was watching him closely. Yet he didn't fire until after the sniper had already shot Trump. The FBI led us to believe the Secret Service shot the shooter alone. It turns out someone else fired first, potentially disarming Crooks, which effectively forced the Secret Service to fire as well.

Again: Why would a Secret Service counter-sniper spot a man with a rifle from 140 yards away and not take the shot? The Secret Service has the authority to use lethal force if necessary to protect the lives of their protectees, and themselves.

When engaging with potential shooters, the Secret Service follows a strict protocol. They begin with detection and assessment, using advanced tools and intelligence to identify threats. Once a threat is identified, agents are trained to position themselves strategically to shield the protectee, often creating a human barrier and swiftly moving the protectee to a secure location. If the threat is imminent, agents are authorized to engage the shooter, using lethal force if necessary. The decision to shoot is based on a split-second assessment of the threat's severity and the immediacy of the danger posed to the protectee. They will first try to visually assess the situation, determine with certainty if there is a credible lethal threat, ensure no one else is in the line of fire, and only discharge their weapons if risk of death or serious injury is imminent. All this, of course, explains why the on-stage Secret Service agents bumrushed Trump and piled onto him in a protective scrum. And yet that need not have happened.

A possible explanation for the counter-sniper hesitation is that he thought it was a police officer. Remember, the local police were

supposed to have control of that building, but there was no communication with them. At events, it's common for someone from one
agency to be mistaken because there are people from various agencies, including many from HSI and other local agencies. With multiple
agencies present, and especially at the RNC where about 130 different
agencies were represented, if there's poor communication because you
didn't attend the meeting and didn't get the radios, then you have no
way of knowing. Consider the hypothetical, "Hey guys, do you have
someone on that building or not? Because I see someone with a rifle
that doesn't look like a police officer and he's aiming his rifle at the
president."

There were not enough people in the right place at the right
time—this is the most lenient explanation we find. "This was a Secret
Service failure. . . . That roof should have been covered," said acting
Secret Service Director Ronald Rowe.[18] So why wasn't it? U.S. Senator
Josh Hawley (R-Mo.) sent Rowe a letter, alleging the Director's role
of scaling back the agency's manpower and retaliating against agents
who voiced their concerns about the security at President Trump's
events.

Senator Hawley's letter dated August 1, was prompted by a heated
exchange with Acting Director Rowe on Tuesday, July 30. During this
exchange, Rowe confirmed that the Secret Service had refused drones
from local law enforcement, a detail uncovered by a whistleblower
who reached out to Hawley's office. Senator Hawley said:

> Whistleblower tells me Secret Service Acting Director Rowe
> personally directed cuts to the USSS agents who do threat
> assessments for events. Whistleblower says those agents were
> NOT present in Butler—and some of them had warned of
> security problems for months.[19]

The whistleblower is not the only one raising alarms; a Secret Service
counter-sniper has also spoken out. On July 29, he emailed the entire
Uniformed Division, vowing to continue speaking out until five
high-level supervisors are either fired or reassigned. He also warned

of another possible assassination attempt before November and expressed his disappointment in the agency's leadership, especially after the Trump rally in Butler on July 13. The sniper called for urgent changes within the agency, criticizing the leadership for failing the officers.

> A Secret Service counter sniper sent an email Monday night to the entire Uniformed Division (not agents) saying he will not stop speaking out until "5 high-level supervisors (1 down) are either fired or removed from their current positions."[20]

The controversies didn't stop there. Dan Bongino exposed more troubling issues within the Secret Service, pointing to a severe level of incompetence, culture of corruption, and cover-ups. Bongino, alongside another agent now on Trump's detail, warned Secret Service management about a suspicious woman, "Anna," hired at the US embassy. Instead of taking action, they were told to keep quiet. The woman was only confirmed as a Russian spy in 2018, exposing the agency's glaring inability to address and manage serious security concerns.

From 2020 to 2022, four Secret Service agents were duped by would-be Trump assassins from Pakistan. Susan Crabtree writing in *RealClearPolitics*:

> [T]wo men of Pakistani heritage were arrested and charged with posing as Department of Homeland Security officers in Washington and duping four Secret Service agents charged with protecting President Biden and his family. According to federal prosecutors, the imposters provided the Secret Service agents with tens of thousands of gifts, including rent-free apartments, in a two-year scheme that began in February 2020 while Trump was still in office.
>
> "Taherzadeh and Ali have attempted to use their false and fraudulent affiliation with DHS to ingratiate themselves with

members of federal law enforcement and the defense community," David Elias, an FBI agent, wrote in the affidavit.

Yet, Elias did not say why the men orchestrated the elaborate plan to impersonate DHS agents and cozy up to members of the presidential protective Secret Service detail. Prosecutors said they used their false identities to obtain security footage of the apartment building, as well as a list of the building's residents and contact information.

The Secret Service agents implicated in the scheme were placed on administrative leave, but it's unclear what disciplinary action, if any, was taken against them.[21]

What are we to make of this track record? As the public clamors for answers, the principle of "innocent until proven guilty" has reasonably flipped, with the Secret Service being presumed guilty until they can prove their innocence. Here's why.

When you look at the government, in criminal justice you have the presumption of innocence. The government has the presumption, the evidence must be on their side. They have to bring the evidence; the burden of proof is on the government because the government is bringing the accusations. We first heard this new standard from Scott Adams, that when it's the government, it's the opposite. The burden of innocence is on the citizens, and the presumption of guilt is on the government. They have to prove they are telling the truth. More on this later.

Our minds are continually pulled pack to two sobering facts. First, no one was on the roof at any point other than apparently this Thomas Matthew Crooks. Second, once all law enforcement around the event knew that there was a problem, knew that something had gone wrong, and Trump was still backstage. The first call to make is to his personal Secret Service detail and say, "Hold him. We have to check this guy out."

But that did not happen. A total and complete review by the authorities—namely, the FBI and the Secret Service—did not happen either, at least not by the time of this writing, despite the investigation being opened. It took nearly six weeks for anything resembling personnel discipline to occur:

> One member of Trump's personal protective team and four members of the Secret Service's Pittsburgh Field Office, including the special agent in charge, have been sidelined nearly six weeks after the incident. The five are still employed but are teleworking and are no longer allowed in the field. They cannot do any investigative work.[22]

Six weeks, when six hours would have been appropriate. As Wisconsin senator Ron Johnson said:

> The FBI and the Secret Service are slow walking and stonewalling the Senate's investigation into the Trump assassination attempt.
>
> If you wanted to raise suspicions and drive conspiracy theories, this is exactly how you'd conduct an investigation.[23]

What else didn't happen that day in Butler, PA? Every male with a healthy testosterone level has already thought about it—about what they would have done. Consider this:

On August 3, Jack conducted a site survey in Butler, Pennsylvania, where the assassination attempt occurred. Jack went live to discuss his observations on *Human Events Daily*, chief among them being just how short the distance appeared in person between the warehouse where Crooks stationed himself on the roof and the very spot where President Trump stood. A sufficiently healthy adult could cover that ground in mere seconds. In a near-last-ditch effort to save the president, imagine literally taking off running across from the rally site to the building. Most of you reading this right now would have risked life and limb to make the run, in the event of radio and phone communication being siloed. You would have done it. You would have booked. Waved. Pointed. Screamed. Assuming you had no rifle to take Crooks out yourself.

Corey Comperatore should still be alive. And Trump should have a perfectly uninjured ear. Daydreams of heroism aside, we return to the obvious and as yet unanswered question: Why was Trump not immediately secured and moved in those critical ninety minutes at any point? Why was there so little responsiveness? So little preparedness?

And on the latter note, we spoke with an Operational Medicine Physician with experience in the Diplomatic Field during our research for this book. "VIP Medic," we'll call this individual, who wished to remain anonymous. But we did receive permission to reprint the encrypted text messages we received:

Not having a BORTAC Medic with President Trump is another substantial security failure considering the uncommon, elevated threat levels he is subjected to as a FPOTUS. These individuals are skilled NREMT certified paramedics, with the vast majority of them having gone through DoD approved Special Operations Medical Training.

While local paramedics were indeed present, the aforementioned professionals possess an elevated level of practical healthcare & emotional integrity necessary to care for a VIP with traumatic injuries in a chaotic, high stress environment.

Being that BORTAC is also under Homeland Security a temporary duty assignment would've been seamless & quick, I can verify that these potential life saving changes are being discussed for the future.

Again, we're left to let our worst fears run free; was this grave lapse another failure by design? Was the intent for a "VIP" to have "traumatic injuries" for which there would be no "elevated levels of practical healthcare & emotional integrity necessary"?

Guilty until proven innocent?

DAY SIX, JULY 18, 2024: THE SPEECH

This chapter is Jack's recollection of the Republican National Convention on **July 18, 2024**:

The air was charged with electricity.

I had been to other political rallies. I'd been to other conventions. Those had enthusiasm, but here? At the 2024 Republican National Convention? Something was different. Something had *changed*. Things were more real, more intense, more focused. This wasn't just some run-of-the-mill collection of speakers, of black-suited and red-tied politicians making promises to voters. I wasn't here for that, and neither were the people next to me. We weren't here to see that.

We were here for a man with a bandage over his ear.

We were here because they tried to kill Donald Trump, the Republican candidate, and they missed. We were here because what was happening *right now* was what they deemed unacceptable. Was what had to be stopped by any means necessary. Was what necessitated putting a "bullseye" on Trump, to use the current president's own words.

The convention hall in Milwaukee was awash with red, white, and blue, the colors of America's flag draped everywhere, from the bunting on the stage to the caps worn by the delegates. I walked along, with my family in tow, navigating through the sea of people, the air thick with anticipation and the scent of freshly printed campaign materials. My wife, Tanya Tay, held onto our two little boys, Jack Jack and AJ, their eyes wide with the excitement of being at such a historic event. And also because I told them Hulk Hogan was coming.

As we found our seats, I took in the grandeur of the Fiserv Forum. The stage, a massive affair, was set against a backdrop of stars and stripes, with large screens flanking either side, ready to broadcast the night's proceedings to the world. The crowd was a mix of the patriotic, the curious, and the hopeful, all waiting for the moment Donald Trump would be officially nominated. The boys kept asking me when Hulk would come. We bought them some snacks at the stand.

Eight years prior, at the 2016 RNC where Trump was nominated, I was in the room as well. The biggest difference? I was there alone. Sure, I had some friends with me, but I didn't have a family yet. Tanya and I had been dating for about a year and a half, but she was overseas during the convention in Cleveland, and we wouldn't be married until November 2017. And now, I was there eight years later with the most important people in the world with me: my family. It was hard not to reflect on all that had happened in the intervening years, and the journey that you go on when you become a parent, a father. Now I had skin in the game. And for them, I wasn't about to back down one inch.

I have to tell you, the atmosphere shifted palpably when the lights dimmed, and the familiar chords of "Real American" filled the arena. Out walked Hulk Hogan, not in his trademark wrestling attire and yellow boots, but in a suit, yet his presence was as commanding as ever as he waved a giant American flag over the crowd. The crowd roared as he approached the center stage, and during his speech, with a dramatic flair, he ripped off his shirt to reveal a "Trump-Vance 2024" tee. The nostalgia hit me like a wave; here was a cultural icon, bridging the gap between the world of wrestling and the political arena, a symbol of America's resilience and showmanship. I was overcome by a powerful wave of patriotic energy and glory, and I almost dropped my three-year-old and was thrown back into a wall. Don't worry, AJ was okay! I've been trying to find footage of the arena from the right angle to see us during this moment, but no luck as of yet.

Hogan's speech was brief but charged, rallying the crowd with tales and physical reminders of America's greatness and Trump's role in restoring it. I felt that surge of pride, not just for the moment, but for the shared American history and culture that Hogan represented. My boys, Jack Jack and AJ, were mesmerized, their hero from the screen now part of their real-life story. They clapped along and cheered.

The night's climax came when Trump himself took the stage. The room, already electric, seemed to pulse with a new energy. Trump's speech was a rollercoaster of emotion, from recounting the assassination attempt to promises of a brighter future. But it was when he brought out the uniform of Corey Comperatore, the slain fire chief, that the mood turned solemn. The stage turned sterling white. The uniform, a stark reminder of sacrifice, was held up for all to see. Trump's voice broke, and across the arena, not a dry eye could be found. I felt Tanya's hand squeeze, her eyes glistening up at me. This wasn't just about politics; it was about the heart of America, the sacrifices made, and the battles fought. She's always been by my side, through every single one, and never once wavered.

Corey's uniform, a symbol of service, stood in stark contrast to the jubilation of the nomination. Trump spoke of Comperatore's bravery, his family's loss, and the nation's debt to its heroes. The room, filled with thousands, became a single entity, mourning together, celebrating together, united in their vision for America.

As Trump concluded his speech, the convention hall erupted into cheers, chants of "USA! USA!" echoing off the walls. Balloons fell from the ceiling, and confetti cannons blasted, but for me, Tanya, and the boys, this moment was more than just a political victory. It was a testament to the enduring spirit of America, seen through the eyes of a cultural icon, a fallen hero, and a leader's vision for the future. We left the event not just as spectators but as participants in a narrative much larger than ourselves, one that would be told for generations to come. And one that would be told well, as long as we won.

DAY SEVEN, JULY 19, 2024:
THE PILE-ON

How do guilty people react when they're caught?

Hold that thought.

How do innocent people respond when they're accused? Let's start there.

The best "tell" for innocence is little to no change in behavior prior to versus immediately following said accusation. An innocent person going about their business, when accused, will give you "the look," tell you to screw off, then go right back to their business. But a guilty person? You know what they do: they change *everything*. It's a deer in the headlights moment, caught in the spotlight, and they *freeze*. Everything grinds to a sudden stop because they got caught and they know it, you know it, everybody knows it.[1, 2]

That sums up what Joe Biden's campaign had been doing since July 13. Before that, to counter the disastrous performance at the debate, his team had been on the offensive. Trump was a threat, was a danger to democracy. Then came the shot, and Biden went silent. The campaign pulled all ads and "outbound communications." Furthermore, we learned that memos were issued mere moments after the shooting, telling staffers to "refrain from issuing any comments on social media or in public."[3]

This was stunning. Keep in mind, the Butler rally was right before the RNC, and that would be the optimal time to ramp up political ads. Counter the messages the Republicans would be putting out during their convention. But to go completely silent?[4]

Did they think their rhetoric contributed? Were they guilty? Well, they sure acted like it. They couldn't have acted guiltier if they had said, "Whoops, my bad, we were trying to incite violence with our anti-Trump content, and it would have worked if it wasn't for you meddling cops!"

But what else had the Biden campaign been doing, if they weren't pumping out counter-messaging?

Prior to the shooting, it seemed to be "stewing in despair."

The debate was bad for Biden, that much a blind monkey could have seen. So, cleanup was necessary. Biden had to do the rounds, meet with top Democrat movers and shakers, do the occasional press conference or two. Except, rather than convincing everyone the debate was a hiccup, it seemed to just be digging a deeper and deeper grave.

Ouch.

But wait, there's more! Not only were his own staffers convinced that he had zero chance (an anonymous staffer told NBC, "No one involved in the effort thinks he has a path,"), they were also convinced he would drag other Democrat candidates down with him.[5]

And they had reason to believe that. Before the shooting, Biden wasn't looking too hot in the polls. Voters were more concerned with his physical and mental capacity (in other words, if he was too weak or dementia-ridden to actually do the job) than they were with Donald Trump's character. And this was after the legal proceedings against Trump![6]

Another poll, from NBC, had Trump leading Biden by 2 points. That same poll also stated that a majority of Democrats wanted someone else to be a nominee.[7]

And after the shooting?

New polls had Trump leading Biden. A sizable minority had said they would consider voting for him after the shooting.[8] Another pollster said that the attempted assassination would have Trump voters "energized."[9] Combine that with a poor debate performance? Team Biden had to be sweating bullets.

It was no wonder, then, that Democrats were calling on Biden to resign.

On **July 19**, Illinois Representative Sean Casten wrote an op-ed for the *Chicago Tribune* that ended with him begging the president to give up election, stating, "It breaks my heart to say it, but Biden is no longer up for that job."[10] He was joined by Representatives Jesús "Chuy" García (IL-04), Mark Pocan, (WI-2), Jared Huffman (CA-2) and Marc Veasey (TX-33).[11] They join Democrat Representatives Mike Quigley (IL -05), Brad Schneider (IL-10), and Eric Sorenson (IL-17).[12] [13] They join over thirty more politicians.[14] These include influential politicians like Adam Schiff (CA-30).[15]

Did Biden listen? No, instead, as of July 17, he said he would consider dropping out of the race if he was diagnosed with a "medical condition."[16] Not merely because people were worried.

He did resume campaigning, but then on the 17th, while in Las Vegas, Biden came down with COVID-19, suffering "mild symptoms," and would be returning to his home in Delaware.[17, 18] This had first been shared by the CEO of Unidos US, Janet Murguia, to "groans in the conference room at the news."[19]

She did, however, assure the group that "We're going to have a chance to hear from him in the future directly."[20] So it seemed that Biden wasn't ready to drop out that day, even when coming down sick.

But then, on July 18, Reuters reported that, though officially denied by the campaign, the *New York Times* reported that Biden was starting to come around to the idea that he'd have to drop out.[21] Why the sudden change? What were they trying to hide?

The news quickly capitalized on the change. The *New York Times* detailed how he was coughing and weak during interviews before he had departed for Delaware.[22]

The next day, Mr. Biden seemed much more frail as he stepped into a dining room at a Mexican restaurant, the Original Lindo Michoacán Desert Inn. Walking more slowly and looking pale, Mr. Biden took group selfies and squeezed next to patrons in a booth as an upbeat Latin song playing over the restaurant speakers . . .

. . . Mr. Biden also sat for an interview with Univision. Fighting through a cough, he articulated the concerns of those who have urged him to drop out.

He then disappeared from public view for nearly two hours while reporters waited outside the restaurant in extreme heat, pacing along the president's motorcade and knocking on the car windows to ask staff members for an update.

Then reporters began to get alerts and text messages from people at the UnidosUS conference, where Mr. Biden had been scheduled to speak in the afternoon.[23]

The pivot took less than a day, as the media turned on Biden. Too sick to run, coincidentally, the one condition that he said he would drop out for. Just as the number of Democrats calling for Biden to step down was reaching critical mass.

It appeared donors were starting to see funds drying up. America Votes reported that fundraising had slowed.[24] At this point, Senator Sherrod Brown of Ohio, running against a Republican (and no doubt in fear of losing his own race) became senator number four to beg Biden to drop out.[25] Later on, two other Democratic Representatives (Morgan McGarvey (KY-03) and Gabe Vasquez (NM-02)) joined the dozens of Democrats calling for Joe Biden to end the campaign.[26]

It was clear what was going on. Joe Biden wasn't just losing his lead in the polls. He was losing the faith of his fellow Democrats.

At this point, it was clear that the Shade War was going hot. On July 2, Jack reported that "Michelle Obama quietly discussing putting together a coalition of wealthy black donors for Kamala Harris." This was the first report that the Obama family had begun to make moves to replace Joe Biden, and was siding firmly with Kamala Harris. The palace coup had begun.

DAY EIGHT, JULY 20, 2024: THE RUMOR

"He needs to drop out. He will never recover from this."[1]

You could be forgiven if you imagined this came from a Republican congressman, talking about President Biden's failing health and recent COVID-19 diagnosis. But that actually came well before Trump survived the bullet. That was said by a member of Biden's own team.[2]

This dissatisfaction with Biden has been in the works for a while. But while Democrats were praying that Biden would drop out of the 2024 presidential race, Republicans went, "Wait a minute, if he's not capable of being president in a few months . . . why would he be capable now?"

That's exactly the point, as vice presidential candidate JD Vance said when he tweeted on **July 20**:

> Everyone calling on Joe Biden to *stop running* without also calling on him to resign the presidency is engaged in an absurd level of cynicism.
>
> If you can't run, you can't serve.
>
> He should resign now.[3]

It's a logical position that shows the absolute clown show that was the Biden Presidency. Biden was the label, not the actual person running it, and *everybody* saw that to the point where the competency of his presidential administration wasn't really called into question.

Because everyone knew it wasn't really his administration.

106

Republicans were jumping onto this blatant hypocrisy, including Bernie Moreno, the man running for Senate in Ohio (a.k.a. the guy threatening Senator Sherrod Brown's grip on power).[4] "Make no mistake, [Senator Sherrod] Brown was fully aware of Joe Biden's mental decline, covered it up," he also said.[5]

Just another example of Joe Biden being the albatross around the neck of anyone with a D next to their name.

But what would Biden do? Would he recognize his own unpopularity and drop out? Save his fellow Democrats and let someone else take the nomination, someone without the baggage of a debate performance that devolved into gibberish?

Nope!

Instead, Biden refused, as of July 20. He "promised to remain in the presidential race and beat his opponent despite growing calls from members of his Democratic Party asking him to withdraw."[6]

This was consistent with his, well, consistently communicated position. On July 5, Biden posted on X:

Let me say this as clearly as I can:
I'm the sitting President of the United States.
I'm the nominee of the Democratic party.
I'm staying in the race.[7]

But the bullet at Butler changed everything.

"Before Biden stepped aside, a majority of Americans thought the attempted assassination of Donald Trump would increase his chances of winning the 2024 election" read one headline for a YouGov poll. [8] The shot that was supposed to put an end to Trump once and for all backfired, and backfired badly. Now, it looked like the damage was done to Biden.

The Democrats realized that Trump's survival meant Biden could not win, and had to go. He was beating them in the polls before the shot, and now? Now he was in the same camp as Ronald Reagan, Andrew Jackson, and Teddy Roosevelt, having survived an assassination. The bullet didn't eliminate him, it practically crowned him.

It must have driven Democrats mad, realizing that people would be mentioning Trump, Roosevelt, Reagan, and Jackson in the same breath. Practically legendary figures in American history.

The only way it could have been worse—more dramatically ironic—is if Biden's people were involved.

Are we suggesting we think the Biden administration, which was responsible for Trump's security, allowed this to happen? It's not outside the realm of possibility. It's just not. We wouldn't necessarily say it was Biden's call, though. That's the part that we might have hesitation on.

One of the weird quirks of our system is that while the Biden administration was the name, that's not actually who's running it. To understand correctly what the situation was, Donald Trump was running not only to remove the Democrats from power, but the regime system itself. And in fact, that same regime also provided for his security.

That's very weird.

So, let's talk hypothetically:

Let's say you knew that security posture wasn't doing well back then. Let's say you knew that the Secret Service was stretched thin. Let's say you knew, for example, that Trump's normal team—the people who are used to the type of threats that come around when Donald Trump is in town and holding a rally—wasn't around him.

Keep that in mind when you're talking about the FBI, when you're talking about loners like this Thomas Matthew Crooks. Our minds keep going back to the Garland, Texas shooting. You might remember this. It was like Pamela Geller, and they did the "Draw Muhammad" event. (Geller was an anti-Muslim activist who had organized the event, with a cash prize for cartoon depictions of the Prophet Mohammed.) Jack actually knew some people who were there. That event was later attacked by a couple of these locally trained, homegrown domestic terrorists who were supposedly in support of ISIS at the time. Well, we know that there were two guys who opened fire and that the two guys were both shot and killed. And we know that they were killed before anyone else was able to be killed inside the Garland, Texas 2015 event.

But did you know about the FBI asset in the car behind them directing the whole thing?

The guy that had texted "Tear Up Texas"? This came out, by the way, because the two terrorists had a third friend who was later charged with financing all of this, and that friend's lawyer uncovered text messages and communications in discovery about an FBI employee as well as multiple informants that were all involved with this mosque that they were attending in the Phoenix area.

One of the assets, or one of the employees, was paid like $132,000 over the course of years to befriend these guys and to push them in this direction of radicalization. And then we were told—and all of this comes out in the lawsuit, but is completely thrown out based on standing grounds, sovereign immunity—that not only is there an FBI guy talking to them, he was saying, "tear up Texas," inciting them to violence, knew that they were going to the event and was sitting in the car behind the two of them when they opened fire.[9]

When that happened, he fled. He was actually stopped by local police and arrested. They asked, "Why are you fleeing the scene?" And he said, "Well, I saw shooting." He was put in handcuffs at one point. Later, and this came out years later, they found out this guy was an FBI asset. He'd been talking to the terrorists the entire time. Comey wiped the entire thing under the rug.

For years, we were told that these were just a couple of nut jobs trying to shoot up a conservative anti-Muslim Draw Muhammad event. In fact, the initial photo that was reported by local law enforcement of the event was taken by the FBI asset who was sitting in the car. That's how he was able to get the photo. Wow. What a great shot.

Think about the Trump rally, of course. Well, the New York Times was there. Obviously, at the beginning of the rally, that's when the photographers always come in. Usually, the photographers leave after a couple of minutes. There's the set period when they come in and then they leave from that directly under the ground shot.

Kind of interesting that that's when the shots were fired.

So there's precedent for this.

And we think January 6 is the perfect example. We've never gotten accounting of how many federal agents were in the crowd, but an enormous number, way disproportionate to any other event we've ever heard of in Washington. And while it was to some extent organic, to some extent it was also a setup. That's our sincere and pretty well-informed opinion of that.

DAY NINE, JULY 21, 2024:
THE PALACE COUP

"We turn now to the co-chairman of the Biden-Harris reelection campaign, Cedric Richmond, and he joins us this morning from New Orleans."[1]

And so began an interview on *Face the Nation*, the morning of **July 21**, where Margaret Brennan squared off with Cedric Richmond, one of the driving forces behind Joe Biden's campaign. She asked about the forty politicians who were calling for Biden to resign, to let someone else take the reins. "Clearly leadership is setting up a permission structure for lawmakers to come out and say these things. Has Joe Biden lost control of the Democratic Party?"[2]

Richmond's answer?

RICHMOND: No, he's not, and he's heard those concerns. And I want to be crystal-clear. He's made a decision, and that decision is to accept the nomination and run for reelection, win reelection, and I think that there are those out there that need to hear it again, that he made a decision. He's going to be the candidate. He's going to be the next president. And now it's time to focus on the threat that Donald Trump poses and what the extreme agenda is on the other side.

BRENNAN: Is the president aware that the calls are only growing in number and not diminishing?

RICHMOND: The president's aware of the calls, and the president has made clear that members should do what they think they need to do. And he's going to do what the American people need him to do, and that's to beat Donald Trump.[3]

No matter what Brennan said, Richmond was insistent. Biden would *not* back down.

> **RICHMOND:** "The voters in Congressman Dean's [a challenger to Biden in the Democratic primary] district wanted the president to be the nominee. And he is the nominee and he's going to be the next president of the United States."[4]

The message that morning was clear. Biden was not going to be stepping down.

Or at least, not *willingly*.

"[A] coup is still a coup."[5]

This sentence headlined an opinion-editorial in *The New York Times* on the eve of the Democrat National Convention in August 2024. For once, the paper of record says the quiet part out loud:

> A coterie of powerful Democrats maneuvered behind the scenes to push an incumbent president out of the race.
>
> . . . it was a jaw-dropping putsch.
>
> But at some point, when the polls cratered, Democratic mandarins decided to put the welfare of the party—and the country—ahead of the president's ego . . . Also, they all could know that Biden was slowing faster than he and his family and his inner circle were acknowledging.[6]

The author named Barack Obama, Nancy Pelosi, Chuck Shumer, and Hakeem Jeffries as some of the apparent chief architects of this "coup." In fact, even Pelosi commented as much, saying that she hoped that her relationship with Joe Biden could "survive" and that "I lose sleep on it, yeah."[7, 8] "I had to do what I had to do. . . . My concern was not about the president, it was about his campaign."[9]

This wasn't something that Biden had been talked into. This was something he had been *forced* into. According to Biden's longtime advisor Ron Klain:

> "I think it was unfortunate because I think that the president had won the nomination fair and square," Klain said. "Fourteen million people had voted for him and the vice president as vice president." He added: "I do think, you know, the president was pushed by public calls from elected officials for him to drop out, from donors calling for him to drop out. And I think that was wrong."[10]

It turns out, not only did Biden's staffers think this was wrong and unjust, but so did Biden. And this seemed to be a resentment that had been steeping for some time.

> The president already resented Obama for shoving him aside for Hillary, and he resented Hillary for squandering that opportunity and losing to Trump. Even though Obama tried to do everything quietly to protect his saintly status, Joe was furious that Obama was sidelining him twice.[11]

Why do this? Why deny Joe Biden his chance to run? In his own words, "[W]hat happened was a number of my Democratic colleagues in the house and Senate thought that I was gonna hurt them in the races."[12]

Meanwhile, as if they really wanted to rub salt in the wound, the Democratic operatives, who had just finished sticking metaphorical knives into Joe Biden's back, went on to praise him. To wash their hands of the figurative blood, they "whitewashed the coup by ornately extolling Biden."[13]

> James Clyburn told CNN that Biden had a record "that no president of the United States could ever match." Pelosi proposed on CBS's "Sunday Morning" that Biden's face should be carved onto Mount Rushmore. "You have Teddy Roosevelt

up there," she said. "And he's wonderful. I don't say take him down. But you could add Biden."[14]

Yes, the same Pelosi who had said that said "I had to do what I had to do. . . . My concern was not about the president, it was about his campaign."[15]

It was ornate . . . but sloppy. One, we have the receipts. And two, on the morning of the DNC convention, the official DNC platform was released . . . with *multiple* references to "President Biden's second term" and other such language.[16]

This has to have been the worst coup in the history of coups, maybe ever. But surely, you say, this has never happened before!

Well, we've got some news for you.

When the Soviets wanted to get rid of Khrushchev in 1964, he was on vacation in what is now the Republic of Georgia, in Abkhazia. He was on the beach while Brezhnev and all the other officials gathered in the Kremlin.

They decided, "Okay, we're done with this guy. He's old. We're pushing him out." This was their moment. They thought, "We're not going to wait for a 'Death of Stalin' situation with him. We're just going to go in and decide we're making the move." They got together with the KGB because Brezhnev had already maneuvered everything so his people were in power. They ran the full unhumans playbook on Khrushchev and decided he was done.

When he flew back to Moscow, they told him, "We have a meeting to discuss agricultural reports." The KGB intercepted Khrushchev at the airport. They brought him in and handed a resignation letter to him, saying, "This is the letter you're going to sign."

At that point, Khrushchev thought, "You know what? I'm old. I always kind of knew this day was going to come." So he just went along with it. He totally gave in. They put him under house arrest for the rest of his life. He was never seen or heard from again, except for a memoir that came out later.

That's the Soviet Union. America is a free and transparent country. And yet, it sounds so similar.

It was at this point that the successor to Joe Biden's campaign was chosen.

If you need more proof that we live in an oligarchy pretending to be a democracy, more proof than the last few years of the regime, here you can see it out in the open. The real business of the oligarchy gets conducted in the shadows . . . normally. They can pretend that everything is happening through democratic processes, but in this case, as Biden is weighing down every other Democrat running, they had to act visibly.

The irony is that Democrats are far more likely to emphasize that we "live in a democracy" even though technically, America was founded as a republic. "They're fighting to protect our democracy" and "Donald Trump is a threat to our democracy!" But the thing is, none of this is real! None of the rhetoric has any shred of truth backing it! At this point, with delegates—lawfully elected to support Joe Biden—immediately switching to Kamala Harris, they're basically saying that the 14 million people who voted . . . don't matter. Who's the threat to democracy?

Donald Trump *is* a threat to the oligarchy. He's a spanner in the works. Obviously, the oligarchy tries to get rid of him. Yes, there's the nuclear option—the 1963 option—but they don't want to begin with that. It's messy, difficult, and you might just turn the victim into a martyr. Instead, it's easier to assassinate someone's character. Break their spirit. That was a lesson the Stasi of East Germany had learned. If you can manage that, then the victim takes themselves out for you. Sometimes they commit suicide, other times they just disappear from life.

Except now, that doesn't work.

Before, you had official channels. You had TV and radio, and you could control the narrative there. Now? Social media has *actually* democratized that. You can't just lie with impunity, because now anybody can call you out. Anyone can go viral with the truth.

What's left is force. Ratcheting up force—midnight raids, lawfare, et cetera—until at last, you're left with the nuclear option. Which, at this point, is what you just saw.

Think about it. They had deep state guys like Bolton and Pompeo, trying to run regime change on Trump while in office. That failed. They pushed Trump out in 2020. And, for good measure, they loaded him up with tons upon tons of bogus lawsuits. That didn't work. *Well, at least Trump will lose his cool in the debate!* And that backfired so spectacularly that, it seems, they were left with no other choice.

And then *that* failed.

"Biden" has to resign. Even though that morning his campaign co-chairman said that he wasn't going to quit. You pull a Khrushchev on Joe. Hunter Biden is facing felony tax charges. You pardon Hunter Biden, clean up the messes, make sure that Jill Biden has enough money to live in Rehoboth for the rest of her life.

But who then succeeds? Well, at this point, they're stuck with the DEI hire. They're stuck with Kamala Harris.

Before George Floyd, Biden was looking at Senator Amy Klobuchar, or even Gretchen Whitmer as his VP pick for the 2020 election. But then George Floyd happened. Kamala Harris was the pick because she checked off so many boxes. And now? That's an integral part of the Democratic platform. They *have* to go with her. Even if nobody really wants her. And nobody does! She's just *not Biden.*

In fact, only after Jack tweeted that Biden's official announcement post didn't endorse Kamala did the official Biden account rush out a photo of the two of them!

The thing is, is it even legal? So many people donated to Joe Biden . . . and now all that money was practically looted by Kamala Harris. In fact, she even registered using Biden's candidate number, muddying the waters further and making it difficult to say whether she doesn't have a claim to Biden's war chest.[17]

In fact, during the DNC, after the coup had taken place, Biden even admitted it was so that the Democrats could focus on House and Senate seats, even though he insisted it was his own decision.[18]

California Governor Gavin Newsom himself slipped up, joking that he was *told* to say the system was inclusive.[19]

"We went through a very open process, a very inclusive process. It was bottom-up, I don't know if you know that. That's what I've been told to say," Newsom said as he laughed during a talk with "Pod Save America" posted Friday.[20]

Joking. You know, the way Hollywood joked about Harvey Weinstein's behavior. An open secret, so obvious that you can make fun of it.

And during the week of the Democratic National Convention, on August 21, the day after President Joe Biden spoke, Trump posted this commentary on Truth Social. We can't say it better ourselves, so we end this chapter here:

I watched Joe Biden Monday night, and was amazed at his ANGER at being humiliated by the Democrats. I was happy to have played a part in his demise in that it all began on the evening of June 27, 2024, THE DEBATE, which I think was heavily pushed and promoted by Comrade Kamala Harris. She knew what was going to happen, and so did everyone else. It led to a first ever COUP of the President of the United States, who is now unhappily sunbathing on a Beach in California, watching the waves, and thinking how much he hates Barack Hussein Obama, Crazy Nancy Pelosi, and Lightweight Movie "Star" George Clooney, who failed to come to Crooked Joe's defense. The good news is that I believe Joe Biden, the Worst President in the History of the United States, who served with the Worst Vice President in the History of the United States, is now seething. I don't know why he gave up, I don't know why he quit. He got 14 Million Votes, she got NONE. He's an angry man now, and he should be![21]

PART III

AFTER THE SHOT

Revelations and Ramifications

ONE INCH FROM
CIVIL WAR

Let's lay out a hypothetical.

What if?

What if Donald Trump had been assassinated?

What if Donald Trump hadn't turned his head at the ultimate moment?

In this hypothetical scenario, we believe that two things would have happened. **First**, a monumental funeral would have been held at Mar-a-Lago, Trump's private residence in Florida. This event would have been unprecedented, surpassing all previous records to become the largest and most-attended (and most-viewed) funeral in the history of the observable universe.

To put it in perspective, the largest funeral in history was that of C.N. Annadurai, the Tamil Chief Minister of Madras State, which drew approximately 15 million mourners in 1969.[1] It would have surpassed the global viewership of Queen Elizabeth II's 2022 funeral, which saw over a million attendees in London and around 4 billion viewers worldwide.[2]

Yet the spectacle of his funeral is only the surface level of what would have come next, which brings us to the **second** and more important point: A one-inch shift to the right in the bullet's trajectory could have sparked massive uprisings all over the country. This headline from Arie Perliger, Director of Security Studies and Professor of Criminology and Justice Studies, UMass Lowell in *The Conversation U.S.* is prescient for that alternate history:

'One inch from a potential civil war'—near miss in Trump shooting is also a close call for American democracy.[3]

Had the Lord not intervened. Had Trump not swiftly tilted his head to view the chart, we would have seen likely violent protests near Mar-a-Lago, with federal informants inciting a grieving mass mob into boiled-over conflict with local law enforcement and counter-protesters. It would have been January 6, 2021, but every day and nationwide.

By Fall 2024 in this alternate history, the election is essentially over. It's not a genuine election anymore—there's no real voting happening. Sure, we would go through the motions the same way the Democratic Party went through the motions to select Kamala Harris as the 2024 nominee. The scenario would involve a manipulated process where the entire opposition has been criminalized nationwide, as there would likely be a domestic terrorist watch list with millions of Trump supporters added to it—by the week.

Undoubtedly, this would lead to conflict and bloodshed. That said, we believe that due to a lack of organization it would unlikely be successful—and contrary to what the media might tell you—Republicans, by and large, are not insurrectionists. People on the right aren't naturally inclined toward such extreme actions.

Contrary to what some might think, Republicans, despite recognizing its flaws, largely believed in the 250-year-old system because it worked better than others. Now, imagining this alternate history we were so close to, dark forces have torn it apart, and it wasn't the right that caused its destruction. The federal government under President Biden would have launched a Patriot Act 2.0 to unconstitutionally and extrajudicially monitor, charge, and punish those millions added to the watch list database. Rule of law would, in effect, have been suspended. We would be told it's "for the greater good," of course. No Republican would be allowed to win federal office again if he or she had been caught on record speaking positively of the late President Donald Trump. And the US military would deploy internally, keeping the peace of course.

Imagine drone strikes on US soil against conservative Christian influencers calling for justice for the assassinated president. That was our future. A future one inch away. And everyone involved would be "just doing their job." Those Trump supporters who were not outright executed or imprisoned would have been isolated into e-gulags, prevented from working, banking, moving, or buying certain goods (like firearms) and services (like retail investing). And there would not have been a single thing they could have done about it. Presumed allies in the institutions would be enemies of the people.

Nothing New under the Sun

Historically, this pattern of infiltration and destruction would not be unique to the United States in this alternate timeline. This is what destructive forces do in any system where they want it to, whether it be pre-revolutionary France, whether it be Bolshevik Russia, whether it be Spain in the 1930s, whether it be of course China in the 1920s, 30s, 40s, all the way up to the founding of the People's Republic of China. This is what they do. These forces infiltrate institutions, incite unrest, and directly target the military. As seen in the Russian Revolution, the military was heavily targeted, with deserters from the Imperial Army becoming the first units of the Red Army. However, instead of facing Germany, these units were redirected towards St. Petersburg under the leadership of the German agent Lenin. And many of these units were used for radicalization.

Imagine all that, on American soil. The regime would metastasize. The oligarchical panopticon would grow in might. The managerial elite would micromanage more. This is what they do. What they would have done. If not for the chart.

Now, assuming there was any semblance of a real election, the two figures of the intramural war on the right for the future of the Republican Party would have been corrupted warmonger Nikki Haley versus the heir himself: Donald Trump Jr., together with his family members and what remained of the Trump empire. Haley would have likely attracted the backing of the oligarchs, the money, and the power players, however. She would have been handed the GOP nomination the same way largely that Kamala had on the DNC side, by establishment Republicans eager to remove Trumpism from the Uniparty system.

There are questions about when it was decided that Nikki Haley was to be added to the Republican National Convention agenda, and she was added to the schedule just two days after the assassination attempt. Initially, she wasn't supposed to be there. Neither was Ron DeSantis, who had also run against Trump in the primary. They were initially not slated to speak at the RNC. But at some point, they were later put on. Nikki Haley would then mention in her speech, "Donald Trump wants me to be here." Then there went viral a clip showing Trump talking to JD Vance, and he mouthed, "She wanted to speak," referring to Haley. So it appears she pushed her way in, and whoever was in charge decided to allow it in the name of unity. That said, forgiveness is a necessary practice in politics. The critical point is about safeguarding oneself. The issue is whether extending forgiveness means allowing those who have caused harm to continue affecting your circumstances. Forgiveness should not equate to self-sabotage or allowing harmful individuals to remain involved in important matters. Forgiveness is something that happens in your heart. It's not, "I'm going to let you in my house now and sit at my table when I know you."

The lesson here is that all of this can end in the blink of an eye. Again, just one inch to the right. And all of it goes away. Then that would have ignited a massive fight, with figures like Nikki Haley and Don Jr. vying for control. But you look at some of this movement right now, and a lot of it is on the precipice of Donald Trump—because of his figure, because of his notoriety, because of his connection with the people—that you take him out and suddenly the whole nation is up for grabs. And anyone associated with Donald J. Trump or his supporters would have been prohibited from grabbing it.

And that's where we would have been. Where we almost were. If not for the chart.

THE HERO'S FUNERAL

On July 14, 2024, conservative Christian commentator John Doyle wrote on X:

> You shoot into a crowd of Trump supporters, like in Butler, you hit hardworking men adored by their families.
> You shoot into a crowd of leftists, like in Kenosha, you hit convicted sex offenders and pedophiles.
> Huh. What are the odds?[1]

Doyle only got one aspect wrong—then-seventeen-year-old Kyle Rittenhouse did not "shoot into a crowd" during the Kenosha, Wisconsin, riots of 2020, but rather opened fire in self-defense. Yet again we find a point of difference between the armed left and the armed right in America. Offense versus defense, respectively.

> **BREAKING:** Kyle Rittenhouse has been acquitted of all charges after pleading self-defense in the deadly Kenosha, Wisconsin, shootings that became a flashpoint in the nation's debate over guns, vigilantism and racial injustice.[2]

In any case, the hardworking men adored by their families included fifty-year-old firefighter Corey Comperatore, who was struck by a bullet from Thomas Matthew Crooks at the Butler rally. He died because he shielded his family from the gunfire.

Comperatore was a committed firefighter up until his passing. He started as a volunteer at the age of sixteen, and eventually, he became a fire chief for Buffalo Township Volunteer Fire Company during the early 2000s before stepping back to dedicate more time to his family.

His daughter Allyson remembered him as a devoted "girl dad," braiding hair, attending cheer competitions, and even impressing the cheer squad with his back handsprings.

He would put my hair in braids if I wanted my hair in braids.

When I was doing competitive cheer, he was the cool dad because he could do back handsprings—and as soon as everybody got wind of that, he had all these little girls begging him to go up and do these back handsprings on the tumble track.[3]

Helen Comperatore shared during interviews that she and her husband were looking forward to their twenty-ninth wedding anniversary when they decided to attend the Trump rally in Butler, Pennsylvania on July 13, 2024, as a family to show their support.

Me and the kids were all there as a family.

He was just excited. It was going to be a nice day with the family.

It was a bad day.

He was a very loving husband.

He was a simple man but he put his wife and kids first all the time. I did nothing here. I didn't lift a finger. He did everything.[4]

When shots rang out, Comperatore instinctively shielded his wife and daughters, sacrificing himself to protect them. He yelled at them to "Get down!" as he pushed Allyson out of the way. These will be his last words. Unfortunately, he was struck by one of the bullets.

Despite the chaos, his thoughts remained on his family's safety until his final moments.

Comperatore's wife recently announced that she is seeking justice and has hired a lawyer, determined to uncover the truth behind the security failures that allowed such a tragedy to occur.

JUST IN: Corey Comperatore's widow DEMANDS ANSWERS for the massive security failures in Butler that took her husband's life, retains attorney.

I know he would want me to get the bottom of it. I want justice for my husband and I am going to get it.[5]

As the Comperatore family grapples with their profound loss, they are demanding accountability from the rally's security team. Kaylee Comperatore's statement reflect the pain and urgency behind their search for answers:

I just want them to know that I really think my dad's blood is on their hands, and I hope they wake up every day thinking about what they took from our family. Because we have to wake up every day and see that image of our father in our head, and no child should ever have to see that.[6]

An online fundraiser for the Comperatore family has surpassed $1 million, far exceeding its initial goal of $7,000.[7] The campaign was organized by Jason Bubb, the owner of Three Fit Six gym in Cabot, where Comperatore's daughter, Allyson, is a long-time member. Jason, who also counts himself as a friend and neighbor to the family, set up the fundraiser to support the family during this difficult time.

After that grim Saturday's shocking events, a memorial site was established outside Buffalo Township Volunteer Fire Department the next day where the local community paid respects to Comperatore. His fire company colleagues displayed his turnout gear and draped it with black ribbons of mourning.

In addition, black bunting was draped solemnly across his fire station locker. Black bunting is a solemn tradition of displaying black fabric to signify mourning when a firefighter or first responder passes away.

A few days later, Helen Comperatore shared on Facebook on Tuesday, July 16—that Trump personally reached out to express his sympathy and assured her he would continue to stay in contact in the days to come.

He was very kind and said he would continue to call me in the days and weeks ahead.

I told him the same thing I told everyone else. He left this world a hero and God welcomed him in. He did not die in vain that day.[8]

On Thursday, July 18, the town of Freeport, Pennsylvania, gathered to pay tribute to Corey Comperatore. The visitation was held at Laube Hall, 115 Community Park Rd. Outside Laube Hall, a row of flags greeted those arriving to pay their respects, a tribute meticulously arranged by Jeff Jones, Dawson Gaillot, and Anthony O'Donnell.[9] The three men, none of whom knew Comperatore personally, were moved by his story and his service as a ten-year Army reservist. They spent their Thursday morning carefully placing each flag, ensuring it was done with precision as a mark of respect. Gaillot said:

> I'm thinking about how there's going to be a nice little procession up here and how people are going to be passing through this.[10]

Jones, on the other hand, commented that he was simply reflecting the community's desire to support Comperatore's loved ones during their time of loss.

> It's all for his family and his daughters and wife, that's all and just a tribute to him. [11]

Meanwhile, O'Donnell said:

> Someone in the community is at a low right now and we need to help pick them up and bring them back up to where they should be.[12]

In response to the tragic event at the rally, a Trump-endorsed GoFundMe campaign was launched by Trump Campaign National

Finance Director Meredith O'Rourke to help the victims and their families. Former President Donald Trump authorized this account to ensure all donations go directly to those affected by the horrific assassination attempt. The shooting not only claimed Corey Comperatore's life but also left two others critically injured—US Marine David Dutch, fifty-seven, and James Copenhaver, seventy-four—both of whom are now recovering at home after their release from the hospital.

As of this writing, the online fundraiser has reached more than $6.5 million, with Dan Newlin contributing $1,000,000 as the top donor, followed by Elon Musk with $100,000, and Kid Rock with $50,000, among many others.

> President Donald Trump has authorized this account as a place for donations to the supporters and families wounded or killed in today's brutal and horrific assassination attempt. All donations will be directed to these proud Americans as they grieve and recover. May God bless and unite our nation.[13]

On Thursday night, July 18, in Milwaukee, former President Donald Trump delivered a powerful RNC acceptance speech that reflected both his vision for America's future and his response to the Butler rally tragedy. He spoke passionately about launching a new era of unity, safety, and prosperity, while also honoring the victims.

He addressed the heartbreaking loss of Corey Comperatore and extended sympathy to David Dutch and James Copenhaver—who were both seriously injured in the attack—as well as their respective families.

Trump paused his speech and took a moment to kiss the fire suit and helmet of Corey Comperatore that was displayed onstage at the Republican National Convention. Comperatore's wife, Helen, said:

> That was a big honor. I'll tell you why. All day at the rally, my husband kept saying, "He's going to call me up on stage, you're going to hear him, he's going to say Corey, get up here."

He was just joking, obviously, but he kept saying that—"He's going to call me up on stage"—and we were all like, there's his moment. He's up on stage. He got his moment on stage.[14]

Eight firefighters carried Comperatore's casket—draped in a US flag, out of the church—while his family and other mourners looked on. The flag was then removed by the firefighters and presented it to his widow, Helen, after which his casket was carefully loaded onto a fire truck draped in black bunting.

On August 13, Trump announced plans to return to Butler, Pennsylvania, for a rally in October, just months after surviving an assassination attempt there though he did not provide a specific date or location for the event. During a social media conversation with Elon Musk, Trump confirmed:

We're going back to Butler and we're going to go back in October. We're all set up.[15]

Helen Comperatore has been invited to join Trump onstage at his October rally in Butler, PA. She said she is considering the offer but will base her decision on the security measures in place.[16]

THE DIRECTOR

The day of the shooting, July 13, 2024, former Secret Service agent Dan Bongino posted on X:

> It is time right now for Kim Cheatle to get her head out of her ass and do the right thing. I could tell you stories for days about her putting politics ahead of presidential protection.[1]

Kimberly Cheatle had not shown herself to be capable of handling the responsibilities that come with leading the United States Secret Service. Cheatle failed at even this simple task.

During her testimony to Congress on July 23, Representative James Comer (R-KY) asked why there were no agents on the sloped roof that the shooter used, pointing out a statement Cheatle made where she said no agents were on that roof because it was sloped. Cheatle's answer? It has to be seen to be believed:

> What I can tell you is that there was a plan in place to provide overwatch, and we are still looking into responsibilities and who was going to provide overwatch. But the Secret Service in general, not speaking specifically to this incident, when we are providing overwatch, whether that be through counter snipers or other technology, **prefer to have sterile rooftops.**[2]

Emphasis ours. But that doesn't make a lick of sense. Secret Service agents are supposed to protect the president in all conditions, rain or shine, day or night. Something like a sloped roof should be a simple problem-solving exercise, not some insurmountable barrier.

Right after that, Comer asked if the Secret Service deployed a drone, since there were reports that the shooter did deploy one. She dodged the question.

Furthermore, requests for additional resources by the Trump campaign were reportedly denied.

Representative Jamie Raskin (D-MD) asked another obvious question: How could a twenty-year-old with his father's AR-15 assault rifle climb onto a roof with a direct 150-yard line of sight to the speaker's podium without the Secret Service or local police stopping him? Even worse, the shooter had no form of ID on their person and was only identified when the AR-15's serial number was checked. While Cheatle took responsibility for the tragedy, she couldn't give a real explanation for this failure.

Representative Jim Jordan (R-OH) caught an inconsistency on Cheatle's part in which she initially denied that the Trump campaign was refused, but then revealed that there were indeed refusals.

Representative Jordan says:

But that's not what he said. He said they were denied certain requests. Some requests. This is your spokesperson, not me talking. This is the Secret Service talking. And what it changed from absolutely false, unequivocally false to, "Oh, by the way, there were some times where we didn't give them what they wanted." That's a huge change in five days, and the fact that you can't answer how many times you did that, that's pretty darn frustrating not just for me but for the country.[3]

Cheatle replied:

I hear your frustration.[4]

Then Representative Jordan asked the following:

Let me ask you this. Were any of those requests denied to President Trump's detail after you knew about the Iranian threat?[5]

To which Cheatle replied:

What I can tell you, again, I don't know the specifics, is that there are times when we can fill a request. It doesn't necessarily have to be with a Secret Service asset or resource, we can fill that request with locally available assets.[6]

Representative Stephen Francis Lynch (D-MA) pointed out another obvious mistake on the Secret Service's part: the failure to isolate the podium from exposure to direct fire, as well as allowing someone deemed by law enforcement to be a 'person of interest' to get anywhere near the rally. Furthermore, local attendees identified the shooter as a suspicious person, yet it was not until the shooter had fired off rounds that the Secret Service took any action.

Representative Virginia Foxx (R-NC) moved on from the failures at the Trump rally to the Secret Service's organizational culture as a whole. She pointed out that in 2022, nearly half the agency's workforce was believed to have left, and that among federal law enforcement agencies, it was ranked dead last. Cheatle countered with claims that the 2022 data was inaccurate and that hiring and staffing had increased. When asked again about the Secret Service's rotten culture, she retreated into platitudes about the agency's commitment to its duty.[7]

Representative Gerald Connolly (D-VA) asked a simple question: Is the Secret Service's mission more difficult because Americans have easy access to guns? Cheatle failed to answer even this simple question in a straightforward way, preferring instead to waffle about:

I think the threat environment for protecting our Secret Service protectees is always difficult and that's dynamic and it's always evolving.[8]

She even tried to use the Second Amendment as a defense, but Representative Connolly recognized the evasion and didn't buy it, hammering home the point that she was refusing to answer even a simple question about threat assessment.

Representative Connolly asked:

We stipulate it's always difficult. Again, this is a simple one. Does the ubiquity of guns make your job easier or more difficult today?[9]

To which Cheatle responded:

I understand the Second Amendment rights of individuals.[10]

Representative Connolly didn't buy this risible attempt at evasion:

I didn't ask that question. I'm not questioning the Second Amendment. I'm asking a simple analysis, Director Cheatle. I can tell you, you're not making my job easier in terms of assessing your qualification for continuing honest director. Please answer the question. You're the head of the Secret Service. You're speaking on behalf of 8,000 members who put their lives on the line. We just had a failure by your own admission. Do guns make your job easier or harder?[11]

Cheatle retreated into platitudes:

I think the job of the Secret Service is difficult on every day and we need to make sure that we are mitigating all threats, whether that be weapons or personnel.[12]

But Representative Connolly got fed up with all the evasions and answered like this:

How else could I feel, Director Cheatle, when you're clearly avoiding a direct answer to a very simple declarative question?

We almost lost a presidential candidate the other day. A 20-year-old had access to his father's AR-15 and got on top of a roof within 500 yards or feet of the podium. I'm asking you, did the availability of that AR-15, which is replicated all across America, make your job harder or easier. You are not willing to answer that question and you wonder why we might have a lack of confidence in your continued ability to direct this agency?[13]

Representative Glenn Grothman (R-MI) cut into another area of concern regarding Cheatle: the idea that she felt there were too many men. Cheatle stated that she selected the best and the brightest she could find.

After more questions from different congressmembers about why the roof used by the shooter was left unguarded, Congressman Pete Sessions (R-TX) grew tired of Cheatle's dodging of questions; a favorite tactic of Cheatle's was stating that the shooting was still under investigation, and thus she didn't want to comment on it. Sessions pointed out that Cheatle had been in the Secret Service for twenty-eight years, yet she didn't want to explain the actual operations of the agency, and she didn't give any analysis either. He then asked how many Secret Service employees were disciplined for the failure at the Trump rally.

Cheatle could not give an answer.

And when Cheatle tried her usual evasive talk, Representative Sessions called her to the carpet for offloading responsibility to other people when she was the one who ran the place. Keep that in mind; **Kimberly Cheatle was the Director of the Secret Service.** That meant that she had detailed information about the agency's operations and a long tenure in the agency, and yet she dissembled and evaded every time she was asked a direct question about why the failure happened. After all, she should know these things—she was the expert with twenty-eight years of experience.

Even Representative Alexandria Ocasio-Cortez (D-NY) took a few shots at her. Earlier, Cheatle said the report about what happened was due in sixty days, but AOC pointed out that the threat to top officials was current, and timely information was needed so that immediate action could be taken.

Cheatle finally gave concrete information—that the usual perimeter around a protectee was 200 yards. However, AOC explained that the AR-15's range is much longer than that, at about 500 yards. Cheatle went right back to her evasiveness, and AOC called her out on it:

> Respectfully, Dr. Cheatle, as well, as a person who has experienced an enormous amount of threat incidents, including incidents that have never been reported publicly, there is a common pattern that happens here, whether it's Secret Service, FBI, Capitol Police, local departments. After a critical security failure, we often hear there will be an independent investigation. That independent investigation gets set up. Usually, the expectation is between two to three months after the incident, and then nothing really occurs from there. The report is usually not satisfactory to the questions that are usually being raised here. And most importantly, corrective action is rarely taken.
>
> If I were to state anything that I think is profoundly important, is that we need to have answers to the public. Ideally, I would encourage you and the agency to be more forthright with the members that still have yet to have their questioning because the public deserves to have full confidence. And the stakes are too high. The violence that could break out in this political moment, regardless of party, in the event of someone getting hurt, constitutes a national security threat to the entire country. Thank you, and I yield back.[14]

And it went on from there. Cheatle eventually realized that she couldn't convince anyone that she knew what she was doing, so she resigned the following day.

Patterns of Failure

On Fox News, Dan Bongino said:

> I am sadly, tragically confident, if we don't change the Secret
> Service directors and other managers there as well, there will be
> another incident. It is not a question of "if"—it's only an issue
> of "when."[15]

It did not matter whether we were talking about Republicans or
Democrats; neither side was satisfied with the performance of the
Secret Service that day, and all the congressmembers got was excuses
and evasions instead of solid explanations about how things normally
work and why certain decisions were made. In the face of such massive criticism from within the government and outside it, Cheatle had
no choice but to leave the agency in shame.

In popular culture, the Secret Service is thought of as a hyper-
competent organization full of action heroes in suits and shades who
can stop any threat before any ordinary person even notices it. This
image is reinforced in countless films and television programs, which
also adds to the agency's prestige.

However, on an interview with Mark Levin on Fox News (the
same one the above quote is taken from), former Secret Service Agent
Dan Bongino explained the following:

> Someone sent me a text message last night; let's just say a friend,
> who is in the know at the entity, that they have BQA'd. That
> stands for "Better Qualified Applicant," meaning they're flush-
> ing people out of the recruiting pipeline with Special Forces
> backgrounds because of DEI-type initiatives in favor of recent
> college grads with no work experience.[16]

Wrap your head around that: People, largely men, with significant
military expertise were being swept aside in favor of the sort of people you'd hire at Starbucks, or the sort of people who'd be hired in
a local police department instead of an agency requiring maximal

competence. While local cops do their best to protect the communities they serve, protecting the president, other elected officials, and foreign dignitaries requires a level of ability that local cops just aren't able to provide. The Secret Service cannot coast on its reputation alone; they have to act when it counts, and with the failed assassination attempt on Trump, they didn't make the grade.

"But the attempt failed," I hear you say. Here's the important thing, though—it failed because Trump turned his head at the right moment, not because of anything the Secret Service did. They only acted after shots were fired and an attendee was killed, so in that respect they *did* fail. **Had the agency been doing its job properly, that shooter wouldn't have gotten on the roof in the first place.**

Never has a reputation as storied as the Secret Service's crashed to Earth so hard. This failure to protect lives at a political rally where a presidential candidate is present may well encourage future attempts, as the entire world has now seen that the United States Secret Service is run by incompetent toadies, not the action heroes people thought they were. Having a reputation for toughness and competence allows you to win without fighting most of the time, because most people would be afraid of you. But after this, what bad actor would be afraid of the Secret Service now?

Through this weak performance, the Secret Service not only endangered Trump, not only endangered Biden, not only endangered Harris, but endangered anyone who may come under their umbrella of protection, now and in the future. Now that the Secret Service has been shown to fail, someone else will try their luck.

All we can do is pray they don't hit the jackpot.

The New Guy Testifies

But the show of incompetence from the Secret Service didn't just stop at Kim Cheatle. The acting director, Ronald Rowe Jr., was brought before Congress as well.[17] Overall, Rowe was contrite about the failures of security, much as Cheatle was.

But much like Cheatle, Rowe was evasive.

Senator Tom Cotton (R-AK) pointed out that no one was covering the roof the shooter used—perhaps the single most obvious issue with how the Secret Service handled the perimeter. Senator Cotton wanted to know why no Secret Service counter-sniper was there.

Rowe responded in a manner that could have been ripped from Wikipedia:

The Secret Service's counter-sniper role is to neutralize those threats that are looking in on us from where the protectee is.[18]

Senator Cotton pointed out further that the Secret Service couldn't even do that much because Trump was hit and one attendee was killed outright, with two others getting injured.

To compound the lack of responsibility, Rowe stated that the agents who failed to act were being interviewed by the FBI and were cooperating with the investigation, but they haven't been relieved of duty. Rowe's reason for not taking this step? *He didn't want to rush to judgment.* Senator Cotton pointed out, with great fervor, that when a presidential candidate was hit with a bullet and a rally attendee was killed, no one in the agency responsible for providing security to the event was held accountable. The failures were plain to see; this was not some he-said she-said incident where the facts were disputed.[19]

Senator Mike Lee (R-UT) noticed something else important: Why was Trump allowed to take the stage after multiple reports of a suspicious individual had come in? Even worse, it was photographic evidence, and the shooter was carrying a rangefinder—something regular people didn't normally use at political rallies. Rowe responded that the agency got no reports of an individual with a gun, but Lee asked if President Biden would be allowed on stage if there were similar amounts of suspicious person reports.

Rowe said he needed more facts, echoing similar evasions by Cheatle.

More damningly, Senator Lee stated that Trump's campaign team had made multiple requests for additional resources, but these resources were denied, though the Secret Service tried to say that no such requests were made in the first place. Rowe had no real answer for this, instead agreeing to submit in writing what requests were made. This is still something; he had to at least admit that the requests were made.[20]

There was also the matter of the two minutes between when the shooter was identified and when the shots were fired. By now the Secret Service had gone from "suspicious person" to "active threat." Senator Lee asks if the Secret Service had a channel of communication where they could take out a person with a gun as soon as that person was identified. Rowe stated that the local police didn't tell the Secret Service that there was a problem, passing the responsibility for the failure on to them.

Senator John Cornyn (R-TX) pointed out that while the *shooter's* drone worked fine, the Secret Service's drones apparently didn't have enough bandwidth, and Cornyn went on to question whether or not the Secret Service had the capability to jam or take down weaponized drones. Rowe answered that the anti-drone system had technical difficulties, which kept it from going operational until after 5:00; by that time, the shooter had his rifle ready. This painted a picture of institutional incompetence, showing that the Secret Service didn't have all its ducks in a row when a presidential candidate was about to give a speech *and* there were credible reports of a suspicious individual.[21]

Continuing this trend, Senator Cornyn asked why an elite law enforcement agency like the Secret Service would delegate key responsibilities to local law enforcement. Rowe pointed out that the agency people assumed that local law enforcement was doing their job and keeping an eye on things.[22]

Ramifications

Overall, we get a picture of an agency in disarray. Sloppy work, evasions of responsibility, and a culture of excuse-making were the orders of the day, and for this reason people got hurt at the rally, with one fatality. Both Cheatle and Rowe were more concerned with protecting their own reputations than owning up to allowing these security failures to take place. It does not raise a whole lot of confidence in an organization that is supposed to protect some of the most powerful and influential individuals on the planet.

But this shameful picture of an elite law enforcement agency acting like clueless amateurs was only the tip of the iceberg. Dan Bongino pointed out that Ronald Rowe, who used to run daily protection operations—the same operations that failed on July 13—was promoted to acting director after Kim Cheatle resigned; from here, he asserted that the Secret Service has not learned its lesson and would allow a similar failure to happen again.

According to a *Washington Times* article titled "Secret Service opens disciplinary probe into agents responsible for securing Trump's July 13 rally":[23]

Unlike his predecessor, Mr. Rowe visited the site of the Butler, Pennsylvania, rally. He said he climbed onto the roof of the building where the would-be assassin fired and laid in the same position as the shooter to understand his view of Mr. Trump.

"What I saw made me ashamed," he said. "I cannot defend why that roof was not better secured."

South Carolina Senator Lindsey Graham, the top Republican on the Judiciary Committee, said if such security failures occurred in the military, many people would have been axed.

"Somebody's got to be fired," he said. "Nothing is going to change until somebody loses their job."

Kentucky Senator Rand Paul, the top Republican on the Homeland Security panel, said he was encouraged to hear the Secret Service opened a disciplinary review, calling the assassination attempt "a monumental failure."

Later in the hearing, Sen. Josh Hawley, Missouri Republican, asked Mr. Rowe who was the lead site agent for the event who made the decision to leave the building the shooter fired from outside the security perimeter—and whether that person was fired.

"This person is operational," Mr. Rowe said, noting the agent is still involved.[24]

A refusal to fire bad performers. Running and hiding instead of own-ing up to inadequacies. Retreating into platitudes when explanations are demanded. How did a law enforcement agency like this one sink into such a mire? What will be the next thing they miss? And why would they miss it?

It's chilling to think that this is what the Secret Service has been reduced to.

THE BIG COVER-UP

"Why are conservatives claiming Google is covering up the shooting of Trump?" asked Al-Jazeera, newsmedia mouthpiece of the Arabian slaver state Qatar.[1]

Well, Al, it's because Google *was* covering up the shooting of Trump.

The article tries to be subtle, and it's another form of malinformation. It implies two lies. First is that it's *just* conservatives claiming Google was covering up the shooting. That there is no "there" there.

The second lie is the insinuation that conservatives are lying. That there's an ulterior motive to their claims. As if by calling out censorship, they're *actually* trying to deceive you.

And yet, what conservatives were claiming is precisely what happened. Search engines were not completing. And then Meta AI was saying the assassination was fiction. And then Leftwing influencers spread that as truth.

"You type in assassination of T-R-U, it doesn't auto-complete Trump," noted JD Vance. "Google is a straight up insane company. It is effectively a left-wing propaganda machine."[2]

But this time, Google hasn't escaped entirely unscathed. Senator Dr. Roger Marshall is now investigating Google for censorship and election interference.[3]

So then, the elite, our oligarchical panopticon, the enlightened few that are just *better* than us, went to work erasing the erasing, when they got caught. And then, they did it again.

JD Vance just said "They Even Tried To Kill Him" about Trump. This is a deeply irresponsible lie and if he had one iota of integrity left he would stop.[4]

It's an "irresponsible lie" to acknowledge he survived an assassination attempt now.

This is what they do.

Those who don't know history are doomed to repeat it; those who allow history to be rewritten are doomed to repeat it sooner.

And now, we humbly submit the closing two chapters as testament and reminder. This is what *we* do.

THE SCENARIOS, REVISITED

Elon Musk shared a popular reframe on X recently. *What's the difference between a conspiracy and the truth? About six months.*

Scenario 1: The Official Narrative

The official narrative is one of chance and happenstance. Thomas Crooks—a twenty-year-old with a bright future, potential mental struggles, and *no discernable motive*—scaled a local building that *just so happened* to be unsecured by Secret Service. He *just so happened* to attempt an assassination—again, for *no discernable reason*—at the one rally where security was so embarrassingly lax it ended up with several officials resigning in shame. All without knowing that this rally would offer him the best chance.

Assessment: Least Likely.

Scenario 2: The Iranian Plot

Iran has been spoiling for revenge against the United States, and Trump in particular, for the drone strike on Qasem Soleimani. In fact, there is a human source that said the Iranians were planning an attack, and the day before the rally, Asif Merchant, an individual with ties to Iran, was arrested for plotting to carry out political assassinations.[1] It was also known that Crooks had encrypted messaging apps on his phone, making it *plausible* that he was in contact with the Iranians.

145

However, there is no evidence that Crooks had any contact with Iran. And Israel is a more likely target of Iran's Revolutionary Guard. Iran has also denied the theory, saying they would rather see Trump tried in court for Soleimani's "murder."

The other motivation behind this could be rooted in the interests of the military-industrial complex, which thrives on sustained military engagement and defense spending. By pinning the assassination attempt on Iran, a long-standing adversary with whom tensions have historically been high, the US could justify a military invasion. This invasion would not only serve as a retaliatory measure but also as a pretext to bolster military presence in the Middle East, thereby ensuring continued or increased defense contracts, maintaining high military budgets, and securing strategic interests like oil routes or countering Iran's influence in the region. Such a scenario would feed into the narrative of Iran as a perpetual threat, necessitating robust military responses, thus fueling the cycle of conflict and defense spending that benefits the military-industrial complex.

Assessment: Unlikely

Scenario 3: The Inside Job

Take a deep-seated resentment for the bureaucratic "deep state" and combine that with the dozens of jaw-dropping, pack-your-bags-you're-fired failures of the US Secret Service, and people start to wonder whether this was intentional. After all, what other conclusion could you draw from the fact that rally attendees were alerting Secret Service to the shooter's presence *minutes* before he took eight shots at Trump, and sadly took the life of Comperatore?

Unlike the other two theories, this one has motive, means, and opportunity. Motive, in that Trump was a spanner in the works, a disrupter; the regime had tried co-opting him, had tried character assassination to keep him down, had tried to throw him in prison, but nothing seemed to be sticking. Means, in that Crooks had encrypted communications platforms. And opportunity, as the federal government would be providing security for an outdoor rally, which is considered one of the most dangerous political events in terms of risk to the politician.

Assessment: Most Likely

The Presumption of Guilt, Say the Odds

The "security failure," which is the official narrative's prime implication, is poison. Because it makes that lone wolf shooter story stronger and moves the focus away from Thomas Matthew Crooks, *his* motives, his secret communications, and what US intelligence knew and when they knew it. This is a strategic misdirection and yes, we do believe it to be strategic. *Oops, we gaffed, sorry Trump, we'll try harder next time*, is thus the conclusion, in effect. How gullible do they think we are? Well, a lot, apparently. Because Trump-friendly commentators, influencers, journalists, and even security experts have been taking the bait hook, line, and sinker. We've even seen such experts form panels to discuss "how I would have done it" to better protect Trump in Butler, PA, when *what if NOT protecting him was the goal?*

You see, this is the same confusion many conservatives have on cultural issues, which we wrote about in *Unhumans*. It is the fried mental model that many Americans have that people in power are basically good people, as most of the rest of us are. So benefit of the doubt is granted when it ought not be. As we wrote earlier, the government is to be presumed guilty until proven innocent. That is the standard, and that is a standard we will uphold until such a time as all government officials, employees, and organizations associated with the events of July 13, 2024, prove themselves to be *not* guilty.

The Twelve "Botches"

We humbly conclude this chapter with more than a legal standard, but with **probability**. Consider the various "security failures" that occurred in Butler, Pennsylvania, that collectively allowed Thomas Matthew Crooks to seep deep into presidential territory and to get off eight shots—eight chances to kill Donald J. Trump. Not one. Eight. Recall that Lee Harvey Oswald needed three to murder President

John F. Kennedy in broad daylight, and the man and his motorcade were *moving*.[2]

In *The Review* chapter, we've called out twelve security "botches" that, had any single one of them been handled with professionalism and care, would have prevented the shooting—and Corey Comperatore would still be alive.

Botch 1, Failure to Attend Security Briefing: Recall that the Secret Service did not attend the security briefing the morning of the rally, leaving local SWAT and sniper teams without crucial coordination and communication.

Botch 2, Inadequate Counter-Sniper Preparedness: Counter-sniper teams showed up only the day before the rally to conduct site casing, rather than weeks prior as is standard. There was no initial plan to provide counter-sniper teams, and even when they were present, their communication tools were insufficient (no radios, only personal cell phones for communication).

Botch 3, Drone Security Refusal: The Secret Service refused drone security offered by local law enforcement, which could have provided crucial aerial surveillance—and made known sooner there was a kid with a gun prowling around within eyesight and earshot of President Trump.

Botch 4, Counter-Sniper Communication Failures: Counter-snipers and local law enforcement had no direct communication, severely hampering the ability to respond to threats in real-time. Radios set aside for Secret Service were never picked up, and there was no established method for cross-agency communication.

Botch 5, Inadequate Manpower: Secret Service agents were instructed not to request additional manpower for the rally, and any such requests were likely to be denied. This directly contradicted testimony from the acting Secret Service director, who claimed that no resources were denied. It seems to us that all they do is lie. Why?

Botch 6, Abandoned Overwatch Post: Officers from the Butler County ESU left their assigned overwatch post, which had a vantage point over the area where the shooter, Thomas Matthew Crooks, eventually fired shots. This abandonment created a significant vulnerability. This fact still has us in disbelief. As in, we are having a hard time believing this was *not* intentional.

Botch 7, Failure to Secure Perimeter and Buildings: The Secret Service failed to secure buildings around the event, specifically the one Crooks used to carry out the attack. There was no surveillance or security presence on the roof from which the shots were fired.

Botch 8, Slow Response to Crooks: Despite being aware of the shooter's suspicious activity ninety minutes before the incident, there was a delay in the Secret Service's response. The counter-sniper hesitated to fire on the shooter, only doing so after a local SWAT officer had engaged.

Botch 9, Failure to Prevent Crooks from Accessing High Ground: Crooks was able to climb onto a roof, bear crawl to a vantage point, and take multiple shots at Trump, all while under the observation of law enforcement. The failure to intercept or neutralize him before the shooting is a significant lapse.

Botch 10, Failure to Secure Trump Immediately after Threat Detected: Trump was not immediately moved to a secure location after Crooks was identified as suspicious. The Secret Service allowed Trump to take the stage even after being aware of a potential threat.

Botch 11, Leadership and Operational Failures: The overall management and operational decisions, including the lack of communication, inadequate preparations, and refusal of additional security measures, indicate systemic failures within the Secret Service, exacerbated by leadership that appeared either negligent, or . . . complicit.

Botch 12, Lack of Specialized Medical Support: The absence of a BORTAC medic, despite the high threat level, is another critical failure in the security plan. This one doesn't seem like a big deal, at first, but consider a worse-case scenario—Trump was hit, but not fatal, and the wound was *bad*. How inconvenient for the president that the most-qualified, most-capable medical personnel would *not* have been present in Butler when the difference between life and death would have been literal seconds. How inconvenient.

These twelve failures reflect a severe breakdown in standard security protocols, coordination, and responsiveness. This is more than a competence issue. It's integrity. And it may be even more than that . . .

What are the odds that all twelve botches could occur on the very same day that there also happens to be an armed man with malicious intent present amid all twelve if-only-one-of-these-hadn't-occured-there-would-have-been-no-shooting as well? Let's think in terms of probability.

Now, neither of us is a statistician, but we *can* run the odds. And we'll do so using *extremely* conservative numbers for the purposes of illustration only, not legal argument. That's OK because you'll get the point anyway. And it's probably all you'll be able to think about for the next month, after you read it.

That said, calculating the precise probability that all twelve security failures occurred simultaneously on the same day as Crooks showing up to the event—and with no knowledge of those twelve security failures—is a wee bit complex. So we'll be armchair statisticians and try to provide a structured approach to estimate the odds, along with the necessary considerations and assumptions. And to estimate the probability mathematically, we need to make several assumptions:

- **Independence**: Each "botch" event occurs independently of the others.
- **Baseline Probabilities**: Assigning an estimated probability to each botch based on general knowledge or analogous situations.
- **Temporal and Contextual Consistency**: All events are considered within the same context (a high-security event) and timeframe (same day).

In reality, these twelve security failures are not entirely independent of one another. The occurrence of one failure likely increases the probability of others (e.g., poor leadership may lead to multiple failures . . . *duh*).

Now, since these types of failures are known to be rare but not theoretically impossible, we'll have to assign probabilities based on a rough estimate of how often they might happen.

As a social experiment, we decided to take this probability question and ask AI what it thought, ChatGPT 4o, specifically. For each individual failure—for each botch—GPT 4 Omni suggested a 1 percent chance ($Pi = 0.01$) that any one of those security botches might occur independently on any given event day. (Every math wiz reading this is shaking their head right now. Yes, we know this estimate is picked out of thin air. AI "knows," too. Doesn't matter. You'll see why.)

Now, the probability of an armed man with malicious intent being present at Butler, given the context of heightened security around Trump, is probably harder to estimate. However, AI suggested we assume that there is a 0.1 percent chance ($Pm = 0.001$) an armed man would be present at a given rally with premeditated intent to kill. Again, we (and AI) are giving the benefit of the doubt, if you could call it that. The odds of this specific situation occurring—someone like Crooks showing up to literally murder someone like Trump—we'd like to think are far less likely than a 0.1 percent chance. Same story with the 1 percent chance for each security botch occurring. We can reasonably believe they are *way* less common than that. Doesn't matter. Again, you'll soon see why.

Because we're going to *calculate the combined probability*. If we assume that all twelve failures and the presence of the armed man are independent events, the probability of all twelve failures happening and the armed man being present on the same day is the product of these probabilities. **Which means we have to multiply each botch by the others.** Like so:

$$P(\text{all failures and armed man}) = P1 \times P2 \times \ldots \times P12 \times Pm$$
Since $P1 = P2 = \ldots = P12 = 0.01$, and $Pm = 0.001$:

$$P(\text{all failures and armed man}) = (0.01)^{12} \times 0.001$$

So now we calculate the combined probability:

$$(0.01)^{12} = 1 \times 10^{-24}$$
$$1 \times 10^{-24} \times 0.001 = 1 \times 10^{-27}$$

This means the probability of all twelve security failures taking place independently from one another yet simultaneously, together with the presence of a capable marksman with intent to kill, is 1×10^{-27}, or one in a septillion (1 followed by 27 zeros).

Let us say that again: The odds of all twelve failures happening on the same day as an armed man with malicious intent happening upon that situation without prior knowledge, assuming these events are independent, are at minimum **1 in 1 septillion**, and again, that is being *extremely* conservative in our estimation. This suggests that the occurrence of all these failures and the presence of the shooter is extraordinarily unlikely by chance alone. And that's just *twelve* of numerous more, and we have already admitted how wildly overestimative we are of these twelve lapses occurring individually and independently. Wow.

OK, but *how "unlikely"*? Well, here's a little perspective:

- The odds of finding a four-leaf clover are about 1 in 5,000.
- The odds of being hit by a meteorite in your lifetime are estimated at 1 in 700,000.
- The odds of being struck by lightning in a given year are about 1 in 1.2 million.
- The odds of being killed by a shark are about 1 in 3.7 million.
- The odds of winning the Powerball jackpot are about 1 in 292 million.
- The odds of flipping a coin and getting heads 93 times consecutively are approximately 1 in 10 septillion. So this is only slightly less likely than 1 in a septillion.

We then asked GPT 4 Omni what it thought, and here's what it concluded:

> This suggests that the occurrence of all these failures and the presence of the shooter is extraordinarily unlikely by chance alone, raising serious questions about whether these events were truly random.

The presumption of guilt.

Where do we go from here?

THE SECOND ATTEMPT

The sun dipped below the horizon, casting long shadows over the Trump International Golf Club in West Palm Beach, Florida, the evening of that near-fateful day, September 15, 2024. Here, in what should have been a serene setting, the tranquility was ended by gunfire—gunshots that echo across the country.

Because it happened again.

Donald Trump was out on the links, enjoying what he might have thought was a routine day of golf. However, unbeknownst to him in his brief respite from the rigors of the campaign trail, a dangerous figure loomed ahead on the course.

Again. After everything. After the debate with Joe Biden . . . the Democrats' desperation . . . the unprecedented security failures aligning to allow Thomas Matthew Crooks eight clean shots at Trump . . . and after the resulting palace coup of a sitting US president and installation of a deeply unpopular alternative, Kamala Harris . . .

And so there was another debate. This one with Harris. The moderators teamed with her to fact-attack Trump. And they lost. The story of pets disappearing from yards across Springfield, Ohio, to be feasted on by unwanted migrants—that's what the global audience of the debate remembered, not any of the so-called "lies" Trump told.

And so the pattern repeated.

Debate loss, assassination attempt . . . debate loss, assassination attempt.

The scene was set with an eerie calm before the storm. A man named Ryan Wesley Routh, equipped with an AK-47 style rifle, a scope for precision, and a GoPro to capture what he perhaps believed would be his moment of historical significance, awaited President Trump. The presence of the GoPro wasn't just for documentation; it was a message, a broadcast of his ideology, a desire to be seen, to be known.

As Trump moved across the golf course, the Secret Service, reeling from the humiliation of Butler, spotted something amiss. The barrel of Routh's rifle, protruding from the foliage, was a stark contrast. An agent reacted with the speed and precision of his training. Gunfire erupted from the Secret Service, aiming to neutralize the threat before it could act.

Routh, his plan unraveling, attempted to flee. The chase that ensued was brief but intense, culminating in his capture on I-95, thanks to an eyewitness's quick thinking in photographing his license plate. This detail, seemingly minor, was pivotal in preventing Routh's escape. When he was pulled over by a patrol unit on I-95, he wasn't armed, and he didn't question why he was pulled over.[1]

The aftermath was a whirlwind of chaos and investigation. The FBI confirmed what many feared: this was an assassination attempt. Routh's background, his radicalization, and his direct ties to foreign conflicts through his activities in Ukraine, painted a picture of a man driven by duty and vengeance. His capture revealed not just a lone wolf but a symptom of deeper, more troubling issues within the fabric of international politics and domestic security.

A heavily radicalized supporter of the global American empire's Ukraine versus Russia war, Routh's mind had been twisted. The motive of the media and the Democratic elite had become his own. And Trump's pleas for peace in Ukraine felt worse than a call for war. To Routh, this was not just policy disagreement; it was betrayal. His radicalization was not a spontaneous combustion but a slow burn, fueled by his experiences as a foreign fighter himself in Ukraine, where he undoubtedly developed ties with national security elements, giving him insights and misguided justifications for his actions.

Routh had been profiled in the *New York Times*. He'd appeared in Semafor. He even appeared in a propaganda video for the neo-Nazi Azov Battalion in Ukraine, a controversial unit of the Ukrainian armed forces that has received direct US arms transfers (and credible accusations of unspeakable war crimes).[2] Routh also claimed he was attempting to recruit Afghan foreign fighters to travel to Ukraine following the US withdrawal from Kabul and the end of the Afghanistan War, Global War On Terror edition. Routh's Ukrainian foreign fighter group was called the International Volunteer Center. At a minimum, his activities in and around Ukraine would have placed him on the radar of US national security agencies, most directly the CIA and FBI.

As such, there is a 1:1 connection between Ryan Routh and the military industrial complex, in Ukraine. Trump, known for his diplomatic foreign policy and criticism of military spending, would pose a threat to the profits of defense contractors if he were to pursue a policy that de-escalates or ends the conflict in Ukraine. The military-industrial complex, comprising defense contractors, lobbyists, and politicians, benefits immensely from prolonged military engagements through increased defense budgets and arms sales. Trump's potential to disrupt this cycle by negotiating peace or reducing military aid could make him a target for those who profit from war.

This second assassination attempt on Trump's life wasn't just an attack on a man; it was another assault on the stability of American politics, a stark reminder of the deep divisions and the potential for violence that lurks beneath the surface of democratic discourse. Trump, once again, emerged unscathed, but the incident left a mark, not on his person, but on the psyche of a nation.

The chapter of this event in West Palm Beach would be written not just in history books—beginning with this one—but in the hearts of every American and citizen of the world. We understand fully the times in which we live.

And what did the mainstream media do in the midst of all this? They did what they always do when it matters most. They spread malinformation. They said technically correct things, framed headlines in ways that were factually accurate but designed to mislead, or to offer a psychological "out" to the potentially painful idea –unbearable for some– that another assassination attempt had just occurred.

CNN, for example, made sure to specify that the FBI was looking into the "apparent assassination attempt."3 Not an assassination attempt, but an apparent assassination attempt. It "appears to be an attempted assassination."4 Because looks can be deceiving, can't say for certain that a man with an AK-47 style rifle lurking outside of the golf course where a controversial presidential candidate was currently golfing was actually trying to assassinate said candidate.

Or take the video they posted. "Hear what law enforcement sources are telling John Miller about shots fired in 'vicinity' of Trump" the headline reads.5 Note the scare-quotes around "vicinity." Technically, it's the word that they were quoting, but to the average reader, it makes it sound like it was up for debate whether any gunshots were anywhere near Trump. Technically true. And maybe, for your average, uninformed and apolitical person, not as misleading. But for those—like Routh—who absolutely despised Trump and would feel mental pain at having to admit that someone tried to hurt the president (as opposed to it being staged, or not even happening in the first place), these headlines give a way out of having to admit uncomfortable truths.

Two movies on one screen.

MSNBC, not to be outdone by CNN, boasted this headline: "Full press conference on what FBI calls apparent Trump assassination attempt."6 Again, note the use of apparent in the headlines. What they'll cite as avoiding a rush to judgment, those seeking any way to avoid thinking Trump was assassinated will use it as an excuse. They then followed it up with a gem of a headline, where "Florida officials identify suspect in Trump golf course shooting incident."7 At this point, it seems that what was an assassination attempt has now been downgraded to an "incident."

Again, technically true, meant to mislead. Apparent attempts aren't officially attempts. And incidents are the kinds of things that you have to write a small report about for HR. Not earth-shattering political news. Two movies on one screen. Malinformation.

The timing of the second assassination attempt unfortunately coincided with an old video of Kamala Harris resurfacing and making the rounds on X, a clip from a sit-down with Ellen DeGeneres where she joked about killing Trump.

> DEGENERES: If you had to be stuck in an elevator with either President Trump, Mike Pence, or Jeff Sessions, who would it be?
> HARRIS: Does one of us have to come out alive?[8]

Again, it's *Trump* who is the threat to democracy. It's *Trump* who's an existential danger to our nation. It's *Trump* whose rhetoric incites violence. And yet it's always his opponents who get caught on camera—or even go on camera—talking about how he must be stopped by any means necessary.

And what did that rhetoric reap?

Routh's own son, Oran Routh, said that his father hates Trump as "every reasonable person does" and admitted to his own dislike of the man.[9] But this was out of character. "'He's my dad and all he's had is couple traffic tickets, as far as I know,' the son said. 'That's crazy. I know my dad and love my dad, but that's nothing like him.'"[10]

(He didn't seem to know about the reported simple drug possession arrest, or the 2002 arrest after Routh barricaded himself in his office after a traffic stop for three hours.[11])

But, according to his son, Routh isn't "crazy" enough to do this.

What *is* he crazy enough to do, though?

Unlike Thomas Crooks, Ryan Routh wore his political heart on his sleeve. His pickup truck in Hawaii had a Biden-Harris bumper sticker. [12] He was a frequent donor to Democratic candidates, donating nineteen times to everyone from Elizabeth Warren to Tulsi Gabbard, as our friend Natalie Winters posted, after some digging.[13] And from a quick scroll through his Twitter/X account, before it was suspended, showed a man utterly obsessed with the current conflict in Ukraine.[14] This includes everything from begging people to help write a "tribute song in English" to raise awareness for Ukraine to asking Elon Musk to give him a rocket to blow up Vladimir Putin with.[15] Routh's "backpacks" were found to contain "ceramic tile," which could very well be expedient body armor plates. This is something he potentially learned to do in Ukraine.[16]

He was a known quantity, having been interviewed several times, having functioned as a sort of foreign recruiter for Ukraine . . . except his efforts seemed to be stymied by the fact that the Ukrainians were not interested, fearing that their ranks might be infiltrated by Russian spies.[17] But he didn't stop there.

The *New York Times*, reporting on the soldiers flocking to Ukraine for dubious and sometimes fraudulent reasons, mentioned him:

> With Legion growth stalling, Ryan Routh, a former construction worker from Greensboro, N.C., is seeking recruits from among Afghan soldiers who fled the Taliban. Mr. Routh, who spent several months in Ukraine last year, said he planned to move them, in some cases illegally, from Pakistan and Iran to Ukraine. He said dozens had expressed interest.[18]

In fact, he went further than merely wanting to move Afghan refugees; he was preparing to commit international fraud to do so. *The New Indian* reported that he planned to try to get said refugees Pakistani passports.[19] "'We can probably purchase some passports through Pakistan since it's such a corrupt country,'" he was reported to have said.[20]

He's not crazy enough to do this. But he is crazy enough to try to commit multiple felonies in multiple countries for the sake of Ukraine.

He also wrote a book, where he asked Iran to assassinate Trump.[21] Robby Starbuck summed it up best:

> Wow. Attempted Trump Assassin Ryan Routh wrote a book on the Ukraine war. In the book he tells Iran to assassinate Trump while praising John Kerry for the Iran Deal. He also calls Trump an idiot and says he "perpetrated" Jan. 6th.
>
> He sounds like a mainstream media addict.[22]

At the time of writing this, Routh is in custody. Florida Governor
Ron DeSantis has come out stating that his state would be doing their
own investigation:

> The State of Florida will be conducting its own investigation
> regarding the attempted assassination at Trump International
> Golf Club.
>
> The people deserve the truth about the would-be assassin
> and how he was able to get within 500 yards of the former
> president and current GOP nominee.[23]

We encourage our readers to keep their eyes out in the coming months.

And with that said, we find our reflection upon the second
assassination attempt bringing us to this: It appears that God has His
hand on Donald Trump. We hope and pray that continues.

THE SHADOW OVER
THE REPUBLIC

The events surrounding the assassination attempt on former President Trump and the palace coup against President Biden have left an indelible mark on the nation's psyche. These incidents, shrouded in darkness and intrigue, compel us to delve into the very essence of power, governance, and the shadowy elite that lurk behind the curtains of public office.

The assassination attempt on Trump, like the assassination of Kennedy, serves as a stark reminder of the fragility of leadership in a country where political figures are often seen as untouchable. They can be removed by the powerful. Similarly, the public palace coup against Biden paints a picture of internal strife within the highest echelons of power. It is not we the people in control. These events force us to question:

Who truly governs America?
The elected officials, or is there a shadow elite pulling the strings? The notion of a shadow government isn't new; it's been whispered about in corridors of power, discussed in conspiracy theories, and occasionally hinted at by those in the know. The military-industrial complex, as Eisenhower warned, has evolved into a broader network of

influence, where corporations, intelligence communities, and perhaps even global entities might hold sway over policy and decision-making.

What is the role of the Military-Industrial Complex?
This complex, as described by Eisenhower, has grown into a behemoth that not only influences defense policies but also shapes economic, foreign, and domestic policies. The intertwining of defense contractors with government contracts, the revolving door between public office and private sector jobs, and the lobbying power of these entities suggest a system where profit and power are deeply intertwined.

What is the media's involvement?
The media's role in these narratives cannot be understated. The way these events were reported, the narratives pushed, and the information withheld or exaggerated, all play into how the public perceives these incidents. This raises questions about media ownership, its alignment with political or corporate interests, and its impact on democracy.

What happens next?
They will try it again. President Trump's security, and all populist political figures, is paramount and must be increased. The polarization in American politics, the rise of extremist groups, and the perceived failure of the system to address grievances might suggest an increase in political violence. However, this also depends on the response of law enforcement, intelligence, and the political will to address underlying issues like inequality, corruption, and the erosion of democratic norms.

Conclusion: Vigilance and Reform
The events discussed here are not just anomalies but symptoms of deeper issues within the American political system. They call for:

- **Transparency:** Greater transparency in government operations, government spending, and government-related industries could mitigate the power of any shadow elite.

- **Education and Awareness:** An informed citizenry is crucial. Education on how government really works, the influence of money in government, and critical media literacy (understanding corporate-controlled media) could empower people to make better decisions.
- **Reform:** Structural reforms in how elections are conducted, how policies are made, and how accountability is enforced might reduce the influence of unseen powers.

As we close this work, the shadow over the republic reminds us that vigilance is not just a virtue but a necessity for self-government. The future might hold more attempts, more coups, or perhaps, a renaissance of the strength of the common man and woman. The choice, ultimately, lies with the American people, who must decide how much shadow they are willing to tolerate in their pursuit of light.

We must fight to defend our nation, or it will surely perish.

OUR PRIVATE
INVESTIGATIVE REPORT

INVESTIGATIVE REPORT - PRIVATE
INVESTIGATIVE FIRM INDEPENDENT REPORT

SUBJECT (Name & Address):		Type of Investigation:		Type of Report:	
Thomas Matthew Crooks ▉▉▉ Bethel Park, PA 15102 (Allegheny County) (DECEASED)	**SUBJECT** (July 13, 2024)	**Pattern of Life**		☐ Initial Report ☐ Interim Report ☐ Final Report	
		Period of Investigation:		Report Date:	
		3 August 2024 - Present		**7 September 2024**	
Date of Birth:	Age:	Social Security #:	File Number:		Assignment Date:
September 20, 2003	**20**	▉▉▉	▉▉▉		**3 August 2024**
Telephone:	Marital Status:	Sex/Race:	Employer/Insured:		
N/A	**Unmarried**	**Male/Caucasian**			
Date of Death:	Place of Employment:				
13 July 2024	**Bethel Park Skilled Nursing & Rehabilitation Center** ▉▉▉				

Date: September 4, 2024

To: Mr. Jack Posobiec and Mr. Joshua Lisec

INTERIM EXECUTIVE SUMMARY

Since this matter was assigned to this agency on August 3, 2024, investigators have expended over 240 hours of investigation to establish a pattern of life of Thomas Matthew Crooks, the twenty-year-old Bethel Park, PA resident who allegedly attempted to assassinate President Donald J. Trump on July 13, 2024, in Butler, Pennsylvania.

Investigators conducted extensive field investigation, surveillance, research of private databases, interviews and other activities to accomplish this task. Investigators conducted these activities in Bethel Park, Pittsburgh, Butler, and surrounding areas in western Pennsylvania.

DISPOSITION OF THOMAS CROOKS REMAINS

According to a source within the Butler County Sheriff's office who requested anonymity, the disposition of Thomas Crooks' remains raised some questions about investigative protocol. According to this source, the body of Crooks was left on the roof of the AGR building until 14 July 2024, at least 15 hours after his death and the official pronouncement of death by the Butler County coroner. As the biological evidence collection, photographic and digital evidence collection should have long been completed, and no threat was posed by movement of his body (regarding any potential IED placement), the reason for allowing his body to remain as such is curious.

It was considered that the FBI might have been conducting laser tests to determine the trajectory of the bullet(s) that might have struck Crooks, however no evidence exists to support this theory.

Also inconsistent with procedure was how rapidly the roof was power washed, reportedly by federal law enforcement, after the body was moved. Although the body was permitted to lay in its final resting position, the cleanup of blood spatter and evidence of a potentially evidentiary forensic value, visible once the body was taken from the scene, was done with inordinate dispatch, according to this source.

Additionally, the body of Thomas Crooks was ultimately moved to the Allegheny Coroner's office, office of the medical examiner, for a complete autopsy. Federal authorities decided to conduct the autopsy in Pittsburgh due to the more expansive resources available at that location, and due to the high profile nature of this case. It is expected, although unconfirmed, that the appropriate tissue and blood samples were collected at that time for proper toxicology screening, yet this has not been confirmed or released.

Upon completion of the autopsy, the body of Thomas Crooks was reportedly transferred back to the Butler County morgue, however the coroner reportedly lost custody, at least temporarily, of Crooks' body. Reportedly unknown to the Butler County coroner, Crooks' remains were allegedly released to the family by federal authorities rather than by the coroner's office. On or about 23 July 2024, Thomas Crooks was cremated by a Bethel Park funeral home and crematorium at the request of his family. However, the Butler County coroner was reportedly not informed of the release and disposition of Crooks' body until on or about 5 August 2024.

Contrary to the Commonwealth of Pennsylvania Open Records Act, Butler County released a rudimentary statement of death in late July. Although the public right-to-know statute appears to apply, the office of the coroner has declined the release of any autopsy findings, including the toxicology reports. This investigator was informed that legal suits are being filed for those records.

Neighborhood Canvas & Interviews

Until his death on July 13, 2024, Thomas Matthew Crooks, 20, resided at an address in Bethel Park, PA 15102-1757. It is a brick structure with an attached mudroom on the east side of the structure, set back from the front. It appears to be used as the primary entrance by the residents.

The dwelling is located in a middle-class area in the town of Bethel Park, PA, a south suburb area of the city of Pittsburgh, PA. The residence and property appear to be lacking normal upkeep, and landscaping is minimal.

Based on our investigative and limited surveillance findings, the subject resided with his mother, father and sister until his sister moved from the residence in 2022. Currently, it appears the only occupants at this address are the parents of Thomas Crooks.

Neighbor Interviews

On Thursday, August 29, 2024, investigator 1 attempted to question the immediate neighbors of the Crooks family. A total of eight-(8) residents in closest proximity to the family residence were personally contacted at their homes. Each contact was performed in the same manner, with Pennsylvania detective credentials consisting of an ID card and badge being shown at the onset of each contact.

Five refused interviews despite being shown this investigator's credentials, with the majority stating that they had already provided statements to federal law enforcement officials and were also "sick of being hounded by media." They declined to provide their names when asked. Despite some understandable hostility, those contacts were terminated by this investigator without incident.

Two nearby residents agreed to talk to this investigator despite already being interviewed by federal investigators. They were cordial but noticeably irritated, and also declined to provide their names. Both admitted living in their homes for at least four years and offered nearly identical descriptions of the Crooks family. They described the family as reclusive and non-interactive to the point of almost being unfriendly. They correctly identified the family vehicles and members of the household, including Thomas Crooks, who appeared to be more active than his parents. Aside from an adult daughter (Katie) who moved away from the home a few years ago, they appeared to have few visitors.

Only one older retired female resident with an unobstructed line of sight to the Crooks residence, including their driveway and front property, who asked to remain anonymous, added that she noticed an increase in activity at the Crooks residence that began in the late winter and early spring of this year. She stated that she had observed at least two vehicles parked on the driveway, usually in the late afternoon or early evening hours, driven, apparently by visitors to the Crooks home.

She described one vehicle as a dark gray "hatchback," and another as a dark colored sedan (unknown make/model). Both vehicles appeared to be present when Thomas Crooks was home, although has not seen either vehicle there recently. She admitted knowing about Thomas Crooks' alleged activities on July 13, 2024, and acknowledged that she wondered aloud whether either visitor "knew about his plans." She added that she had not seen either vehicle at the Crooks residence since the shooting.

Regarding the operators of the two different vehicles, she stated she only saw one, which she identified as the driver of the dark colored sedan. She saw him when he walked from his vehicle, describing him as a Caucasian male having short, light-colored hair, who appeared to be "clean-cut and older looking than the younger Crooks," estimating his age as late twenties. She added that she assumed that he was visiting Thomas Crooks, although never saw them together outside of the house. She estimated that this individual visited that residence 1-3 times a week since late spring, She observed nothing remarkable about the visitor, and was unable to provide a more precise description of this man or either vehicle. She declined to provide her name and asked for anonymity as she lives alone and "wants no trouble" from anyone. She added that she had provided the same information to the police when she was questioned the weekend of the assassination attempt.

Bethel Park Public Library
5100 W. Library Road
Bethel Park, PA 15102

Figure 2 Bethel Park High School Yearbook with Crooks and one other student photo cut out

On Wednesday, August 14, 2024, investigators conducted research of the city and county directories located within the reference section of the public library. Yearbooks from Bethel Park High School were also researched for information pertaining to the subject or any other relevant information.

Research of historical issues of the Cole and Criss Cross directories provided no relevant information about the subject's residence, family, or Crooks himself.

Continued research found that Thomas Matthew Crooks' picture was published in only one of four yearly issues. When accessed, investigators noted that his class photograph was cut from the yearbook with scissors. Interestingly, a second photograph was removed in the same manner.

A subsequent inquiry with the manager of the reference desk was made by Investigator 1 on August 27, 2024. This source stated that she personally opened the yearbook for a news reporter on or about July 15, 2024, and permitted the reporter to photograph the book and page that contained the portrait of Thomas Matthew Crooks. She told this investigator that she replaced the yearbook later that day after the reporter left, and the book was undamaged. She was surprised and visibly irritated that between July 15, 2024, and late August, someone had damaged the yearbook as shown above.

Due to the layout of the portraits, it was unclear whether the actor's intent was to remove the photograph on the same page as Crooks (the classmate's photograph) or the photograph on the reverse.

Clairton Sportsmen's Club
Thomas Crooks (member #1133) was a frequent user of the club's rifle and pistol ranges.

Open-source news reports determined that Crooks frequented the range 43 times between 10 August 2023 and the day before his 12 July 2024 alleged assassination attempt.

 It is noted, however, that on at least one occasion, an individual checked in on the same date and at the same time as Crooks. While this could be purely coincidental, a complete redaction and access to all logs is necessary. Such records would require an authoritative body with subpoena power.

It has been verified that the Clairton Sportsmen's Club has retained legal counsel.

Club officers:
Bill Sellitto, President

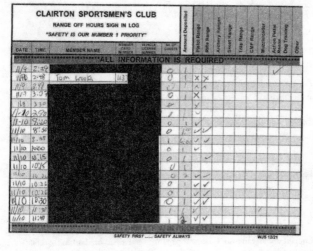

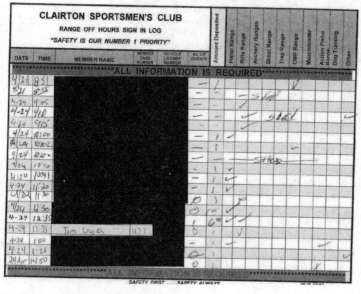

At 1440 hours on Tuesday, August 20, 2024, Investigator 1 arrived at the Clairton's Sportsmen's Club at the above listed address. The main structure is situated at the end of a narrow, winding road about a quarter of a mile from the main road. It consists of a large meeting room, bar, kitchen, and offices.

This investigator was met by a man who did not identify himself by name but stated that he is in charge of the club. He was seated at a table toward the rear of the meeting room, near the side entrance. He was noted to be a heavyset Caucasian male, 55-65 years-old, with gray hair. Prior to this contact, this investigator confirmed that at least one federal law enforcement agency has a contractual relationship with the club for shooting exercises.

This investigator presented proper credentials, using the pretext of mitigating claims exposure for a large insurance carrier holding coverage for municipal, county and state property. The July 13, 2024, shooting at the Butler, PA grounds was identified as the claim of concern. This investigator assured this source that the questions had nothing to do with his club, club members, or any proprietary information, and was merely a request for advice about who might know whether the alleged shooter, Thomas Crooks, might have been accompanied by anyone else at the Butler County property for claim exposure mitigation purposes.

This source immediately presented with a hostile response, telling this investigator to "get the fuck off [his] property." This investigator expressed sympathy for the man and his club, acknowledging that he was obviously inundated by people who likely treated his club as a point of curiosity in high profile case. Despite the assurances by this investigator that only his professional advice and direction was requested, he rapidly became much more belligerent and vocal, threatening to call the police.

Miscellaneous

Fat Angelo's Pizza
Bethel Park, PA 15102

Investigator 2 interviewed the owner of this establishment as it was identified in an *BBC News* article published on July 19, 2024, as a business whose employees knew Thomas Crooks. The owner identified in that article was identified as Sara Petko.

NOTE: The closest pizza shop to the home of Thomas Crooks (with Angelo's in the name) operates as "Fat Angelo's at the above listed location, which is about 1-1/2 miles from the Crooks residence. Although there is a pizza shop known only as "Angelo's," it is situated northeast of the city of Pittsburgh, about a 30-minute drive from Crooks' home.

Contact with the owner/operator (identified above) of Fat Angelo's Pizza at the Library Road location, revealed that they received a lot of attention because of the *BBC News* article, which was also picked up by *ABC News*. Haley stated that no one from this location knows Thomas Crooks either personally or as a customer. They have received numerous inquiries from other news reporters and curious citizens, and even "had issues" with vendors selling Trump merchandise in front of this establishment in the days and weeks following the shooting. Finding that the vendors increased their food and drink sales, they allowed them to remain. Nonetheless, she insisted that neither she nor her employees had any relationship or even contact with Crooks or his family, adding that "[they] never even delivered to his address."

INVESTIGATION USING LOCATION-BASED TECHNOLOGY

In addition to field investigation, surveillance and utilization of proprietary databases, this agency used location-based technology, most commonly known as geofencing, to conduct an investigation to identify individuals that could be associated with Thomas Matthew. Geofencing is a location-based service by which an app or other software program uses radio frequency identification (RFID), Wi-Fi, GPS, or cellular data when a mobile device or RFID tag enters or exits a virtual geographic boundary, known as a geofence.

NOTE: We are aware that the Heritage Foundation Oversight Project utilized the same technology on the evening of July 13, 2024. Considering that the information about the assassination attempt was limited at that time, investigators believe that the data points, or the source locations, were also limited.

Using information developed from this agency's field investigation complimented by database searches, this agency used several additional and specific locations, thus broadening the scope of devices and the area of the geofence. Our analysis of the data retrieved indicated a much more robust "pattern of life" related to Crooks.

It is from this analysis, combined and confirmed with additional field investigation, that investigators found unexpected intersectionality before, during, and *after* July 13, 2024. What was unforeseen and is of extreme interest and concern is the overwhelming amount of data that connects Crooks' house, his employer, and a suspicious third location in a local Bethel Park public facility.

Specifically, a device appeared at the home of Thomas Matthew Crooks during time when he returned to his residence after his initial appearance at the Butler rally site on July 13, 2024. According to the timeline established by police, Crooks returned to his residence at or about 2:00 pm on July 13, 2024. The individual/device appeared at his residence at that time and during his presence there, before Crooks returned to the rally site to allegedly shoot President Donald J. Trump. This analysis is firm and unequivocal. The device has the characteristics of a "burner device" and was activated in December 2023. Perhaps most disturbing is that this device appears to remain active in and around Bethel Park.

Additionally, the analysis of the data found layers of activity involving individuals and locations that if revealed, could compromise our ongoing investigative efforts. Our initial analysis of the electronic data, combined with on-site inspections of the identified locations by investigators, suggest that Thomas Matthew Crooks had a network of support that will be identified when our investigation is complete.

Source: FBI

Further analysis is expected to lead to the identification of assets who might have provided material or technical assistance in the construction and possible materials acquisition involved in the construction of two explosive devices found in the vehicle used by Thomas Crooks. Initial reports that these explosive devices were crude have been publicly debunked by the FBI, despite their initial characterizations. They were indeed more advanced than initially reported and could have been functional but for the fact that the receivers to activate detonation were turned off. The relevance of the construction will become much clearer once additional field investigation – using, in part, the geolocation data, is completed to determine if these additional locations and individuals were connected to the construction of explosive devices.

AUTHORS' ASSESSMENT: While initial investigations and public statements lean towards Crooks acting alone, the complexity of his operational planning and execution,

combined with insights from this investigation, suggests the possibility of a local support network or at least a community environment that might have indirectly facilitated his actions. Transparency in further investigations, coupled with community outreach, is crucial to either confirm or dispel these hypotheses. This assessment underscores the need for continued vigilance and thorough investigation into the social and operational networks of individuals like Crooks to prevent future incidents.

THE TEXT MESSAGES[1]

July 8, 2024: Beaver County Emergency Services Unit (ESU) Team Leaders receive a request to cover the July 13 Trump rally

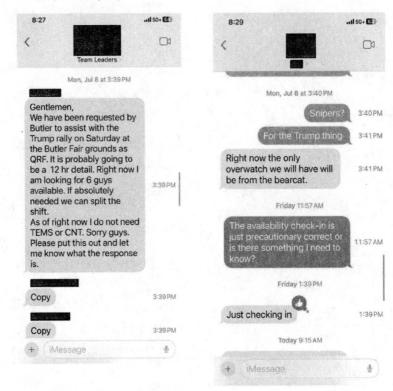

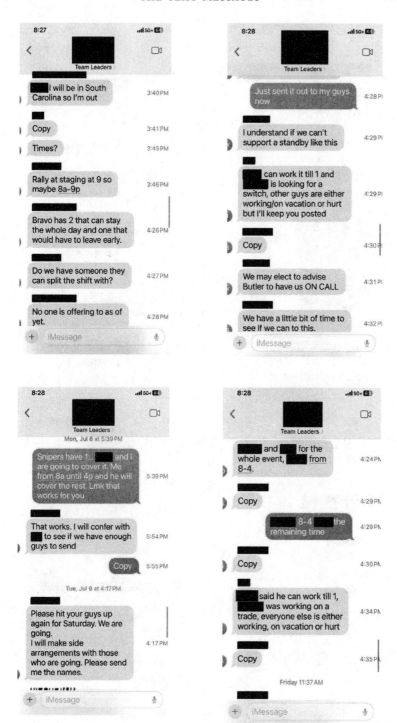

Screen 1 (8:27 — Team Leaders):

▮ I will be in South Carolina so I'm out — 3:40 PM

▮ Copy — 3:41 PM

Times? — 3:45 PM

▮ Rally at staging at 9 so maybe 8a-9p — 3:46 PM

Bravo has 2 that can stay the whole day and one that would have to leave early. — 4:26 PM

▮ Do we have someone they can split the shift with? — 4:27 PM

▮ No one is offering to as of yet. — 4:28 PM

iMessage

Screen 2 (8:28 — Team Leaders):

Just sent it out to my guys now — 4:28 PM

▮ I understand if we can't support a standby like this — 4:29 PM

▮ can work it till 1 and is looking for a switch, other guys are either working/on vacation or hurt but I'll keep you posted — 4:29 PM

Copy — 4:30 PM

We may elect to advise Butler to have us ON CALL — 4:31 PM

▮ We have a little bit of time to see if we can to this. — 4:32 PM

iMessage

Screen 3 (8:28 — Team Leaders):

Mon, Jul 8 at 5:39 PM

Snipers have 1. ▮ and I are going to cover it. Me from 8a until 4p and he will cover the rest. Lmk that works for you — 5:39 PM

That works. I will confer with ▮ to see if we have enough guys to send — 5:54 PM

Copy — 5:55 PM

Tue, Jul 9 at 4:17 PM

Please hit your guys up again for Saturday. We are going.
I will make side arrangements with those who are going. Please send me the names. — 4:17 PM

iMessage

Screen 4 (8:28 — Team Leaders):

▮ and ▮ for the whole event, ▮ from 8-4. — 4:24 PM

Copy — 4:29 PM

▮ 8-4 ▮ the remaining time — 4:29 PM

Copy — 4:30 PM

▮ said he can work till 1, ▮ was working on a trade, everyone else is either working, on vacation or hurt — 4:34 PM

Copy — 4:35 PM

Friday 11:37 AM

iMessage

July 10, 2024: Beaver County ESU finalizes assignments for the July 13 Trump rally

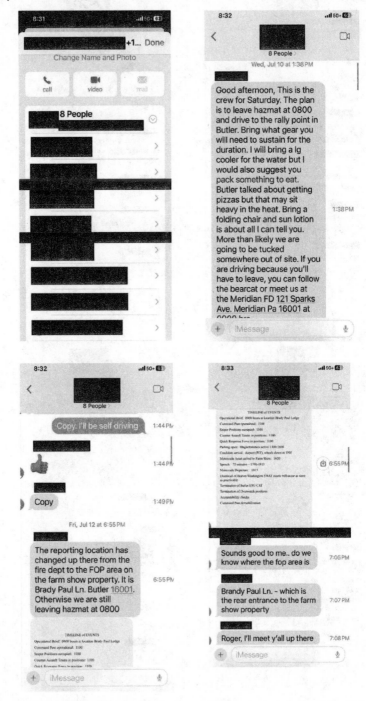

July 13, 2024: 1:03 p.m.: Beaver, Butler and Washington County snipers connect via group chat

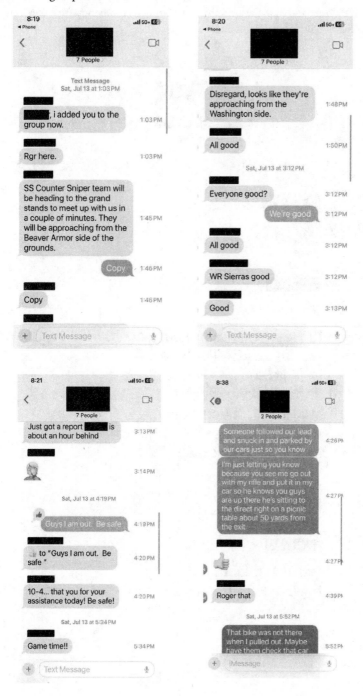

5:38 p.m.: A Beaver County sniper sends photos of Crooks to the Beaver, Butler and Washington snipers group chat. The Beaver sniper notes Crooks was using "a range finder looking towards the stage" and recommends that they notify Secret Service snipers to "look out"

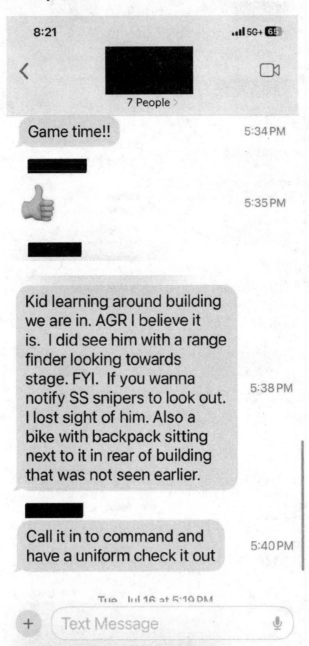

5:45 p.m.: A Beaver County sniper sends photos of Crooks to the Beaver County ESU group chat. Beaver law enforcement recommends they alert "command"

███ if you wanna send this to whoever at command if you have cell # — 5:45PI

███

Sent — 5:51PI

███

They're asking for a direction of travel — 5:59PI

███

Not sure. He was up against the building. If I had to guess towards the back. Away from the event. — 6:00PI

iMessage

FPOTUS AFTER ACTION BEAVER COUNTY ESU/SWAT[1]

FPOTUS After Action
Beaver County ESU/SWAT

Materials Provided by Butler
Command

Materials Provided by Butler Command

Sector #1 - Main Stage/Audienc
Sector #2 - Barns/Motorcade
Sector #3 - Entrance to Event
Sector #4 - Ponds
Sector #5 - Parking

Timeline

- 0900 – Briefing by Butler Co. ESU
  - Washington Co. ESU
  - Beaver Co. ESU
  - Butler Co. ESU
  - State Police – no input
  - Bravo Team Leader Gives Assignments
- 10:15 – Beaver Co ESU in place
- 10:30 – Vendor dispute at Main Entrance handled by Butler Co Sheriff ███
- 10:30 – Snipers in place
- 17:10 – First Observed Suspect by ███
  - Walked by window
- 17:14 – Picture of Suspect (time taken)
- 17:28 – Picture of Bike (time taken)
- 17:32 – Suspect spotted looking at phone, news feeds, and range finder confirmed through monoculars

Timeline

- 17:34 (approx.) – Butler Co. Sniper texts Butler Team(assumed)
- 17:38 – ▇▇ sends text to group text to Sniper Group about suspect
- 17:40 – Response text to ▇▇ "Call into command"
- 17:41 – Called into command by ▇▇ about suspect (Butler 4 Command Frequency)
  - 4 Sierra 2 to Command – communicated description and range finder lurking around AGR Building
- 17:45 – Text sent to Beaver ESU Group Command about Suspect and to relay to command
- 17:49 – ▇▇ communication to ▇▇ regarding suspect and pictures
- 17:55 – ▇▇ acknowledges receipt to ▇▇ and passing it on to command
- 17:59 – ▇▇ to ▇▇ sent to Command and asking for direction of travel
- 18:00 – ▇▇ to ▇▇ asking for direction of travel for suspect
- 18:00 – ▇▇ to ▇▇ unsure of direction of travel
- 18:05 – Approx suspect at picnic tables and moving direction of Sheetz, he has a back pack (communicated by ▇▇) via radio
  - Bulter Sniper stayed in place at original position

Timeline

- 18:06 – 18:12:
  - ▇▇ goes downstairs of building 1 to meet patrol to let them know suspect is around building on side of fairgrounds
    - 1 Marked vehicle and unmarked vehicle pull in together
- 18:12 – Shots Fired
- Unknown Time: Shooter Down
- 18:23 – (approx.) ▇▇ and ▇▇ climb black tactical ladder to L of Building 3 door to access roof
- 18:25 – Pronounced DOA by ▇▇
- 18:25 – General clearing by Beaver County ESU with other agencies of surrounding buildings
- 18:32 – DOA Photo sent by ▇▇ sent to ▇▇ and ▇▇
- 18:35 – ▇▇ sends confirmation picture to command to confirm dead
- 18:46 – ▇▇ from Washington Co. ESU pats suspect down finds cellphone and device
- 18:48 – Cellphone and remote found in deceased's right pocket sent to ▇▇
- 19:45 – Device and Face sent by ▇▇. Number provided by EOD.
  - ▇▇ sent phone number
- 19:46 – Facial recognition photo sent by ▇▇ to ▇▇

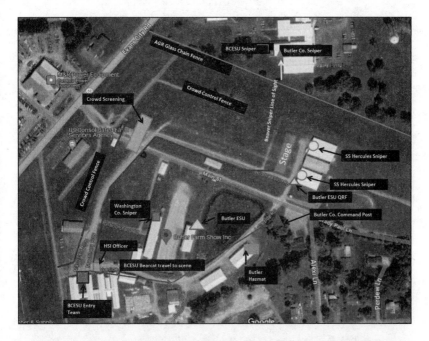

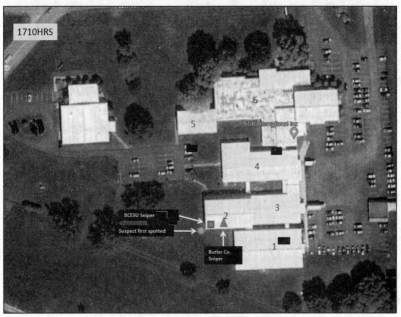

Suspect Photo
Taken by:
Captured: 07/13/2024 17:14
Sent to: Sniper Group and BCESU
Commander Group

Photo of Bicycle and Backpack
Taken by:
Captured: 07/13/2024 17:28
Sent to: BCESU Commander Group

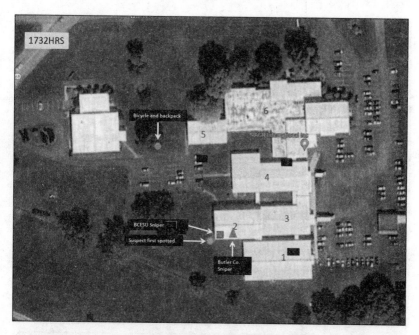

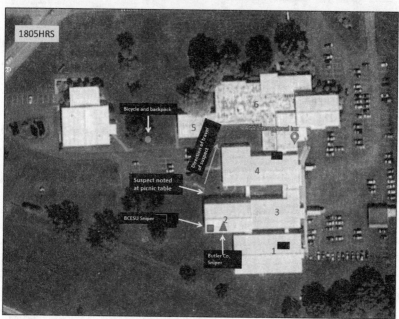

SHOTS FIRED
18:12HRS

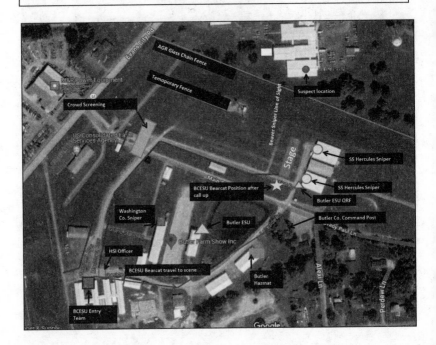

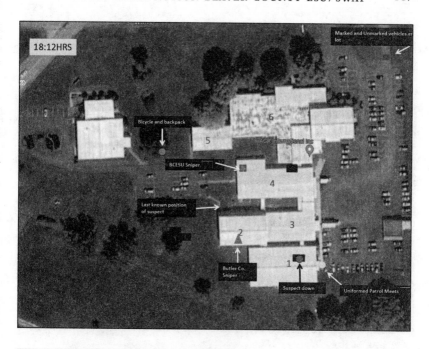

and ██████ make access to Roof
Time: 18:23 approx.

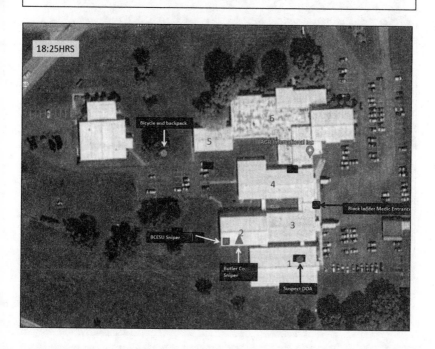

DOA Confirmation Photos
Taken by: ███████
Captured: 07/13/2024 18:32
Sent to: ███████████

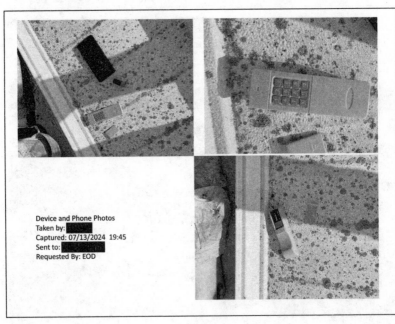

Device and Phone Photos
Taken by: ███████
Captured: 07/13/2024 19:45
Sent to: ███████████
Requested By: EOD

Facial Recognition Photo
Taken by: ▮▮▮▮▮
Captured: 07/13/2024 19:46
Sent to: ▮▮▮▮▮
Requested By: EOD

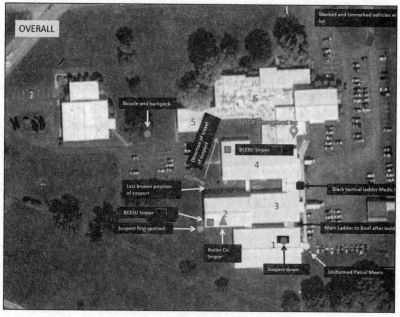

OVERALL

Marked and Unmarked vehicles en lot

Bicycle and backpack

5

6

AGR International Inc.

BCESU Sniper

4

Direction of travel of suspect

Last known position of suspect

Black tactical ladder Medic

3

BCESU Sniper

2

Suspect first spotted

Main Ladder to Roof after incid

Butler Co. Sniper

1

Suspect down

Uniformed Patrol Meets

Duties

- ■ Monitor Channel 4 – Butler Police ESU Command
- ■ Monitor Channel 3 – Butler Police Patrol
- Sniper:
  - ■
- Operators
  - ■
  - ■
  - ■
  - ■
  - ■
  - ■
  - ■
- Medic
  - ■

NOTES

THE TIMELINE

1   Trump, Donald (@realDonaldTrump). "Thank you to everyone for your thoughts and prayers yesterday, as it was God alone who prevented the unthinkable from happening. We will FEAR NOT, but instead . . . " Truth Social, July 14, 2024. https://truthsocial.com/@realDonaldTrump/posts/112784638860095397.

THE SCENARIOS

1   Weinthal, Benjamin. "Iran's Assassination Plot against Trump Latest Attempt to Kill Americans on US Soil." Fox News, July 17, 2024. https://www.foxnews.com/world/irans-assassination-plot-against-trump-latest-attempt-kill-americans-us-soil.

2   Reuters, and Jerusalem Post Staff. "US Received Intel of Iranian Plot to Assassinate Trump, CNN Reports." *The Jerusalem Post* | JPost.com, July 16, 2024. https://www.jpost.com/breaking-news/article-810587.

3   AFP. "Trump: 'If Iran Assassinates Me, US Must Wipe It off the Face of the Earth' | the Times of Israel." *The Times of Israel*, July 26, 2024. https://www.timesofisrael.com/trump-if-iran-assassinates-me-us-must-wipe-it-off-the-face-of-the-earth/.

4   Crabtree, Susan. "Secret Service Agents Placed on Leave after Trump Assassination Attempt | Realclearpolitics." RealClear Politics, August 22, 2024. https://www.realclearpolitics.com/articles/2024/08/22/secret_service_agents_placed_leave_after_trump_assassination_attempt__151502.html.

THE MOTIVE

1   Cillizza, Chris. "Analysis: How Donald Trump's 'perfect' Phone Call Foretold His 2020 Loss | CNN Politics." CNN, November 11, 2020. https://www.cnn.com/2020/11/11/politics/donald-trump-biden-ukraine-call/index.html.

2   Ballard, Jamie, and David Montgomery. "What Americans Believe about the Attempted Assassination on Donald Trump." YouGov, July 24, 2024. https://today.yougov.com/politics/articles/50154-what-americans -believe-about-attempted-assassination-donald-trump-poll.

3   Solana, Mike. "Thoughts and Prayers for 'Literally Hitler.'" Pirate Wires, July 16, 1970. https://www.piratewires.com/p/thoughts-and -prayers-trump-assassination.

4   Stelter, Brian (@brianstelter). "Trump's repeated use of the word "fascist" today reminded me of this—@NewRepublic's new cover package about "what American fascism would look like". . ." X (formerly Twitter), May 31, 2024. https://x.com/brianstelter/status/1796644798570348769.

5   Elliott, Tim. "America Is Eerily Retracing Rome's Steps to a Fall. Will It Turn around before It's Too Late? - Politico." Politico, November 3, 2020. https://www.politico.com/news/magazine/2020/11/03/donald -trump-julius-caesar-433956.

6   Junker, Andrea (@Strandjunker). "Have you ever wondered why Germans didn't do anything about Hitler? Well, the rest of the world is wondering exactly that about Americans and Trump." X (formerly Twitter), March 3, 2024. https://x.com/Strandjunker/status /1764387799963242578.

7   Barrow, Bill, and Lisa Mascaro. "With 'Gestapo' Comment, Trump Adds to Numerous Past Nazi Germany References." PBS, May 6, 2024. https://www.pbs.org/newshour/politics/with-gestapo-comment -trump-adds-to-numerous-past-nazi-germany-references.

8   McCarthy, Mia. "'I'm a Never Trump Guy': All of J.D. Vance's Trump Quotes That Could Come Back to Bite Him." Politico, July 15, 2024. https://www.politico.com/news/2024/07/15/jd-vance-donald -trump-comments-00168450.

9   Slattery, Gram, and Helen Coster. "J.D. Vance Once Compared Trump to Hitler. Now They Are Running Mates | Reuters." Reuters, July 15, 2024. https://www.reuters.com/world/us/jd-vance-once-compared-trump -hitler-now-they-are-running-mates-2024–07-15/.

10   Levin, Bess. "Donald Trump, Who Has Been Likened to Hitler by His Own Running Mate, Claims Tim Walz as VP Pick Is 'Insulting to Jewish People.'" Vanity Fair, August 7, 2024. https://www.vanityfair.com/news /story/trump-claims-tim-walz-as-vp-pick-is-insulting-to-jewish-people.

11   Stelter, Brian. "Experts Warn That Trump's 'Big Lie' Will Outlast His Presidency | CNN Business." CNN, January 11, 2021. https://www .cnn.com/2021/01/11/media/trump-lies-reliable-sources/index.html.

12   "Joseph Goebbels: On The 'Big Lie.'" Jewish Virtual Library. Accessed September 1, 2024. https://www.jewishvirtuallibrary.org/joseph-goebbels -on-the-quot-big-lie-quot.

13 Moosa, Tauriq. "The 'Punch A Nazi' Meme: What Are the Ethics of Punching Nazis? | Tauriq Moosa." *The Guardian*, January 31, 2017. https://www.theguardian.com/science/brain-flapping/2017/jan/31/the-punch-a-nazi-meme-what-are-the-ethics-of-punching-nazis.

14 Hayes, Christal. "Biden Admits Trump 'Bullseye' Comments a Mistake." BBC News, July 16, 2024. https://www.bbc.com/news/articles/cd1rzde0n4do.

15 Thaler, Shannon. "Linkedin Billionaire Reid Hoffman Visited Jeffrey Epstein's Private Island, Planned to Visit NYC Mansion." *New York Post*, May 3, 2023. https://nypost.com/2023/05/03/linkedins-reid-hoffman-visited-jeffrey-epsteins-private-island/.

16 Propper, David. "LinkedIn Co-Founder, Dem Donor Tries to Clean up Comment Wishing Trump Was an 'Actual Martyr.'" *New York Post*, July 14, 2024. https://nypost.com/2024/07/14/us-news/linkedin-co-founder-reid-hoffman-clarifies-trump-actual-martyr-comment/#:~:text=%E2%80%9CYeah%2C%20I%20wish%20I%20had,martyr%2C%E2%80%9D%20Hoffman%20reportedly%20replied.&text=In%20light%20of%20the%20attempt,wished%20Trump%20a%20quick%20recovery.

17 Aitken, Peter. "Biden Admits 'Bull's-Eye' Comment about Trump Was a 'Mistake' after Assassination Attempt." Fox News, July 15, 2024. https://www.foxnews.com/politics/biden-admits-bulls-eye-comment-about-trump-mistake-after-assassination-attempt.

18 Lorenz, Taylor. "How Libs of TikTok Became a Powerful Presence in Oklahoma Schools." *Washington Post*, February 24, 2024. https://www.washingtonpost.com/technology/2024/02/24/libs-tiktok-oklahoma-nonbinary-teen-death/.

19 Dr RollerGator PHD. "Stochastic Terrorism - a Game of Rhetorical Asymmetry." Stochastic Terrorism—A game of rhetorical asymmetry, October 1, 2022. https://drrollergator.substack.com/p/stochastic-terrorism-a-game-of-rhetorical.

20 Fiallo, Josh. "'A Lot of Hatred': What Trump Said When Dr. Phil Asked If Harris Wanted Him Shot." *The Daily Beast*, August 28, 2024. https://www.thedailybeast.com/dr-phil-asks-donald-trump-if-joe-biden-and-kamala-harris-were-ok-with-him-being-shot.

21 Ibid.

22 Associated Press. "De Niro: I'd Like to Punch Trump in the Face." YouTube, October 8, 2016. https://www.youtube.com/watch?v=dfW2TiPAKsw.

23 "Johnny Depp: 'When Was the Last Time an Actor Assassinated a President?'" CBS News, June 23, 2017. https://www.cbsnews.com/news/johnny-depp-when-was-the-last-time-an-actor-assassinated-a-president/.

24 Itkowitz, Colby. "Madonna Says She's Thought about 'Blowing up the White House'—*Washington Post*." *Washington Post*, January 21, 2017. https://www.washingtonpost.com/local/2017/live-updates/politics /womens-march-on-washington/madonna-says-shes-thought-about -blowing-up-the-white-house/.

25 Lopez, George (@georgelopez). "Image." X (formerly Twitter), February 28, 2016. https://x.com/georgelopez/status/703826891354968069.

26 TMZ Staff. "Mickey Rourke—Donald Trump's a 'Bitch Bully' . . . 'I Like the Black Dude.'" TMZ. Accessed September 1, 2024. https: //www.tmz.com/watch/0-z26ev8w9/.

27 Broman Entertainment. "Marilyn Manson SAY10 Teaser." YouTube, November 8, 2016. https://www.youtube.com/watch?v=EAsebDGZWko.

28 Hays, Gabriel. "Weeks after Assassination Attempt, Pelosi Compares 'Threat' of Trump to Revolutionary, Civil War." Fox News, August 23, 2024. https://www.foxnews.com/media/weeks-after-assassination-attempt -pelosi-compares-threat-trump-revolutionary-civil-war.

29 Panreck, Hanna. "Sen. Booker Pressed on 'New Chapter' Campaign Message for Kamala Harris at DNC: 'She's the Incumbent VP.'" Fox News, August 25, 2024. https://www.foxnews.com/media/sen-booker -pressed-new-chapter-campaign-message-kamala-harris-dnc-shes -incumbent-vp.

30 Hawkins, David R., and Fran Grace. *The map of Consciousness explained: A proven energy scale to actualize your ultimate potential.* Carlsbad, CA: Hay House, Inc, 2020.

THE RACE

1 Adams, Scott (@ScottAdamsSays). "I also predicted in 2020 that Biden wouldn't last one term. (That wasn't a hard one.) But I didn't predict Michelle Obama as his replacement, and still do not . . . " X (formerly Twitter), June 29, 2024. https://x.com/ScottAdamsSays /status/1807027896567075119.

2 Adams, Scott (@ScottAdamsSays). "Which means they don't expect her to stay "vice" for long—Explained: The role and responsi- bilities of Kamala Harris, the new US Vice President . . . " X (for- merly Twitter), January 25, 2021. https://x.com/ScottAdamsSays /status/1353789857554829312.

3 Adams, Scott (@ScottAdamsSays). "We've seen what happens when the president has a plan but the situation on the ground deteriorates faster than the plan anticipated. I'm talking about Biden's . . . " X (formerly Twitter), August 23, 2021. https://x.com/ScottAdamsSays /status/1429803297871851522.

4   Adams, Scott (@ScottAdamsSays). "Biden won't be serving a second
    term. That question has been answered. But watch the faces of the
    Democrats defending Biden today. It's hilarious and educational." X (for-
    merly Twitter), August 1, 2023. https://x.com/ScottAdamsSays/status
    /1686341913581088768.
5   Victory, Kelly (@DrKellyVictory). "Biden's obvious signs of
    Parkinsonian dementia:1) Shuffling gait 2) Stiff "tin soldier" arms 3)
    Difficulty initiating forward gait 4) Difficulty changing . . . " X (for-
    merly Twitter), July 1, 2024. https://x.com/DrKellyVictory/status/180
    7842497873563952?t=jQjcUZBtuC7dBMTYFLhrAg&s=19.

THE DEBATE

1   Valverde, Miriam. "Brit Hume Falsely Calls Biden Senile." @politifact,
    October 1, 2020. https://www.politifact.com/factchecks/2020/oct/01
    /brit-hume/geriatrics-experts-say-brit-humes-claim-joe-biden-/.
2   Mason, Jeff, and Trevor Hunnicutt. "Biden Is 'Fit for Duty' after
    Annual Physical, Works out Five Days a Week, Doctor Says." Reuters,
    February 28, 2024. https://www.reuters.com/world/us/biden-81-undergo
    -annual-physical-exam-2024-02-28/.
3   Widakuswara, Patsy. "Biden Deemed 'Healthy, Active, Robust' during
    Annual Physical Exam." Voice of America, February 28, 2024. https:
    //www.voanews.com/a/no-new-concerns-in-biden-s-annual-check-up
    -white-house-says/7507324.html.
4   Reuters. "'I'm in Good Shape': Joe Biden Defends His Health |
    REUTERS." YouTube, July 11, 2024. https://www.youtube.com/watch
    ?v=nWGSzaXnjTk.
5   Foster, Robin. "'No New Concerns' for Biden's Health After Annual
    Physical." US News, February 29, 2024. https://www.usnews.com/news
    /health-news/articles/2024-02-29/no-new-concerns-for-bidens
    -health-after-annual-physical.
6   Wyatt, Dennis. "Biden's Detractors Saying 79 Years Old Is Too Old to
    Be Riding a Bicycle: Come on, Man." Manteca/Ripon Bulletin, January
    23, 2022. https://www.mantecabulletin.com/opinion/local-columns
    /bidens-detractors-saying-79-years-old-is-too-old-to-be-riding-a
    -bicycle-come-on-man/.
7   The All-In Podcast (@theallinpod). "The Media is Not Doing its Job
    @chamath breaks down the viral "sharp as a tack" clip: "Six minutes
    of 100 spokespeople and proxies, and they all had the same . . . "
    X (formerly Twitter), July 5, 2024. https://x.com/theallinpod
    /status/1809248157139628481.
8   Creitz, Charles. "Joe Is 'Not Fine': Watters Rips Media's Latest Cleanup
    for Biden after Bike Tumble." Fox News, June 20, 2022. https:
    //www.foxnews.com/media/joe-not-fine-watters-rips-medias-latest
    -cleanup-biden-bike-tumble.

9   Danner, Chas. "Biden Survives Bike Fall after Failed Backpedaling
     Attempt." *New York Magazine*, Intelligencer, June 18, 2022. https:
     //nymag.com/intelligencer/2022/06/biden-survives-bike-fall-after
     -failed-backpedaling-attempt.html.

10   Caralle, Katelyn. "White House Photographer Blows Whistle on
     Biden's Cognitive Health as He Reveals Aides Knew for Months He
     Was Not Fit for Office." *Daily Mail* Online, June 30, 2024. https:
     //www.dailymail.co.uk/news/article-13585781/white-house-photographer
     -biden-cognitive-health-aides-revelation.html.

11   "Donald Trump Speaks in Detroit at Turning Point Event." Rev,
     June 17, 2024. https://www.rev.com/blog/transcripts/donald-trump-speaks
     -in-detroit-at-turning-point-event.

12   Ibid.

13   Long, Colleen, Zeke Miller, Michael Balsamo, Aamer Madhani, and
     Sylvie Corbet. "Biden at 81: Often Sharp and Focused but Sometimes
     Confused and Forgetful." Associated Press, July 4, 2024. https://www
     .ap.org/news-highlights/elections/2024/biden-at-81-often-sharp-and
     -focused-but-sometimes-confused-and-forgetful/.

14   CNN Staff. "Read: Biden-Trump Debate Transcript | CNN Politics."
     CNN, June 28, 2024. https://www.cnn.com/2024/06/27/politics/read
     -biden-trump-debate-rush-transcript/index.html.

15   Sforza, Lauren. "Trump Jabs Biden: 'I Really Don't Know What He
     Said at the End of That Sentence.'" *The Hill*, June 27, 2024. https:
     //thehill.com/homenews/campaign/4744753-trump-jabs-biden-really
     -dont-know-what-he-said/.

16   Adams, Scott (@ScottAdamsSays). "After the debate debacle,
     Democrats changed their messaging from "Biden is fine" to "He's
     better than a liar." Biden is literally the most dangerous liar in . . . "
     X (formerly Twitter), June 28, 2024. https://x.com/ScottAdamsSays
     /status/1806773504014270778.

17   Politico Staff. "Full Text: Trump's Comments on White Supremacists,
     'Alt-Left' in Charlottesville." *Politico*, August 15, 2017. https://www
     .politico.com/story/2017/08/15/full-text-trump-comments-white
     -supremacists-alt-left-transcript-241662.

18   Shivaram, Deepa. "Biden Uses Charlottesville to Talk about Political
     Violence. but He Hasn't Been There." NPR, November 27, 2023.
     https://www.npr.org/2023/11/27/1214460025/biden-uses-charlottes
     ville-to-talk-about-political-violence-but-he-hasnt-been-th.

19   DeBerry, Jarvis. "Trump's Charlottesville Statement Was Repugnant—
     No Matter How You Parse It." MSNBC, July 9, 2024. https://www
     .msnbc.com/opinion/msnbc-opinion/trump-biden-charlottesville
     -snopes-rcna160508.

20   Nava, Victor. "Trump Gives Brutally Candid Assessment of Biden, Harris after Debate Disaster, Leaked Golf Course Video Shows." *New York Post*, July 3, 2024. https://nypost.com/2024/07/03/us-news /trumps-brutally-candid-take-on-biden-harris-after-debate-disaster -video/.

DAY ONE, JULY 13, 2024: THE SHOT

1   The Public Square. "TPS 60: Eye Witness Interview from Trump Assassination Attempt." Spotify, July 18, 2024. https://open.spotify.com /episode/1s9B2HnPh9ueu9Ewjt3O0R?si=LOzFEjRyQJS9CS Geh-pgGg&nd=1&dlsi=27cce6b80f954e8b.

2   Lace, Alec (@AlecLace). "WATCH: Full Interview with Sean Parnell @SeanParnellUSA joined me on The Alec Lace Show today Sean spoke on stage prior to Donald Trump on July 13th and was . . . " X (formerly Twitter), July 16, 2024. https://x.com/AlecLace/status /1813355672299340144.

3   Hecker, Ivory. "Trump Shooting Witness on What Really Happened." YouTube, July 14, 2024. https://www.youtube.com/watch?v=MXfeVEF Y4bw.

4   Lace, Alec (@AlecLace). "WATCH: Full Interview with Sean Parnell @SeanParnellUSA joined me on The Alec Lace Show today Sean spoke on stage prior to Donald Trump on July 13th and was . . . " X (formerly Twitter), July 16, 2024. https://x.com/AlecLace/status /1813355672299340144.

5   Daily Caller (@DailyCaller). "A video shared on social media Saturday shows a live BBC News interview with a witness, who said he tried to warn police prior to the assassination attempt on . . . " X (formerly Twitter), July 15, 2024. https://x.com/DailyCaller/status/1812930884 770930997?t=uNSW-5P3j1Ne-QpT4bxzxg&s=19.

6   Human Events Daily with Jack Posobiec. "Brick Suit's First Hand Account of the Trump Assassination Attempt." Rumble, July 16, 2024. https://rumble.com/v578f5x-brick-suits-in-person-account-of-the- trump-assassination-attempt.html.

7   TENET Media (@watchTENETnow). "'He Was THIS Close:' Eyewitness On Trump Assassination Attempt Lauren Southern speaks to Blake Marnell, known as @Brick_Suit, who describes his experience at . . . " X (formerly Twitter), July 16, 2024. https://x.com/watch TENETnow/status/1813337211871584581.

8   Human Events Daily with Jack Posobiec. "Brick Suit's First Hand Account of the Trump Assassination Attempt." Rumble, July 16, 2024. https://rumble.com/v578f5x-brick-suits-in-person-account-of-the -trump-assassination-attempt.html.

9 Lace, Alec (@AlecLace). "WATCH: Full Interview with Sean Parnell @SeanParnellUSA joined me on The Alec Lace Show today Sean spoke on stage prior to Donald Trump on July 13th and was . . . " X (formerly Twitter), July 16, 2024. https://x.com/AlecLace/status /1813355672299340144.

10 The Public Square. "TPS 60: Eye Witness Interview from Trump Assassination Attempt." Spotify, July 18, 2024. https://open.spotify. com/episode/1s9B2HnPh9ueu9Ewjt3O0R?si=LOzFEjRyQJS9CS Geh-pgGg&nd=1&dlsi=27cce6b80f954e8b.

11 Hecker, Ivory. "Trump Shooting Witness on What Really Happened." YouTube, July 14, 2024. https://www.youtube.com/watch?v=MXfeV EFY4bw.

12 Parker, Rachel (@Emmanuel_Rach). ""Everybody hit the ground." Michael gives his eye witness account of what transpired during the assassination attempt on former US President Donald Trump's life." X (formerly Twitter), July 13, 2024. https://x.com/Emmanuel_Rach /status/1812285770121515421.

13 Hecker, Ivory. "Trump Shooting Witness on What Really Happened." YouTube, July 14, 2024. https://www.youtube.com/watch?v=MXfeV EFY4bw.

14 Lace, Alec (@AlecLace). "WATCH: Full Interview with Sean Parnell @SeanParnellUSA joined me on The Alec Lace Show today Sean spoke on stage prior to Donald Trump on July 13th and was . . . " X (formerly Twitter), July 16, 2024. https://x.com/AlecLace/status /1813355672299340144.

15 Dr Steve Turley. "Here's an Eyewitness Account of Trump's Assassination-Attempt!!!" Rumble, July 16, 2024. https://rumble.com /v576hwx-heres-an-eyewitness-account-of-trumps-assassination -attempt.html?e9s=rel_v1_b.

16 Human Events Daily with Jack Posobiec. "Brick Suit's First Hand Account of the Trump Assassination Attempt." Rumble, July 16, 2024. https://rumble.com/v578f5x-brick-suits-in-person-account-of-the -trump-assassination-attempt.html.

17 The Public Square. "TPS 60: Eye Witness Interview from Trump Assassination Attempt." Spotify, July 18, 2024. https://open.spotify .com/episode/1s9B2HnPh9ueu9Ewjt3O0R?si=LOzFEjRyQJS9CS Geh-pgGg&nd=1&dlsi=27cce6b80f954e8b.

18 Dr Steve Turley. "Here's an Eyewitness Account of Trump's Assassination-Attempt!!!" Rumble, July 16, 2024. https://rumble.com /v576hwx-heres-an-eyewitness-account-of-trumps-assassination-attempt .html?e9s=rel_v1_b.

19   Human Events Daily with Jack Posobiec. "Brick Suit's First Hand Account of the Trump Assassination Attempt." Rumble, July 16, 2024. https://rumble.com/v578f5x-brick-suits-in-person-account-of-the -trump-assassination-attempt.html.

20   Posobiec, Jack, and Tom Natoli. Personal, August 31, 2024.

21   The Public Square. "TPS 60: Eye Witness Interview from Trump Assassination Attempt." Spotify, July 18, 2024. https://open.spotify .com/episode/1s9B2HnPh9ueu9Ewjt3O0R?si=LOzFEjRyQJS9CS Geh-pgGg&nd=1&dlsi=27cce6b80f954e8b.

22   Human Events Daily with Jack Posobiec. "Brick Suit's First Hand Account of the Trump Assassination Attempt." Rumble, July 16, 2024. https://rumble.com/v578f5x-brick-suits-in-person-account-of-the -trump-assassination-attempt.html.

23   Ibid.

24   Prime Time with Alex Stein. "EXCLUSIVE EYEWITNESS: What REALLY Happened at Trump's Butler, PA Rally | Ep 221." YouTube, August 7, 2024. https://www.youtube.com/live/xKtAWnPOpUk.

25   Convention of States Project. "Firsthand Account of Trump Shooting | The BattleCry." YouTube, July 21, 2024. https://www.youtube.com /live/Nu1Gha3xF3o.

26   Ibid.

27   Hecker, Ivory. "Trump Shooting Witness on What Really Happened." YouTube, July 14, 2024. https://www.youtube.com/watch?v=MXfeV EFY4bw.

28   The Public Square. "TPS 60: Eye Witness Interview from Trump Assassination Attempt." Spotify, July 18, 2024. https://open.spotify .com/episode/1s9B2HnPh9ueu9Ewjt3O0R?si=LOzFEjRyQJS9CS Geh-pgGg&nd=1&dlsi=27cce6b80f954e8b.

29   "Donald Trump Speaks at 2024 Republican National Convention," Rev.com, July 19, 2024, https://www.rev.com/blog/transcripts/donald -trump-speaks-at-2024-republican-national-convention.

30   Boyle, Matthew, and Alexander Marlow. "Exclusive: Trump Unveils Dramatic Details of Assassination Attempt." Breitbart, August 25, 2024. https://www.breitbart.com/politics/2024/08/25/exclusive-donald -trump-unveils-dramatic-details-assassination-attempt-moment -happened-whos-blame-why-he-got-up-yelled-fight-fight-fight/.

31   Ibid.

32   Conklin, Audrey, and Fox News. "Marine David Dutch Walked from Trump Assassination Attempt with Gunshot Wounds, Friends Say." Fox News, July 17, 2024. https://www.foxnews.com/us/marine-david -dutch-walked-from-trump-shooting-scene-gunshot-wounds-friends -say.

33   6abc Digital Staff. "Trump Rally Shooting Victim Released from Hospital; 2nd Survivor Remains Hospitalized." ABC7 Chicago, July 25, 2024. https://abc7chicago.com/post/trump-rally-shooting-victim-david-dutch-released-hospital/15093250/.

34   Conklin, Audrey, and Fox News. "Trump Assassination Attempt Victim James Copenhaver 'Sad' with State of 'Political Division' in US." Fox News, August 1, 2024. https://www.foxnews.com/us/trump-assassination-attempt-victim-james-copenhaver-sad-state-political-division-us.

35   Ibid.

36   "Moon Township Man Shot at Trump Rally Released from Hospital." WTAE, July 28, 2024. https://www.wtae.com/article/trump-rally-shooting-james-copenhaver-discharged/61719557.

37   Wright, Michelle. "'He Definitely Was a Hero': Corey Comperatore's Wife and Daughters Talk about Deadly Shooting." WTAE, August 17, 2024. https://www.wtae.com/article/corey-comperatore-family-butler-shooting/61891232.

38   Wright, Michelle. "'He Definitely Was a Hero': Corey Comperatore's Wife and Daughters Talk about Deadly Shooting." WTAE, August 16, 2024. https://www.wtae.com/article/corey-comperatore-family-butler-shooting/61891232.

39   Ibid.

40   Ibid.

41   Brumbaugh, Jocelyn. "Trump Makes Entrance to RNC Speech with Fire Gear of Rally Shooting Victim." WTAE, July 19, 2024. https://www.wtae.com/article/trump-entrance-rnc-corey-comperatore/61641130.

42   "REMINDER: Donald 'Dictator on "Day One"' Trump Is an Existential Threat To Our Democracy." Democrats, June 27, 2024. https://democrats.org/news/reminder-donald-dictator-on-day-one-trump-is-an-existential-threat-to-our-democracy/.

43   Keith, Tamara, and Steve Inskeep. "Biden Meets with Democratic Governors as Questions Swirl around the Viability of His Candidacy." NPR, July 3, 2024. https://www.npr.org/2024/07/03/nx-s1–5028506/biden-meets-with-democratic-governors-as-questions-swirl-around-the-viability-of-his-candidacy.

44   "Remarks by President Biden at a Campaign Reception." The White House, June 30, 2024. https://www.whitehouse.gov/briefing-room/speeches-remarks/2024/06/29/remarks-by-president-biden-at-a-campaign-reception-east-hampton-ny/.

45   Taylor, Grant (@grantltaylor). "Steve Bannon & Bernard Kerik Both Warn: Trump May Be Assassinated (Kerik is a former NYPD Commissioner)" X (formerly Twitter), August 11, 2022. https://x.com/grantltaylor/status/1557791741008289792.

46 Ibid.

47 Chief Nerd (@TheChiefNerd). "Tucker Carlson Says They Will Do Anything to Stop Trump from Being President Again 'If you begin with criticism, then you go to protest, then you go to . . . '" X (formerly Twitter), August 30, 2023. https://x.com/TheChiefNerd /status/1696852029723865263.

48 Adams, Scott (@ScottAdamsSays). "Half of the so-called "news" this week looks like a coordinated op to jail or kill Trump and Musk. How crazy that idea would sound a few years ago. Democrats . . . " X (formerly Twitter), September 12, 2023. https://x.com/ScottAdamsSays /status/1701575559162265696.

49 Hibberd, James. "Bill Maher Pushes Back on Joe Rogan: Trump Is a 'Crazy, Stupid Criminal.'" *The Hollywood Reporter*, September 6, 2023. https://www.hollywoodreporter.com/news/politics-news/joe-rogan -bill-maher-trump-biden-1235581529/.

50 Bruni, Frank. "Old Is Workable. Depravity Is a Dead End." *New York Times*, September 7, 2023. https://www.nytimes.com/2023/09/07/opinion /trump-biden-2024-election.html.

51 Sagal, Peter. "The End Will Come for the Cult of MAGA." *The Atlantic*, September 12, 2023. https://www.theatlantic.com/ideas/archive /2023/08/trumpism-maga-cult-republican-voters-indoctrination /675173/.

52 Kaloi, Stephanie. "NBC's Glenn Kirschner Says Donald Trump Should Be Imprisoned before Going to Trial Due to 'demonstrated Danger' for Witnesses (Video)." *TheWrap*, September 2, 2023. https://www .thewrap.com/donald-trump-msnbc-glenn-kirschner-jail-prison -witnesses-video/.

53 Commander, Anna. "Trump Poses 'Danger' to Witnesses, Threat Must Be Neutralized: Kirschner." *Newsweek*, September 3, 2023. https: //www.newsweek.com/trump-poses-danger-witnesses-threat-must -neutralized-kirschner-1824195.

54 "Lawsuit Filed to Remove Trump from Ballot in CO under 14th Amendment—Crew: Citizens for Responsibility and Ethics in Washington." CREW | Citizens for Responsibility and Ethics in Washington, September 7, 2023. https://www.citizensforethics.org/news /press-releases/lawsuit-filed-to-remove-trump-from-ballot-in-co -under-14th-amendment/.

55 The Post Millennial (@TPostMillennial). "Alex Jones: 'They are going to try to assassinate President Trump . . . We have got to pray for President Trump many times a day.'" X (formerly Twitter), June 16, 2024. https://x.com/TPostMillennial/status/1802386793674727908.

56 Klaidman, Daniel. "Silicon Shift? Major Tech Titans Throw Financial, Political Support to Trump." CBS News, July 19, 2024. https://www.cbsnews.com/news/trump-jd-vance-silicon-valley-support/.

57 Ibid.

58 Yu, Yifan. "Who in Silicon Valley Is Supporting Trump—and Why?" Nikkei Asia, August 1, 2024. https://asia.nikkei.com/Politics/U.S.-elections-2024/Who-in-Silicon-Valley-is-supporting-Trump-and-why.

59 Lee, Wendy, Laura J. Nelson, and Hannah Wiley. "Why Some Silicon Valley Investors Are Backing the Trump-Vance Campaign." *Los Angeles Times,* July 18, 2024. https://www.latimes.com/entertainment-arts/business/story/2024-07-18/why-some-silicon-valley-investors-are-backing-the-trump-vance-campaign.

60 Concha, Joe. "Media Kept Bias on Full Display after Trump Assassination Attempt." *New York Post,* July 15, 2024. https://nypost.com/2024/07/14/opinion/lefty-media-kept-bias-on-full-display-after-trump-was-shot/.

61 *USA Today.* "Former President Donald Trump was rushed off stage by U.S. Secret Service after popping noises rattled the crowd in Pennsylvania." Facebook, July 13, 2024. https://www.facebook.com/usatoday/posts/former-president-donald-trump-was-rushed-off-stage-by-us-secret-service-after-po/1018450849951068/.

62 USA TODAY Network staff. "Trump Wounded at Rally in Assassination Attempt; Gunman Killed." *USA Today,* July 14, 2024. https://www.usatoday.com/story/news/politics/elections/2024/07/13/donald-trump-rushed-off-stage-secret-service-rally/74396110007/.

63 Associated Press. "BREAKING: Donald Trump has been escorted off the stage by Secret Service during a rally after loud noises ring out in the crowd." Facebook, July 13, 2024. https://www.facebook.com/APNews/posts/breaking-donald-trump-has-been-escorted-off-the-stage-by-secret-service-during-a/870413591613218/.

64 Tommy G. "Investigating the Trump Assassination Conspiracies." YouTube, August 13, 2024. https://www.youtube.com/watch?v=WtCR3wqj4kY.

65 Farhi, Paul. "How the Media's Wait for the Facts in Trump Shooting Fed a Backlash." *Washington Post,* July 15, 2024. https://www.washingtonpost.com/style/media/2024/07/15/media-backlash-trump-shooting/.

66 Lisec, Joshua (@JoshuaLisec). "MASS FORMATION HYPNOSIS FBI Chief Chris Wray is using a subtle yet noticeable technique to cast doubt on the official story. Notice that in the hearing . . . " X (formerly Twitter), July 26, 2024. https://x.com/JoshuaLisec/status/1816869885995315435?t=f24wR1kaQhJRWlr3_v6cAw&s=19.

DAY TWO, JULY 14, 2024: THE SHOOTER

1 Perry, Ryan, and Alex Diaz. "I Sat next to Donald Trump Shooter as He Honed His Gun Skills on Range." *The US Sun*, July 20, 2024. https://www.the-sun.com/news/11976797/donald-trump-shooter-thomas-crooks-shooting-range/.

2 Bethel Park School District. "A Statement from the BPSD (Updated: July 20, 2024)." Bethel Park School District, July 14, 2024. https://www.bpsd.org/apps/news/article/1942738.

3 Seldin, Jeff. "New Information Emerges on Trump Shooting Suspect." Voice of America, July 15, 2024. https://www.voanews.com/a/new-information-emerges-on-trump-shooting-suspect/7697793.html.

4 Ibid.

5 Tommy G. "Investigating the Trump Assassination Conspiracies." YouTube, August 13, 2024. https://www.youtube.com/watch?v=WtCR3wqj4kY.

6 BLUX. "BlackRock Ad w/ Shooter Thomas Crooks (Full) | #blux." YouTube, July 15, 2024. https://www.youtube.com/watch?v=SoJ7HHkvtBE.

7 Cochrane, Emily, Steve Eder, William K. Rashbaum, Amy Julia Harris, Jack Healy, and Glenn Thrush. "From Honor Student to the Gunman Who Tried to Kill Donald Trump." *New York Times*, July 19, 2024. https://www.nytimes.com/2024/07/19/us/gunman-thomas-crooks-trump-shooting.html.

8 TribuneReview. "Awards and Recognition Program Honors Bethel Park Graduates." TribLIVE.com, July 14, 2024. https://triblive.com/local/awards-and-recognition-program-honors-bethel-park-graduates/.

9 Cochrane, Emily, Steve Eder, William K. Rashbaum, Amy Julia Harris, Jack Healy, and Glenn Thrush. "From Honor Student to the Gunman Who Tried to Kill Donald Trump." *New York Times*, July 19, 2024. https://www.nytimes.com/2024/07/19/us/gunman-thomas-crooks-trump-shooting.html.

10 "Suspected Trump Shooter Graduated from Community College with 'High Honors.'" ABC News, July 15, 2024. https://abcnews.go.com/Politics/live-updates/donald-trump-rally-shooting-assassination-attempt/?id=111916828&entryId=111974110.

11 Flaherty, Anne. "Gunman Planned to Attend Local 4-Year University This Fall." ABC News, July 16, 2024. https://abcnews.go.com/Politics/live-updates/donald-trump-rally-shooting-assassination-attempt/?id=111916828&entryId=111985581.

12 Wendling, Mike. "FBI: Trump Gunman Acted Alone, but Motive Still Unknown." BBC News, August 28, 2024. https://www.bbc.com/news/articles/c785vyg55xyo.

13   Marino, Joe, Larry Celona, and Chris Nesi. "Trump Shooter Thomas Crooks Might Have Been Battling Undiagnosed Mental Illness: Sources." *New York Post*, July 18, 2024. https://nypost.com/2024/07/18/us-news /trump-shooter-thomas-crooks-may-have-suffered-from-mental-illness/.

14   Keane, Isabel. "Failed Assassin Thomas Matthew Crooks Researched Trump and Biden, and Even a UK Royal, before Shooting." *New York Post*, July 18, 2024. https://nypost.com/2024/07/18/us-news /thomas-crooks-researched-trump-and-biden-and-a-uk-royal/.

15   Lybrand, Holmes, Hannah Rabinowitz, and Devan Cole. "Takeaways from FBI Testimony: Trump Shooter Searched Details of JFK Assassination and Flew Drone near Rally Site | CNN Politics." CNN, July 24, 2024. https://www.cnn.com/2024/07/24/politics/fbi-wray -house-hearing-trump-shooting/index.html.

16   Daly, Michael. "Thomas Crooks Searched for Porn before Shooting Trump: FBI." *The Daily Beast*, July 20, 2024. https://www.thedaily beast.com/donald-trump-shooter-thomas-crooks-final-search-on-samsung -phone-was-for-porn.

17   Lybrand, Holmes, Hannah Rabinowitz, and Devan Cole. "Takeaways from FBI Testimony: Trump Shooter Searched Details of JFK Assassination and Flew Drone near Rally Site | CNN Politics." CNN, July 24, 2024. https://www.cnn.com/2024/07/24/politics/fbi-wray -house-hearing-trump-shooting/index.html.

18   Wendling, Mike. "FBI: Trump Gunman Acted Alone, but Motive Still Unknown." BBC News, August 28, 2024. https://www.bbc.com/news /articles/c785vyg55xyo.

19   Marino, Joe, and Chris Nesi. "Exclusive: Thomas Crooks Used Fake Name to Gear up with Dozens of Purchases from Gun Stores a Year before Trump Assassination Attempt: Sources." *New York Post*, July 29, 2024. https://nypost.com/2024/07/29/us-news/thomas-crooks-used-alias-to -buy-gun-parts-a-year-before-trump-shooting-sources/.

20   Ibid.

21   Rojek, Kevin. "Remarks by FBI Pittsburgh Special Agent in Charge Kevin Rojek at Press Briefing on the Investigation of the Butler, Pennsylvania, Assassination Attempt." FBI, July 29, 2024. https://www .fbi.gov/news/speeches/remarks-by-fbi-pittsburgh-special-agent-in -charge-kevin-rojek-at-press-briefing-on-the-investigation-of-the-but ler-pennsylvania-assassination-attempt.

22   Krayden, David. "Breaking: FBI Releases Details of Thomas Matthew Crooks' Search History, New Photos of Gun, Backpack, Explosives." *The Post Millennial*, August 28, 2024. https://thepostmillennial.com /breaking-fbi-releases-details-of-thomas-matthew-crooks-search-history -new-photos-of-gun-backpack-explosives?utm_campaign=64483.

23   Human Events Daily with Jack Posobiec. "The Shooter's Explosive Devices and the Logistical Failures of July 13th." Rumble, July 27, 2024. https://rumble.com/v58lsg5-who-shot-donald-trump.html.

24   Ibid.

25   Rojek, Kevin. "Remarks by FBI Pittsburgh Special Agent in Charge Kevin Rojek at Press Briefing on the Investigation of the Butler, Pennsylvania, Assassination Attempt." FBI, July 29, 2024. https://www.fbi.gov/news/speeches/remarks-by-fbi-pittsburgh-special-agent-in-charge-kevin-rojek-at-press-briefing-on-the-investigation-of-the-butler-pennsylvania-assassination-attempt.

26   Human Events Daily with Jack Posobiec. "The Shooter's Explosive Devices and the Logistical Failures of July 13th." Rumble, July 27, 2024. https://rumble.com/v58lsg5-who-shot-donald-trump.html.

27   Faulders, Katherine, Mike Levine, and Alexander Mallin. "FBI, in Private Meeting with Trump, Revealed New Details about His Would-Be Assassin: Sources." ABC News, August 9, 2024. https://abcnews.go.com/US/fbi-private-meeting-trump-revealed-new-details-assassin/story?id=112714355.

28   Ford, Nicole. "WPXI Exclusive Photos Show Cell Phone, Transmitter Found next to Trump Shooter's Body." WPXI, July 17, 2024. https://www.wpxi.com/news/local/wpxi-exclusive-photos-show-cell-phone-transmitter-found-next-trump-shooters-body/CDQGAB4ZXNCINEGXNAYHAKTJFQ/.

29   Land, Olivia. "Inside What Trump's Would-Be Assassin Thomas Matthew Crooks Did in the 24 Hours before Rally Shooting." New York Post, July 18, 2024. https://nypost.com/2024/07/16/us-news/inside-what-trumps-would-be-assassin-thomas-matthew-crooks-did-in-the-24-hours-before-rally-shooting/.

30   Christenson, Josh. "Trump Shooter Thomas Crooks Had Encrypted Messaging Accounts in Belgium, Germany, New Zealand." New York Post, August 23, 2024. https://nypost.com/2024/08/21/us-news/trump-shooter-thomas-crooks-had-encrypted-messaging-accounts-in-belgium-germany-new-zealand/.

31   Revolver News. "The Plot Thickens: Damning New Details Emerge in Jan 6 Pipe Bomb Cover Up." Revolver News, February 7, 2024. https://revolver.news/2024/01/plot-thickens-damning-new-details-emerge-in-jan-6-pipe-bomb-cover-up/.

32   Kelly, Julie (@julie_kelly2). "NEW: Recently discovered video from Jan 6 shows an individual believed to be police carrying a bag toward the location where "pipe bomb" was found at DNC. This . . . " X (formerly Twitter), August 14, 2024. https://x.com/julie_kelly2/status/1823783318300557761.

33 Forbes Breaking News. "Eli Crane Plays Video Of Trump Shooting Site, Asks PA Police Commish About Second Shooter Theory." YouTube, July 23, 2024. https://www.youtube.com/watch?v=G4mkaa4WSiY.

34 Coulter, Christina, and Fox News. "Exclusive: Trump Shooter's Father Returns to Public Life, Says 'We Just Want to Try to Take Care of Ourselves.'" Fox News, July 23, 2024. https://www.foxnews.com/us /exclusive-trump-shooters-father-returns-public-life-says-we-just-want -try-take-care-ourselves.

35 Conklin, Audrey, and Fox News. "Trump Shooter Thomas Crooks' Parents Unlikely to Face Criminal Charges, Experts Say." Fox News, July 30, 2024. https://www.foxnews.com/us/trump-shooter-thomas -crooks-parents-unlikely-face-criminal-charges-experts-say.

36 Cohen, Zachary, Evan Perez, and Holmes Lybrand. "Trump Rally Shooter Researched Michigan Mass Shooter Ethan Crumbley and His Family Prior to Attack | CNN Politics." CNN, July 19, 2024. https: //www.cnn.com/2024/07/19/politics/trump-rally-shooter-searches /index.html.

37 Collins, Laura. "Exclusive: Father of Trump Shooter Thomas Matthew Crooks Hires Powerhouse Criminal Lawyer as FBI Intensifies Investigation into His Role in Son's Assassination Attempt." *Daily Mail* Online, August 26, 2024. https://www.dailymail.co.uk/news /article-13765351/Father-Trump-shooter-Thomas-Matthew-Crooks -hires-criminal-attorney.html.

38 "The Monica Crowley Podcast: A Newsmaking Talk with President Donald Trump." The Monica Crowley Podcast, August 29, 2024. https: //rumble.com/v5cvr3v-the-monica-crowley-podcast-a-newsmaking -talk-with-president-donald-trump.html?e9s=src_v1_upp.

39 Moore, Henry. "Thomas Crooks' Father 'Called Police on the Day of the Trump Rally Shooting.'" LBC, July 17, 2024. https://www.lbc .co.uk/news/thomas-crooks-father-called-police-on-the-day-of-donald -trump-rally-shooting/.

40 Forbes Breaking News. "Eli Crane Plays Video Of Trump Shooting Site, Asks PA Police Commish About Second Shooter Theory." YouTube, July 23, 2024. https://www.youtube.com/watch?v=G4mkaa4WSiY.

41 Enheim, R. P. "Basically the insinuation would be that assets scrubbed all DNA evidence that may connect someone outside the family to the home. This would tie into public . . . " X (formerly Twitter), 24AD. https://x.com/RPEnheim/status/1816168593467244606.

42 Oversight Project (@OversightPR). "ASSASINATION INFO DROP We found the assassin's connections through our in-depth analysis of mobile ad data to track movements of Crooks and his associates. To . . . " X (formerly Twitter), July 22, 2024. https://x.com/OversightPR/status /1815446054428352591?ref=404media.co.

43 Oversight Project (@OversightPR). "Someone who regularly visited Crooks home and work also visited a building in Washington, DC located in Gallery Place. This is in the same vicinity of an @FBI . . . " X (formerly Twitter), July 22, 2024. https://x.com/OversightPR/status /1815446057829974267.

44 Marino, Joe, and Chris Nesi. "Exclusive: Thomas Crooks Used Fake Name to Gear up with Dozens of Purchases from Gun Stores a Year before Trump Assassination Attempt: Sources." *New York Post*, July 29, 2024. https://nypost.com/2024/07/29/us-news/thomas-crooks-used -alias-to-buy-gun-parts-a-year-before-trump-shooting-sources/

45 Mathias, Christopher. "Right-Wing Group Makes Questionable Claims about Man Who Shot at Donald Trump." Yahoo! News, July 26, 2024. https://www.yahoo.com/news/wing-group-makes-questionable -claims-200323600.html?guccounter=1&guce_referrer=aHR0cHM 6Ly93d3cuZ29vZ2xlLmNvbS8&guce_referrer_sig=AQAAANtw5I- QBBI2f7AG7mLOUAGYtxYOvew4PW21djdSDWkavZ5BejQYV HrmzDdAaS0fwvd0wOcg5uM4iyZOCngGPFeI_tZbDT-ypLrxJzB pmM4EsS3jGlIe1OhB0gC1qZrQk98-k1o5Xrrycy2YTzf6x1A_bO4I e7c1rj005W8EJOutw.

46 Faulders, Katherine, Mike Levine, and Alexander Mallin. "FBI, in Private Meeting with Trump, Revealed New Details about His Would-Be Assassin: Sources." ABC News, August 9, 2024. https://abcnews.go .com/US/fbi-private-meeting-trump-revealed-new-details-assassin /story?id=112714355.

47 "Gell-Mann Amnesia Effect—Wiktionary, The Free Dictionary." Wiktionary, July 5, 2024. https://en.wiktionary.org/wiki/Gell-Mann _Amnesia_effect#:~:text=(see%20quotation).-,Proper%20noun,that %20person%20is%20knowledgeable%20about.

48 Cohen, Zachary, Evan Perez, and Holmes Lybrand. "Trump Rally Shooter Researched Michigan Mass Shooter Ethan Crumbley and His Family Prior to Attack | CNN Politics." CNN, July 19, 2024. https: //www.cnn.com/2024/07/19/politics/trump-rally-shooter-searches /index.html.

49 "Biden Campaign Enlists First Lady, Vice President at Pa. Events." *Pittsburgh Post-Gazette*, July 14, 2024. https://www.post-gazette.com /news/election-2024/2024/07/13/first-lady-jill-biden-pittsburgh-vice -president-kamala-harris-italian-sons-and-d/stories/202407130065.

50 McEntyre, Nicholas. "Thomas Crooks' Cellphone and Transmitter Seen next to His Body after Trump Shooting—as Details Emerge He Told His Boss He Needed the Day off Work." *New York Post*, July 17, 2024. https://nypost.com/2024/07/17/us-news/thomas-matthew -crooks-cell-phone-and-transmitter-found-next-to-trump-would-be -assassin-body/.

51 Daly, Michael. "Thomas Crooks Searched for Porn before Shooting Trump: FBI." *The Daily Beast*, July 20, 2024. https://www.thedailybeast .com/donald-trump-shooter-thomas-crooks-final-search-on-samsung -phone-was-for-porn.

52 Keane, Isabel. "Failed Assassin Thomas Matthew Crooks Researched Trump and Biden, and Even a UK Royal, before Shooting." *New York Post*, July 18, 2024. https://nypost.com/2024/07/18/us-news /thomas-crooks-researched-trump-and-biden-and-a-uk-royal/.

53 Trump, Donald (@DonaldJTrumpJR). "Just to underscore how crazy this all is, I was once prevented flying MY OWN drone off of the beach at Mar-a-Lago by USSS because my father was inside the house . . . " X (formerly Twitter), July 19, 2024. https://x.com/DonaldJTrumpJr /status/1814459544380060034.

54 Luna, Anna (@realannapaulina). "I have just obtained a photo that was taken by individual at rally in PA of Crooks with the gun used to shoot at President Trump walking around building prior . . . " X (formerly Twitter), August 15, 2024. https://x.com/realannapaulina /status/1824081386807922689.

55 Higgins, Clay. "Preliminary Investigative Report to Chairman Mike Kelly." House.gov, August 12, 2024. https://clayhiggins.house.gov/wp-content/uploads/2024/08/Preliminary-Investigative-Report-8.12.24 .pdf.

56 Ibid.

57 Willis, Haley, Aric Toler, David A. Fahrenthold, and Adam Goldman. "Gunman at Trump Rally Was Often a Step Ahead of the Secret Service." *New York Times*, July 28, 2024. https://www.nytimes.com/2024/07/28 /us/politics/trump-shooting-thomas-crooks-secret-service.html.

58 Oliveira, Alex, and David Propper. "Graphic Video Shows Thomas Crooks Dead Moments after Trump Assassination Attempt, Confirms Secret Service Was Warned." *New York Post*, July 23, 2024. https: //nypost.com/2024/07/23/us-news/graphic-new-video-shows-trump -gunman-thomas-matthew-crooks-dead-on-roof-moments-after-assassination -attempt-confirms-secret-service-was-warned/.

59 ironcladusa. "Terrifying moment . . . looking back at my videos from the PA Butler Trump rally on 7/13/24. We were there just trying to sell our patriotic hats from my small . . . " TikTok, July 23, 2024. https: //www.tiktok.com/@ironcladusa/video/7394850830802816298.

60 Spunt, David, Jake Gibson, Michael Dorgan, Audrey Conklin, and Fox News. "Multiple Secret Service Agents Put on Leave Following Trump Assassination Attempt." Fox News, August 23, 2024. https: //www.foxnews.com/us/multiple-secret-service-agents-put-on-leave -following-trump-assassination-attempt?intcmp=tw_fnc.

61 Willis, Haley, Aric Toler, David A. Fahrenthold, and Adam Goldman. "Gunman at Trump Rally Was Often a Step Ahead of the Secret Service." *The New York Times*, July 28, 2024. https://www.nytimes.com/2024/07/28/us/politics/trump-shooting-thomas-crooks-secret-service.html.

62 Ibid.

63 Ibid.

64 Donlevy, Katherine. "Trump's Secret Service Detail Complaining It Wasn't Warned of Suspicious Person Ahead of Assassination Attempt." *New York Post*, July 28, 2024. https://nypost.com/2024/07/28/us-news/trumps-secret-service-claims-it-wasnt-warned-of-suspicious-person-at/.

65 Gosk, Stephanie, and Rich Schapiro. "Gunman Pointed Rifle at Butler Police Officer before Firing on Trump, Local Official Says." NBCNews.com, July 16, 2024. https://www.nbcnews.com/politics/donald-trump/trump-shooting-butler-building-security-secret-service-rcna161921.

66 Vago, Steven, and David Propper. "Exclusive: Local COP Who Interrupted Thomas Crooks but Failed to Stop Him Is a Hero Who Saved Trump's Life, Sheriff Says." *New York Post*, July 17, 2024. https://nypost.com/2024/07/17/us-news/local-cop-who-interrupted-thomas-crooks-but-failed-to-stop-him-is-a-hero-who-saved-trumps-life-sheriff-says/.

67 Posobiec, Jack (@JackPosobiec). "BREAKING: Bodycam footage of Thomas Matthew Crooks jumping from roof to roof just minutes before he shot President Trump and the crowd in Butler, PA." X (formerly Twitter), August 19, 2024. https://x.com/JackPosobiec/status/1825683293330632869.

68 Burnett, Sara, Michael Tarm, and Ed White. "Lawyers: FBI Lured Men for Michigan Gov. Whitmer Kidnap Plot." AP News, March 9, 2022. https://apnews.com/article/whitmer-kidnap-plot-trial-a7dd7bc1a4e5917c3e2c78f599ebc17f#:~:text=March%209%2C%202022-,GRAND%20RAPIDS%2C%20Mich.,never%20meant%20what%20they%20said.

69 USA v. Fox, Croft, Garbin, Franks, Harris, Caserta, Justice.gov (2020).

70 Julie Kelly (@julie_kelly2). "There is no way to convince me Crooks acted alone . . ." X (formerly Twitter), July 21, 2024, https://x.com/julie_kelly2/status/1815041819840794924?t=TUqpPJa2QivwhHrD7ZjkQg&s=19.

71 Rugg, Collin (@CollinRugg). "NEW: Maria Bartiromo says a mystery man in a gray suit climbed on top of the structure where Crooks had shot from to apparently confirm Crooks' de*th, told . . ." X (formerly Twitter), July 21, 2024. https://x.com/CollinRugg/status/1815040597943779641.

72 Crane, Emily. "Trump Shooter Thomas Matthew Crooks' Father Speaks out for First Time after Son Tried to Assassinate Former President." *New York Post*, July 23, 2024. https://nypost.com/2024/07/23/us-news/trump-shooter-thomas-matthew-crooks-father-speaks-out-for-first-time-after-son-tried-to-assassinate-former-president/.

73 Higgins, Clay. "Preliminary Investigative Report to Chairman Mike Kelly." House.gov, August 12, 2024. https://clayhiggins.house.gov/wp-content/uploads/2024/08/Preliminary-Investigative-Report-8.12.24.pdf.

74 Wendling, Mike. "FBI: Trump Gunman Acted Alone, but Motive Still Unknown." BBC News, August 28, 2024. https://www.bbc.com/news/articles/c785vyg55xyo.

75 Emmons, Libby, and Jack Posobiec. "Scoop: US Attorney Has Empaneled Grand Jury to Consider Criminal Charges in Trump Assassination Investigation." Human Events, August 28, 2024. https://humanevents.com/2024/08/28/scoop-us-attorney-has-empaneled-grand-jury-to-consider-criminal-charges-in-trump-assassination-investigation.

76 Posobiec, Jack (@JackPosobiec). "Receipts:" X (formerly Twitter), August 28, 2024. https://x.com/JackPosobiec/status/1828860468888515069?t=9bCOZKQ9Vp_roaEFUwpmjA&s=19.

77 Posobiec, Jack (@JackPosobiec). "MIKE DAVIS: WE NEED TO BE VERY CAREFUL WITH CHARGING PARENTS WITH THE ACTIONS OF THEIR CHILDREN LETS SEE WHERE THIS INVESTIGATION LEADS JUST BC HE HIRED AN . . . " X (formerly Twitter), August 28, 2024. https://x.com/JackPosobiec/status/1828865786535956698?t=fkGScZqj8XALFlpHGYqSPQ&s=19.

78 Boyle, Matthew, and Alexander Marlow. "Exclusive: Trump Unveils Dramatic Details of Assassination Attempt." Breitbart, August 25, 2024. https://www.breitbart.com/politics/2024/08/25/exclusive-donald-trump-unveils-dramatic-details-assassination-attempt-moment-happened-whos-blame-why-he-got-up-yelled-fight-fight-fight/.

DAY THREE, JULY 15, 2024: THE PICK

1 Cernovich, Mike (@Cernovich). "Trumps VP choice is more important than ever, after last night. He must choose his vice president with one issue in mind. ASSASSINATION INSURANCE. The regime . . . " X (formerly Twitter), June 28, 2024. https://x.com/Cernovich/status/1806718148491522207?t=d1bLNNWuA5Kf14HQWmFV_w&s=19.

2 KFYR Staff. "Trump Announces Vance as VP Pick." https://www.kfyrtv.com, July 15, 2024. https://www.kfyrtv.com/2024/07/15/trump-announces-vance-vp/.

3   "About JD Vance." J.D. Vance, November 28, 2023. https://www
     .vance.senate.gov/about/.

4   Vance, JD *Hillbilly Elegy*. New York, NY: HarperCollins Books, 2016.

5   "Hillbilly Elegy." IMDb, November 24, 2020. https://www.imdb.com
     /title/tt6772802/.

6   Vance, JD *Hillbilly Elegy*. New York, NY: HarperCollins Books, 2016.

7   Ibid.

8   "The Inaugural Address." National Archives and Records Administration,
     January 20, 2017. https://trumpwhitehouse.archives.gov/briefings-statements
     /the-inaugural-address/.

9   "6 Books to Help Understand Trump's Win." *New York Times*,
     November 9, 2016. https://www.nytimes.com/2016/11/10/books/6
     -books-to-help-understand-trumps-win.html.

10   "Sen. J.D. Vance: National Pro-Life Scorecard." SBA Pro-Life America,
     August 9, 2024. https://sbaprolife.org/senator/jd-vance.

11   "Trump Sparks Backlash from Anti-Abortion Group Susan B. Anthony
     Pro-Life America." NBCNews.com, April 20, 2023. https://www
     .nbcnews.com/politics/donald-trump/trump-sparks-backlash-anti-abortion
     -group-susan-b-anthony-life-america-rcna80771.

12   Vance, JD (@JDVance.) "For pro lifers, last night was a gut punch.
     No sugar coating it. Giving up on the unborn is not an option.
     It's politically dumb and morally repugnant. Instead . . . " X (for-
     merly Twitter), November 8, 2023. https://x.com/JDVance/status
     /1722311695140298978.

13   Joseph, Cameron. "JD Vance Compared Abortion to Slavery." VICE,
     July 7, 2024. https://www.vice.com/en/article/ohio-republican-jd-vance
     -abortion-slavery/.

14   Everett, Burgess. "J.D. Vance Wants a Border Wall Battle with Biden—
     Politico." Politico, October 19, 2022. https://www.politico.com/news
     /2022/10/19/j-d-vance-border-wall-biden-ohio-00062603.

15   Timsit, Annabelle, and Leo Sands. "Where J.D. Vance Stands on Key
     Issues: Abortion, Guns, Ukraine and More." *Washington Post*, July 16,
     2024. https://www.washingtonpost.com/politics/2024/07/16/jd-vance
     -key-issues-trump-vp-pick/.

16   Dreher, Rod. "J.D. Vance Becomes Catholic." The American
     Conservative, August 11, 2019. https://www.theamericanconservative
     .com/j-d-vance-becomes-catholic/.

17   Elie, Paul. "J. D. Vance's Radical Religion." *The New Yorker*,
     July 24, 2024. https://www.newyorker.com/news/daily-comment/j-d
     -vances-radical-religion.

18   "Abortion." The Roman Catholic Diocese of Phoenix, 2024. https:
     //dphx.org/respect-life/know-the-issues/abortion/.

19   "Fact Sheet: White House Releases First-Ever Comprehensive
     Framework for Responsible Development of Digital Assets." The White
     House, September 16, 2022. https://www.whitehouse.gov/briefing
     -room/statements-releases/2022/09/16/fact-sheet-white-house
     -releases-first-ever-comprehensive-framework-for-responsible-development
     -of-digital-assets/.

20   Bitcoin Magazine (@BitcoinMagazine). "BREAKING: President Biden
     vetoes bill that would allow highly regulated financial firms to custody
     #Bitcoin and crypto." X (formerly Twitter), May 31, 2024. https://x
     .com/BitcoinMagazine/status/1796676018284953832.

21   Asgari, Nikou. "A Major Ad-Vance for Crypto." Financial Times,
     Subscribe to read, July 19, 2024. https://www.ft.com/content/c1789
     1f6–0cbb-40d4–92cc-62e148eedfeb.

22   Klaidman, Daniel. "Silicon Shift? Major Tech Titans Throw Financial,
     Political Support to Trump." CBS News, July 19, 2024. https://www
     .cbsnews.com/news/trump-jd-vance-silicon-valley-support/.

23   "Trump's Running Mate, JD Vance, Is A True Second Amendment
     Champion." NRA, July 22, 2024. https://www.nraila.org/articles
     /20240722/trump-s-running-mate-jd-vance-is-a-true-second-amendment
     -champion.

24   "Everytown, Moms Demand Action Respond to Trump Announcing
     Vance as His Pick for Vice President." Everytown, July 15, 2024.
     https://www.everytown.org/press/everytown-moms-demand-action
     -respond-to-trump-announcing-vance-as-his-pick-for-vice-president/.

25   Vance, JD (@JDVance. "Joe Biden's ATF is illegally collecting information
     on the gun transactions of millions of law-abiding citizens & putting
     them into a digital database. As . . . " X (formerly Twitter), February 1,
     2024. https://x.com/JDVance/status/1488680895695446017.

26   Stein, Jeff. "J.D. Vance Pick Unnerves GOP's Business Elite, Thrills
     Populists." Washington Post, July 15, 2024. https://www.washingtonpost
     .com/business/2024/07/15/vance-trump-economy-gop/.

27   Ibid.

28   Ball, Molly. "The Secret Bipartisan Campaign That Saved the 2020 Election."
     Time, February 4, 2021. https://time.com/5936036/secret-2020-election
     -campaign/.

29   Douthat, Ross. "What J.D. Vance Believes." The New York Times, June 13,
     2024. https://www.nytimes.com/2024/06/13/opinion/jd-vance-interview
     .html?searchResultPosition=1.

30   Vance, J.D. "J.D. Vance: The Math on Ukraine Doesn't Add Up." New
     York Times, April 12, 2024. https://www.nytimes.com/2024/04/12
     /opinion/jd-vance-ukraine.html.

31   Ibid.

32 "Senator Vance Introduces Legislation to Ban Gender Reassignment Procedures on Minors." JD Vance, July 18, 2023. https://www.vance .senate.gov/press-releases/senator-vance-introduces-legislation-to-ban -gender-reassignment-procedures-on-minors/.

33 Ibid.

34 Filipkowski, Ron (@RonFilipkowski). "JD Vance says women who haven't given birth like Kamala Harris are "childless cat ladies who are miserable at their own lives," and have "no direct stake" in . . . " X (formerly Twitter), July 22, 2024. https://x.com/RonFilipkowski /status/1815503440983867598.

35 Garcia, Nicole. "Bill Kristol Reflects on the Republican Party's Deep Transformation." GBH, July 18, 2024. https://www.wgbh.org/news /national/2024–07-18/bill-kristol-reflects-on-the-republican-partys -deep-transformation.

36 The Associated Press. "Donald Trump selected Ohio Sen. JD Vance as his vice presidential pick. He announced the decision on his Truth Social Network on Monday. Trump and Vance were . . . " X (formerly Twitter), July 15, 2024. https://x.com/AP/status/1813017348460441850.

37 Carlson, Tucker (@TuckerCarlson). "Lindsey Graham is a liar. No one lobbied harder against JD Vance than he did, and in the sleazi- est, most vicious way. He was doing it this morning. This is why . . . " X (formerly Twitter), July 15, 2024. https://x.com/TuckerCarlson /status/1812980770904182891.

38 Swan, Jonathan. "Former White House Doctor Describes Tending to Trump's Wounded Ear." *New York Times*, July 16, 2024. https://www .nytimes.com/2024/07/16/us/politics/trump-shooting-ear-ronny -jackson-doctor.html.

39 Ewe, Koh. "Why Republicans Are Wearing Fake Ear Bandages." *Time*, July 18, 2024. https://time.com/7000028/ear-bandage-fashion-trend -republicans-convention-rnc-trump-shooting/.

40 Parker, Ashley, Meryl Kornfield, and Josh Dawsey. "Meet the RNC Delegates Who Have Adopted Trump's Bandage for Their Own Ears." *Washington Post*, July 18, 2024. https://www.washingtonpost.com /politics/2024/07/18/rnc-delegates-trump-ear-bandages/.

41 Ibid.

42 Posobiec, Jack (@JackPosobiec). "BREAKING: We asked over 100 leftists yesterday if they would condemn the Trump shooting Not one would You have to understand, leftist revolutionaries don't see . . . " X (formerly Twitter), July 16, 2024. https://x.com/JackPosobiec/status /1813191911194136869.

43 Human Events Daily with Jack Posobiec. "ANTIFA Tries to BLOCK the RNC Entrance." Rumble, July 15, 2024. https://rumble.com

/v573ok5-breaking-antifa-has-arrived-at-the-rnc-attempting-to-block
-the-entrance-to-.html.

44 Ibid.

DAY FOUR, JULY 16, 2024: THE BACKLASH

1 DiscussingFilm (@DiscussingFilm). "Jack Black says "all future creative plans" for Tenacious D are on hold and the tour is cancelled.
This is all due to a comment that Kyle Gass made on stage . . . " X
(formerly Twitter), July 16, 2024. https://x.com/DiscussingFilm/status
/1813202026488066257.

2 Weprin, Alex. "Jack Black Cancels Tenacious D Tour after Being
'Blindsided' by Partner Kyle Gass' Trump Comment." *The Hollywood
Reporter*, July 16, 2024. https://www.hollywoodreporter.com/news
/politics-news/jack-black-cancels-tenacious-d-world-tour-kyle-gass
-trump-comment-1235949644/?utm_source=twitter&utm_medium
=social.

3 New York Post (@nypost). "Tenacious D's Kyle Gass deletes Instagram
apology for Donald Trump shooting comment https://trib.al/wGB
MnZl" X (formerly Twitter), July 21, 2024. https://x.com/nypost/status
/1815046023741395405.

4 Sortor, Nick (@nicksortor). "Green Day had a concert here in DC
last night. They decided it'd be a good idea to hold up a severed
Trump head. Just TWO WEEKS after he was sh*t in the head . . . "
X (formerly Twitter), July 30, 2024. https://x.com/nicksortor/status
/1818292038439207075.

5 Kaufman, Eric. "Third of Democrats Wish Donald Trump Had Been
Killed." UnHerd, July 21, 2024. https://unherd.com/newsroom/third
-of-democrats-wish-donald-trump-had-been-killed/#:~:text=A%20
third%20of%20Democratic%20voters,assassination%20and%20
which%20do%20not.

6 Ushe, Naledi, and Brendan Morrow. "Jack Black Reveals Fate of
Tenacious D Following Controversial Trump Comments." *USA Today*,
August 7, 2024. https://www.usatoday.com/story/entertainment/music
/2024/08/07/jack-black-tenacious-d-kyle-gass-future/74700812007/.

7 Ibid.

8 "Tenacious D | The Spicy Meatball Tour—Cancelled." Frontier Touring,
July 7, 2024. https://www.frontiertouring.com/news/tenacious-d-the
-spicy-meatball-tour-cancelled.

9 Sharf, Zack. "Jack Black Cancels Tenacious D Tour and 'all Future
Creative Plans' after Kyle Gass' Remark on Trump Assassination
Attempt: 'I Was Blindsided by What Was Said.'" *Variety*, July 16,
2024. https://variety.com/2024/music/news/jack-black-cancels-tenacious
-d-tour-trump-assassination-kyle-gass-1236073486/.

10 Tupelo Honey. "Our Story: Tupelo Honey Southern Kitchen & Bar." Tupelo Honey, August 5, 2024. https://tupelohoneycafe.com/our -story/.

11 McVicar, Brian. "Tupelo Honey Worker Loses Job after Trump Assassination Attempt Comment." mlive, July 17, 2024. https://www .mlive.com/news/grand-rapids/2024/07/tupelo-honey-worker-loses -job-after-trump-assassination-attempt-comment.html.

12 Ibid.

13 Raichik, Chaya (@ChayaRaichik10). "Chaya Raichik (@ChayaRaichik10)" X (formerly Twitter), November 2022. https://x.com/ChayaRaichik10.

14 WATROBSKI, KRISTINA. "Colorado Teacher Sparks Outrage with Trump Assassination Attempt Post: 'Now He's a Martyr.'" CBS Austin, July 16, 2024. https://cbsaustin.com/news/nation-world/colorado-teacher -sparks-outrage-with-trump-assassination-attempt-post-now-hes-a -martyr-jennifer-ripper-jeffco-public-schools-semper-elementary-donald -trump-butler-pennsylvania-rally-crisis-in-the-classroom.

15 Ibid

16 Libs of TikTok (@libsoftiktok). "Meet Jennifer Ripper, a teacher at Semper Elementary School in @JeffcoSchoolsCo. She's very sad that the sh**ter missed. Any comment @JeffcoSchoolsCo?" X (formerly Twitter), July 15, 2024. https://x.com/libsoftiktok/status/18128870 18403139910.

17 Libs of TikTok (@libsoftiktok). "UPDATE: In response to our reporting of a teacher lamenting that the sh**ter missed, @Jeffco SchoolsCo sent this email reminding parents of their social media . . . " X (formerly Twitter), July 15, 2024. https://x.com/libsoftiktok/status /1812977009871442129.

18 "Is a Career as a Behavior Specialist Right for You?" PaTTAN, February 2024. https://www.pattan.net/assets/PaTTAN/2e/2efd1e23–7f6b-425c -a1ee-92471d20dadd.pdf.

19 WATROBSKI, KRISTINA. "Teachers Who Cheered Trump Assassination Attempt Disciplined by School Officials." The National Desk, July 17, 2024. https://thenationaldesk.com/news/americas-news -now/teachers-nationwide-disciplined-over-trump-assassination-attempt -posts-irresponsibility-donald-trump-rally-shooting-sioux-falls-south -dakota-ardmore-oklahoma-jefferson-county-colorado-crisis-in-the -classroom.

20 Sioux Fall Schools (@SFSchools). "given the public trust in our responsibility to educate the children of our community and serve as positive role models. The staff member's statement does not . . . " X (formerly Twitter), July 16, 2024. https://x.com/SFSchools/status /1813230847941628145.

21　Libs of TikTok (@libsoftiktok). "Meet Alison Scott, a teacher at @
　　Ardmore_Tigers. She appears sad the sh**ter missed and "wishes" he
　　had a better scope. These are the people educating your kids . . . ",
　　X (formerly Twitter), July 16, 2024. https://x.com/libsoftiktok/status
　　/1813244367295094931.

22　Walters, Ryan (@RyanWaltersSupt). "This is unacceptable. SDE is
　　investigating. We will not allow teachers to cheer on violence against @
　　realDonaldTrump." X (formerly Twitter), July 16, 2024. https://x.com
　　/RyanWaltersSupt/status/1813309802363400433.

23　Walters, Ryan (@RyanWaltersSupt). "I have investigated it enough. I
　　will be taking her teaching certificate. She will no longer be teaching
　　in Oklahoma." X (formerly Twitter), July 16, 2024. https://x.com/Ryan
　　WaltersSupt/status/1813382084745982176.

24　Libs of TikTok (@libsoftiktok). "Meet John James. A professor at @
　　bellarmineU. He's very sad that the sh**ter missed.@bellarmineU
　　any comment?" X (formerly Twitter), July 14, 2024. https://x.com
　　/libsoftiktok/status/1812605890274693233.

25　Bellarmine University (@bellarmineU). X (formerly Twitter), July 15,
　　2024. https://x.com/bellarmineU/status/1812962873506676981.

26　Bellarmine University (@bellarmineU). "UPDATE: This individual is
　　no longer a Bellarmine employee." X (formerly Twitter), July 16, 2024.
　　https://x.com/bellarmineU/status/1813326105337647377.

27　Vaccone, Joe. Facebook, image. July 14, 2024. https://www.facebook.
　　com/photo?fbid=1916648328759081&set=pcb.3934296776792246.

28　Prospect Park Fire Company. "Prospect Park Fire Chief Resigns."
　　Facebook, July 15, 2024. https://www.facebook.com/ProspectParkFC/
　　posts/pfbid02nfxNjANeZbaFVfCTP3Bi5ZgoGZ2Tnc4vUoa2K
　　LFz4cQYRU8oaT8ZAkfEhBewgPDEl?ref=embed_post.

29　MacAulay, Jessica. "Prospect Park Fire Chief Resigns after Sharing
　　'Unprofessional Post' Following Trump Assassination Attempt." CBS
　　News, July 16, 2024. https://www.cbsnews.com/philadelphia/news
　　/prospect-park-fire-chief-jim-simmonds-resigns-pennsylvania.

30　Libs of TikTok (@libsoftiktok). "This is what she posted on Facebook
　　@HomeDepot." X (formerly Twitter), July 15, 2024. https://x.com
　　/libsoftiktok/status/1812707740109684745.

31　The Home Depot (@HomeDepot). "Hi, this individual's comments
　　don't reflect The Home Depot or our values. We can confirm she no
　　longer works at The Home Depot." X (formerly Twitter), July 16,
　　2024. https://x.com/HomeDepot/status/1813291845318746134.

32　"Reddit Lies." X (formerly Twitter), October 2015. https://x.com
　　/reddit_lies.

33   Reddit Lies (@reddit_lies). "This is why Trump was almost assassi-
     nated. Because "MAGA would do it to us." X (formerly Twitter), July
     15, 2024. https://x.com/reddit_lies/status/1813020211714388313.
34   Ibid.
35   Reddit Lies (@reddit_lies). "Reddit moments after Trump was shot:" X
     (formerly Twitter), July 15, 2024. https://x.com/reddit_lies/status
     /1813032806500737533.
36   itsagundam (@GundamIsHere). "This is a tremendously bad take,
     the guy died shielding his wife and daughter from bullets. He was a
     fire fighter that lived in service of others. "BuT He WaS aT . . . " X
     (formerly Twitter), July 16, 2024. https://x.com/GundamIsHere/status
     /1813262865484206513.
37   Ibid.

DAY FIVE, JULY 17, 2024: THE REVIEW

1   "DHS Office of Inspector General Announces Reviews of Secret Service
    Process for Securing Trump Campaign Event on July 13, 2024, and
    Secret Service Counter Sniper Preparedness and Operations." DHS,
    17AD. https://www.oig.dhs.gov/sites/default/files/assets/pr/2024/071724
    -dhs-oig-usss-press-release.pdf.
2   Gillum, Jack, James V. Grimaldi, James Fanelli, and C. Ryan Barber.
    "Videos Show Police at Trump Rally Airing Frustration With Secret
    Service." Wall Street Journal, August 8, 2024. https://www.wsj.com
    /us-news/videos-show-police-at-trump-rally-airing-frustration-with
    -secret-service-47c62e12?mod=e2tw.
3   Bongino, Dan. *Protecting the President: An Insider's Account of the
    Troubled Secret Service in an Era of Evolving Threats.* Washington, DC:
    WND Books, 2017.
4   Laila, Cristina. "Dan Bongino: Whistleblowers Confirm Secret Service
    Is Hiding a Big Secret (Video): The Gateway Pundit: By Cristina Laila."
    The Gateway Pundit, August 2, 2024. https://www.thegatewaypundit
    .com/2024/08/dan-bongino-whistleblowers-confirm-secret-service-is
    -hiding/.
5   Morin, Rebecca, and John Bacon. "Pressure Mounts on Secret Service;
    Agency Had Denied Requests for Extra Trump Security." *USA Today*, July
    21, 2024. https://www.usatoday.com/story/news/nation/2024/07/21
    /trump-shooting-updates-secret-service/74488849007/.
6   "New Whistleblower Allegation: Secret Service Prevented Extra Security
    Assets for Trump Rally." Josh Hawley, August 23, 2024. https://www
    .hawley.senate.gov/new-whistleblower-allegation-secret-service-prevented
    -extra-security-assets-for-trump-rally/.
7   Ibid.

8   Cernvich, Mike (@Cernovich). "It was an assassination plot by the deep state." X (formerly Twitter), August 23, 2024. https://x.com /Cernovich/status/1827016666993320219?t=7w4w583HNO7jEfZT KMbnMA&s=03.

9   U.S. Secret Service Media Relations. "Statement from U.S. Secret Service Director Kimberly Cheatle." Statement From U.S. Secret Service Director Kimberly Cheatle | United States Secret Service, July 15, 2024. https://www.secretservice.gov/newsroom/releases/2024/07 /statement-us-secret-service-director-kimberly-cheatle.

10   Watters, Jesse (@JesseBWatters). "BREAKING: @dbongino says sources tell him there were very few actual Secret Service agents posted at the Butler rally site. He says a lot of them were temp . . . " X (formerly Twitter), July 14, 2024. https://x.com/JesseBWatters/status/1812653 990150078756.

11   @amuse. "I don't know what shocked me more, finding out that the Secret Service had never provided Trump counter sniper protection until the Butler rally or that they . . . " X (formerly Twitter), August 4, 2024. https://x.com/amuse/status/1820073799368241617?s=52.

12   Entin, Brian (@BrianEntin). "Secret Service counter-snipers did not have direct communication with the local police snipers at the Trump rally. They had no way to communicate before . . . " X (formerly Twitter), July 31, 2024. https://x.com/BrianEntin/status/1818666427596906612.

13   Devine, Curt, Holmes Lybrand, Isabelle Chapman, and Zachary Cohen. "New Bodycam Video Shows Moment Police Officer Saw Trump Shooter Just before Assassination Attempt | CNN Politics." CNN, August 8, 2024. https://www.cnn.com/2024/08/08/politics /police-body-cam-video-trump-shooting/index.html.

14   Lybrand, Holmes, Zachary Cohen, and Majlie de Puy Kamp. "Forgotten Radios and Missed Warnings: New Details Emerge about Communication Failures before Trump Rally Shooting | CNN Politics." CNN, August 23, 2024. https://www.cnn.com/2024/08/23/politics /trump-rally-shooting-communication-failures/index.html.

15   Posobiec, Jack (@JackPosobiec). "This video proves that the acting Secret Service Director lied yesterday. The shooter wasn't prone the whole time at all, he was running around." X (formerly Twitter), July 31, 2024. https://x.com/JackPosobiec/status/1818707616417149030? t=W1T8bJITkz47SZ7WqBWMVA&s=19.

16   Higgins, Clay. "Preliminary Investigative Report to Chairman Mike Kelly." House.gov, August 12, 2024. https://clayhiggins.house.gov/wp -content/uploads/2024/08/Preliminary-Investigative-Report-8.12.24 .pdf.

17   Signal Contributor, "Investigation: Local officer shot Trump rally shooter
     first," *The Signal*, August 19, 2024, https://signalscv.com/2024/08
     /investigation-local-officer-shot-trump-rally-shooter-first/.
18   Rabinowitz, Hannah, and Tierney Sneed. "Secret Service Should
     Have Watched Roof Used by Trump Rally Shooter, Acting Director
     Says | CNN Politics." CNN, August 2, 2024. https://www.cnn
     .com/2024/08/02/politics/secret-service-trump-assassination-attempt
     -briefing-ronald-rowe/index.html.
19   Hawley, Josh (@HawleyMO). "Whistleblower tells me Secret Service
     Acting Director Rowe personally directed cuts to the USSS agents who
     do threat assessments for events. Whistleblower says . . . " X (formerly
     Twitter), August 1, 2024. https://x.com/HawleyMO/status/18190941
     75096176770?t=6vtOtv4QAvD-lIhrTp4erw&s=19.
20   Crabtree, Susan (@susancrabtree). "EXCLUSIVE: A Secret Service
     counter sniper sent an email Monday night to the entire Uniformed
     Division (not agents) saying he will not stop speaking out until . . . " X
     (formerly Twitter), July 30, 2024. https://x.com/susancrabtree/status/1
     818291679469965647?t=0X4wlzw-dJKKAzNq1IOqgQ&s=19.
21   Crabtree, Susan. "Secret Service Agents Placed on Leave after Trump
     Assassination Attempt | Realclearpolitics." *RealClear Politics*, August 22,
     2024.   https://www.realclearpolitics.com/articles/2024/08/22/secret
     _service_agents_placed_leave_after_trump_assassination_attempt__151502
     .html.
22   Spunt, David, Jake Gibson, Michael Dorgan, and Audrey Conklin.
     "Multiple Secret Service Agents Put on Leave Following Trump
     Assassination Attempt." Fox News, August 23, 2024. https://www
     .foxnews.com/us/multiple-secret-service-agents-put-on-leave-following
     -trump-assassination-attempt?intcmp=tw_fnc.
23   Johnson, Ron (@SenRonJohnson). "The FBI and the Secret Service
     are slow walking and stonewalling the Senate's investigation into the
     Trump assassination attempt. If you wanted to raise . . . " X (formerly
     Twitter), August 25, 2024. https://x.com/SenRonJohnson/status/1827
     773093625934225?t=nBE9TbUpS2Ze62DubsFrvA&s=03.

DAY SEVEN, JULY 19, 2024: THE PILE-ON

1   Evolve Therapy. "How Does an Innocent vs Guilty Person React When
     Accused of Cheating?" *Evolve Therapy*, March 23, 2023. https://www
     .evolvetherapymn.com/post/how-does-an-innocent-vs-guilty-person
     -react-when-accused-of-cheating.
2   Kreutz, Adrian. "Are We All Guilty at Heart?" *Psychology Today*, October
     4, 2023. https://www.psychologytoday.com/us/blog/the-dyslexic-academic
     /202310/are-we-all-guilty-at-heart.

3   Abdul-Hakim, Gabriella, Will McDuffie, and Fritz Farrow. "After Trump Assassination Attempt, Biden Campaign Pauses Ads, Events, Attacks." ABC News, July 14, 2024. https://abcnews.go.com/Politics /after-trump-assassination-attempt-biden-campaign-pauses-ads /story?id=111930384#:~:text=The%20assassination%20attempt%20 on%20the,according%20to%20a%20campaign%20official.

4   Ibid.

5   Allen, Jonathan, Natasha Korecki, and Carol E. Lee. "'No One Involved in the Effort Thinks He Has a Path': Biden Insiders Say the Writing Is on the Wall." NBCNews.com, July 11, 2024. https://www .nbcnews.com/politics/2024-election/biden-reelection-insiders -no-path-debate-rcna161296.

6   Lord Ashcroft. "Before the Shooting, Biden's Capacity Had Become a Bigger Factor than Trump's Character: My Latest Us Polling." Lord Ashcroft Polls, July 14, 2024. https://lordashcroftpolls.com/2024/07 /before-the-shooting-bidens-capacity-had-become-a-bigger-factor -than-trumps-character-my-latest-us-polling/.

7   Murray, Mark. "Poll: Debate Aftermath Damages Biden and Democratic Party—but One-on-One Matchup with Trump Is Unchanged." NBCNews.com, July 15, 2024. https://www.nbcnews .com/politics/2024-election/poll-debate-aftermath-damages-biden -democratic-party-matchup-trump-unc-rcna161154.

8   Irwin, Lauren. "Trump Expands Lead on Biden after Shooting: Polls." The Hill, July 18, 2024. https://thehill.com/homenews/campaign /4780683-trump-expands-lead-on-biden-after-shooting-polls/.

9   Ma, Jason. "'Trump's Voters Are Energized, Biden's Voters Are Demoralized' after the Shooting, and Democrats Will Shy Away from Attacks, Polling Expert Says." Fortune, July 14, 2024. https://fortune .com/2024/07/14/presidential-election-forecast-donald-trump-vs-joe -biden-voter-turnout-assassination-attempt-frank-luntz/.

10 Casten, Sean. "Rep. Sean Casten: It's Time for Joe Biden to Pass the Torch." Chicago Tribune, July 19, 2024. https://www.chicagotribune .com/2024/07/19/opinion-joe-biden-presidential-candidacy-pass-the -torch/.

11 Marzano, Peter. "Sean Casten, Chuy García Join Growing Calls for President Biden to Withdraw from Presidential Race." NBC Chicago, July 19, 2024. https://www.nbcchicago.com/news/local/sean-casten- chuy-garcia-join-growing-calls-for-president-biden-to-withdraw-from- presidential-race/3495462/.

12 The Associated Press. "Rep. Mike Quigley Calls on President Joe Biden to Drop out of Presidential Race." NBC Chicago, July 6, 2024. https://www.nbcchicago.com/news/local/chicago-politics/rep-mike

-quigley-calls-on-president-joe-biden-to-drop-out-of-presidential
-race/3482238/.

13   NBC Chicago Staff. "2 More Illinois House Democrats Call on
     President Biden to Withdraw from Race." NBC Chicago, July 11, 2024.
     https://www.nbcchicago.com/news/local/2nd-illinois-house-democrat
     -calls-president-biden-withdraw-race/3486794/.

14   CNBC, and Dan Mangan. "Senate Finance Chair Sherrod Brown Calls
     on Biden to Drop out, Joins over 30 Lawmakers." NBC Chicago, July
     19, 2024. https://www.nbcchicago.com/news/business/money-report
     /five-more-house-democrats-urge-biden-to-drop-out-campaign-says
     -presidents-in-this-race/3495345/.

15   Hubbard, Kaia, and Melissa Quinn. "Here Are the Democratic
     Lawmakers Calling for Biden to Step aside in the 2024 Race." CBS
     News, July 21, 2024. https://www.cbsnews.com/news/joe-biden-2024
     -race-democrats-who-want-him-to-step-aside/.

16   Saric, Ivana. "Biden Says He Would Drop out of 2024 Race If Diagnosed
     with Medical Condition." Axios, July 17, 2024. https://www.axios
     .com/2024/07/17/biden-drop-out-presidential-campaign-bet-news.

17   Madhani, Aamer. "President Joe Biden Tests Positive for COVID-19
     While Campaigning in Las Vegas, Has 'Mild Symptoms.'" AP News,
     July 18, 2024. https://apnews.com/article/biden-covid-las-vegas
     -ff29bb071f18b993d20dedccbe2c8fbf#:~:text=President%20Joe%20
     Biden%20tests%20positive,Vegas%2C%20has%20%27mild%20
     symptoms%27&text=President%20Joe%20Biden%20tested%20
     positive,infection%2C%20the%20White%20House%20said.

18   Lane, Tiffany. "News 3 Was with President Biden's Press Pool When
     He Tested Positive for Covid." News3, July 17, 2024. https://news3lv
     .com/news/local/news-3-was-with-president-bidens-press-pool-when
     -he-tested-positive-for-covid.

19   Al Jazeera. "Biden Tests Positive for COVID, Cancels Las Vegas
     Campaign Event." Al Jazeera, July 18, 2024. https://www.aljazeera
     .com/news/2024/7/17/biden-tests-positive-for-covid-cancels-las-vegas
     -campaign-event.

20   Ibid.

21   Reuters. "Biden Begins to Accept He May Have to Drop out of Race,
     New York Times Reports | Reuters." Reuters, July 18, 2024. https:
     //www.reuters.com/world/us/biden-begins-accept-he-may-have-drop
     -out-race-new-york-times-reports-2024–07-18/.

22   Kanno-Youngs, Zolan. "From Buoyant to Frail: Two Days in Las
     Vegas as Biden Tests Positive." *New York Times*, July 18, 2024. https:
     //www.nytimes.com/2024/07/18/us/politics/biden-covid-democrats

.html#:~:text=Biden%27s%20motorcade%2C%20who%20quickly
%20rushed,p.m.%20in%20Las%20Vegas%2C%20Mr.

23 Ibid.

24 Shear, Michael D., and Peter Baker et al. "Election Highlights: Biden
Maintains Public Defiance as More Lawmakers Call for His Exit from
Race." *New York Times*, July 23, 2024. https://www.nytimes.com
/live/2024/07/19/us/biden-election-news.

25 Ibid.

26 Ibid.

DAY EIGHT, JULY 20, 2024: THE RUMOR

1   Allen, Jonathan, Natasha Korecki, and Carol E. Lee. "'No One
Involved in the Effort Thinks He Has a Path': Biden Insiders Say
the Writing Is on the Wall." NBCNews.com, July 11, 2024. https:
//www.nbcnews.com/politics/2024-election/biden-reelection-insiders
-no-path-debate-rcna161296.

2   Ibid.

3   Vance, JD (@JDVance). "Everyone calling on Joe Biden to *stop running* without also calling on him to resign the presidency is engaged in
an absurd level of cynicism. If you can't . . . " X (formerly Twitter), July
20, 2024. https://x.com/JDVance/status/1814657912762966064.

4   Kight, Stef W. "GOP Builds New Case for Biden Resignation."
Axios, July 20, 2024. https://www.axios.com/2024/07/20/republicans
-biden-resign-white-house-election-2024.

5   Ibid.

6   Al Jazeera. "Biden Vows to Stay in Race as More Democrats Ask Him to
Drop Out." Al Jazeera, July 20, 2024. https://www.aljazeera.com/news
/2024/7/20/biden-vows-to-stay-in-race-as-more-democrats-ask-him
-to-drop-out.

7   Biden, Joe (@JoeBiden). "Let me say this as clearly as I can: I'm the sitting President of the United States. I'm the nominee of the Democratic
party. I'm staying in the race." X (formerly Twitter), July 5, 2024.
https://x.com/JoeBiden/status/1809310761933525304?lang=en.

8   Ballard, Jamie, and David Montgomery. "What Americans Believe
about the Attempted Assassination on Donald Trump." YouGov, July
24, 2024. https://today.yougov.com/politics/articles/50154-what-
americans-believe-about-attempted-assassination-donald-trump-poll.

9   Hussain, Murtaza. "FBI Agent Goaded Garland Shooter to 'Tear up
Texas,' Raising New Alarms about Bureau's Methods." The Intercept,
August 9, 2016. https://theintercept.com/2016/08/09/fbi-agent-goaded
-garland-shooter-to-tear-up-texas-raising-new-alarms-about-bureaus-
methods/.

DAY NINE, JULY 21, 2024: THE PALACE COUP

1   CBS News. "Biden Campaign Co-Chair Cedric Richmond Says President 'Has Heard Those Concerns' of Democrats." CBS News, July 21, 2024. https://www.cbsnews.com/video/biden-campaign-co-chair -cedric-richmond-says-president-has-heard-those-concerns-of-democrats/.

2   Ibid.

3   Ibid.

4   Ibid.

5   Dowd, Maureen. "The Dems Are Delighted. but a Coup Is Still a Coup." *New York Times*, August 17, 2024. https://www.nytimes.com /2024/08/17/opinion/election-dnc-convention.html.

6   Ibid.

7   Ibid.

8   Guest, Steve (@SteveGuest). "WATCH: CNN's Jake Tapper: Have you talked to Joe Biden? Nancy Pelosi: "I did what I had to do. . . . My concern was not about the president, it was about his campaign."" X (formerly Twitter), August 19, 2024. https://x.com/SteveGuest /status/1825693490115653917.

9   Ibid.

10 Dowd, Maureen. "The Dems Are Delighted. but a Coup Is Still a Coup." *The New York Times*, August 17, 2024. https://www.nytimes.com/2024 /08/17/opinion/election-dnc-convention.html.

11 Ibid.

12 Rugg, Collin (@CollinRugg). "NEW: President Joe Biden confirms he was pushed out of the race by top Democrats who apparently staged a coup on him. "But what happened was a number of my . . . " X (formerly Twitter), August 11, 2024. https://x.com/CollinRugg/status/18 22628391360835825?t=dLVAS7tboXXEI6_lybsmyg&s=19.

13 Dowd, Maureen. "The Dems Are Delighted. but a Coup Is Still a Coup." *The New York Times*, August 17, 2024. https://www.nytimes .com/2024/08/17/opinion/election-dnc-convention.html.

14 Ibid.

15 Guest, Steve (@SteveGuest). "WATCH: CNN's Jake Tapper: Have you talked to Joe Biden? Nancy Pelosi: "I did what I had to do. . . . My concern was not about the president, it was about his campaign."" X (formerly Twitter), August 19, 2024. https://x.com/SteveGuest /status/1825693490115653917.

16 Democratic National Committee. "Final Master Platform." Democrats.org, August 2024. https://democrats.org/wp-content/uploads/2024/08 /FINAL-MASTER-PLATFORM.pdf.

17 Powell, Laura (@LauraPowellEsq). "UPDATE: Last night, Kamala Harris personally filed an updated Statement of Candidacy (aka Form

2) to designate Tim Walz as her running mate. Since she used . . . " X (formerly Twitter), August 7, 2024. https://x.com/LauraPowellEsq/stat us/1821369361904628057?t=DHUCZYE_D5rOiP4yseA1xg&s=19.

18 Posobiec, Jack (@JackPosobiec). "BREAKING: Biden just slipped up and admitted that he dropped out of the race so the Democrats could focus on House and Senate seats He knows Kamala isn't their . . . " X (formerly Twitter), August 20, 2024. https://x.com/JackPosobiec /status/1825923060437790937.

19 Cortes, Steve (@CortesSteve). "Wow. Gavin Newsom mocks the Democrats' coronation of Kamala Harris: Host: "How are you feeling about the switch?"Newsom: "We went through a very open process . . . " X (formerly Twitter), August 24, 2024. https://x.com/CortesSteve /status/1827335460433093048.

20 Flood, Brian. "Gavin Newsom Jokes about Harris Landing Nomination without Primary, Laughs He Was 'Told' to Call It Inclusive." Fox News, August 23, 2024. https://www.foxnews.com/media/gavin-newsom-jokes -about-harris-landing-nomination-without-primary-laughs-he-told -call-inclusive.

21 Trump, Donald (@realDonaldTrump). "I watched Joe Biden Monday night, and was amazed at his ANGER at being humiliated by the Democrats. I was happy to have played a part in his demise in that it . . ." Truth Social, August 21, 2024. https://truthsocial.com/@real DonaldTrump/posts/113000664138401136.

ONE INCH FROM CIVIL WAR

1 Morbid Knowledge (@Morbidful). "The most attended funeral ever in history was for C.N Annadurai, a politician from India. Over 15 million people gathered in Chennai to see him off in 1969, . . ." X (formerly Twitter), October 22, 2023. https://x.com/Morbidful/status /1716039987223835070.

2 Super TV (@superTV247). "NEW It has been confirmed that The Queen's Funeral was viewed by 37.5 MILLION people in the UK on Monday, across over 50 channels on TV. It is the UK's . . . " X (formerly Twitter), September 23, 2022. https://x.com/superTV247 /status/1573317943680712704.

3 The Conversation U.S. (@ConversationUS). "'One inch from a poten- tial civil war'—near miss in Trump shooting is also a close call for American democracy." X (formerly Twitter), July 14, 2024. https://x .com/ConversationUS/status/1812494274266636734.

THE HERO'S FUNERAL

1   Doyle, John (@ComradeDoyIe). "You shoot into a crowd of Trump
      supporters, like in Butler, you hit hardworking men adored by their
      families. You shoot into a crowd of leftists, like in Kenosha . . . " X
      (formerly Twitter), July 14, 2024. https://x.com/ComradeDoyIe/status
      /1812528195863711979?t=qGWwfhdF5tDxfsp9JODRTw&s=03.

2   NEWSMAX (@NEWSMAX). "BREAKING: Kyle Rittenhouse has
      been acquitted of all charges after pleading self-defense in the deadly
      Kenosha, Wisconsin, shootings that became a flashpoint . . . " X (for-
      merly Twitter), November 19, 2021. https://x.com/NEWSMAX
      /status/1461761727104790531.

3   WTAE-TV Pittsburgh. "Corey Comperatore's Wife, Daughters Talk about
      Deadly Shooting." YouTube, August 16, 2024. https://www.youtube
      .com/watch?v=RMCM9cgnERk.

4   Vago, Steven, and Jorge Fitz-Gibbon. "Exclusive: Hero Firefighter
      Corey Comperatore's Widow Reveals His Final Words as He Shielded
      Family at Trump Rally." *New York Post*, July 15, 2024. https://nypost
      .com/2024/07/15/us-news/corey-comperatores-widow-reveals-his
      -final-words-before-he-was-killed-at-trump-rally/.

5   Callesto, Chuck (@ChuckCallesto). "JUST IN: Corey Comperatore's
      widow DEMANDS ANSWERS for the massive security failures
      in Butler that took her husbands life, retains attorney. "I know he
      would . . . " X (formerly Twitter), August 16, 2024. https://x.com
      /ChuckCallesto/status/1824533025696219473.

6   Wright, Michelle. "'He Definitely Was a Hero': Corey Comperatore's
      Wife and Daughters Talk about Deadly Shooting." WTAE, August 16,
      2024. https://www.wtae.com/article/corey-comperatore-family-butler
      -shooting/61891232.

7   "Donate to Support Allyson after Tragic Loss–Corey Comperatore,
      Organized by Jason Bubb." gofundme.com, July 14, 2024. https:
      //www.gofundme.com/f/support-allyson-after-tragic-loss.

8   Swift, Megan. "Corey Comperatore's Widow Takes Call from Trump;
      Report Says She Turned down Call from Biden." TribLIVE.com, July 16,
      2024. https://triblive.com/local/regional/corey-comperatores-widow
      -turned-down-biden-phone-call-report-says/.

9   Flores, Carlos Cristian, Marcie Cipriani, and Yazmin Rodriguez.
      "Viewing Held for Corey Comperatore, Firefighter Killed at Trump
      Rally." WTAE, July 18, 2024. https://www.wtae.com/article/corey
      -comperatore-flags-placed-visitation/61635109.

10   Ibid.

11   Ibid.

12   Ibid.

13   "Donate to Support for Butler Pa Victims - President Trump Authorized, Organized by Meredith Orourke." gofundme.com, July 13, 2024. https://www.gofundme.com/f/president-trump-seeks-support-for -butler-pa-victims?utm_source=twitter&utm_medium=social&utm _campaign=bcgfm_president-trump-seeks-support-for-butler-pa-victims.

14   Wright, Michelle. "'He Definitely Was a Hero': Corey Comperatore's Wife and Daughters Talk about Deadly Shooting." WTAE, August 17, 2024. https://www.wtae.com/article/corey-comperatore-family-butler -shooting/61891232.

15   GOP (@GOP). ""We're going back to Butler"-President Trump." X (formerly Twitter), August 12, 2024. https://x.com/GOP/status /1823173694799163753.

16   Wright, Michelle. "'He Definitely Was a Hero': Corey Comperatore's Wife and Daughters Talk about Deadly Shooting." WTAE, August 16, 2024. https://www.wtae.com/article/corey-comperatore-family-butler -shooting/61891232.

THE DIRECTOR

1   Bongino Report (@BonginoReport). "It is time right now for Kim Cheatle to get her head out of her ass and do the right thing. I could tell you stories for days about her putting politics ahead . . . " X (formerly Twitter), July 13, 2024. https://x.com/BonginoReport /status/1812296491974725835.

2   "Secret Service Director Cheatle Testifies on Capitol Hill." Rev, July 23, 2024. https://www.rev.com/blog/transcripts/secret-service-director-cheatle -testifies-on-capitol-hill.

3   Ibid.
4   Ibid.
5   Ibid.
6   Ibid.
7   Ibid.
8   Ibid.
9   Ibid.
10   Ibid.
11   Ibid.
12   Ibid.
13   Ibid.
14   Ibid.
15   wyntre (Wyntre999). "I am sadly, tragically confident, if we don't change the Secret Service directors and other managers there as well . . . " X (formerly Twitter), July 21, 2024, https://x.com/Wyntre999/status/1 815012717574426715?t=22PdV3fVmYxu7llEdOZw2Q&s=19.

16 Ibid.
17 The National Desk. "Takeaways from Heated Senate Hearing on Trump Rally Shooting." YouTube, July 30, 2024. https://www.youtube.com /watch?v=S899OXKrOtI.
18 Ibid.
19 Ibid.
20 Ibid.
21 Ibid.
22 Ibid.
23 McPherson, Lindsey. "Secret Service Opens Disciplinary Probe into Agents Responsible for Securing Trump's July 13 Rally." *Washington Times*, July 30, 2024. https://www.washingtontimes.com/news/2024 /jul/30/secret-service-opens-probe-into-agents-responsible/.
24 Ibid.

THE BIG COVER-UP

1 Hale, Erin. "Why Are Conservatives Claiming Google Is Covering up the Shooting of Trump?" Al Jazeera, July 30, 2024. https://www .aljazeera.com/news/2024/7/30/why-are-conservatives-claiming -google-is-covering-up-the-shooting-of-trump.
2 Full Send Podcast (@fullsendpodcast). "JD Vance on Google trying to hide the Trump Assassination attempt." X (formerly Twitter), August 2, 2024. https://x.com/fullsendpodcast/status/181937729326700155 6?s=46.
3 Becker, Kyle (@kylenabecker). "BREAKING. "Google, the largest Search Engine Operator in the world, has become a propaganda wing of the Left." @RogerMarshallMD is launching an investigation . . . " X (formerly Twitter), July 31, 2024. https://x.com/kylenabecker/status/1 818758037848371513?t=rLvB3d0ULHaf9IPAvGjOmA&s=19.
4 Miller, Tim (@Timodc). "JD Vance just said "They Even Tried To Kill Him" about Trump. This is a deeply irresponsible lie and if he had one iota of integrity left he would stop." X (formerly Twitter), August 3, 2024. https://x.com/Timodc/status/1819856970108584314?t=vU-Vytj4so8TxTbm6KLD7g&s=190.

THE SCENARIOS, REVISITED

1 Crabtree, Susan. "Secret Service Agents Placed on Leave after Trump Assassination Attempt | Realclearpolitics." *RealClear Politics*, August 22, 2024. https://www.realclearpolitics.com/articles/2024/08/22/secret_service _agents_placed_leave_after_trump_assassination_attempt__151502.html.
2 "JFK Assassination Records." National Archives. https://www.archives. gov/research/jfk/select-committee-report/part-1a.html.

THE SECOND ATTEMPT

1   Cunningham, Hayden. "Breaking Update: Trump Targeted by Man with Gun at West Palm Beach Golf Course: Officials." The Post Millennial, September 15, 2024. https://thepostmillennial.com/breaking-gunshots-fired-near-president-trump-outside-his-west-palm-beach-golf-club?utm_campaign=64466.

2   SAVE AZOV (@save_mrpl). "This video is a message to the world from the Mariupol defenders.They are grateful for our support and ask us to keep on fighting."Thank you to everyone who..." X (formerly Twitter), May 1, 2022. https://x.com/save_mrpl/status/1520721566077698049.

3   Shen, Michelle, Paul LeBlanc, Isabelle D'Antonio, Jack Forrest, and Maureen Chowdhury. "The Latest on the 2024 Presidential Race | CNN Politics." CNN, September 15, 2024. https://www.cnn.com/politics/live-news/trump-harris-election-09-15-24/index.html.

4   Ibid.

5   CNN. "Hear What Law Enforcement Sources Are Telling John Miller about Shots Fired in 'vicinity' of Trump | CNN Politics." CNN, September 15, 2024. https://www.cnn.com/2024/09/15/politics/video/trump-gunshots-vicinity-florida-digvid-nr.

6   MSNBC. "Full Press Conference on What FBI Calls Apparent Trump Assassination Attempt." MSNBC, September 15, 2024. https://www.msnbc.com/msnbc/watch/full-press-conference-on-what-fbi-calls-apparent-trump-assassination-attempt-219403333549.

7   MSNBC. "Florida Officials Identify Suspect in Trump Golf Course Shooting Incident." MSNBC, September 15, 2024. https://www.msnbc.com/msnbc/watch/florida-officials-identify-suspect-in-trump-golf-course-shooting-incident-219405381600.

8   GOP War Room. "Democratic Senator Kamala Harris Jokes About Killing President Donald Trump." YouTube, April 5, 2018. https://www.youtube.com/watch?v=_KlwYaipwl4.

9   Cohen, Shawn. "Exclusive: Son of Alleged Would-Be Assassin Says His Dad Hates Trump like 'all Reasonable People' but He's Never Owned a Gun and Wouldn't Do Anything Bats*** Crazy." Daily Mail Online, September 15, 2024. https://www.dailymail.co.uk/news/article-13853755/Son-alleged-assassin-says-dad-hates-Trump-like-reasonable-people-hes-never-owned-gun-wouldnt-bats-crazy.html?ns_mchannel=rss&ns_campaign=1490&ito=social-twitter_mailonline.

10 Ibid.

11 Colton, Emma, and Brooke Curto. "Who Is Ryan Wesley Routh: Alleged Gunman at Trump Golf Club." Fox News, September 15, 2024. https://www.foxnews.com/politics/who-ryan-wesley-routh-alleged-gunman-trump-golf-club.

12   Pollak, Joel B. "REPORT: Would-be Trump Assassin Had Biden-Harris Bumper Sticker." Breitbart, September 16, 2024. https://www.breitbart.com/politics/2024/09/16/report-would-be-trump-assassin-had-biden-harris-bumper-sticker/.

13   Winters, Natalie (@nataliegwinters). "EXC - FEC Records show suspected Trump sh**ter Ryan Routh made 19 political donations - all to Democrats. Recipients include Elizabeth Warren, Beto, Andrew Yang..." X (formerly Twitter), September 15, 2024. https://x.com/nataliegwinters/status/1835448595438502046.

14   Billboard Chris (@BillboardChris). "Here is a screen recording with all of attempted assassin @RyanRouth's posts, in case his account gets deleted." X (formerly Twitter), September 15, 2024. https://x.com/BillboardChris/status/1835452723929457000.

15   Ibid.

16   Birle, Jack. "What We Know About Ryan Wesley Routh, Suspect in Trump Assassination Attempt." *Washington Examiner*, September 16, 2024. https://www.washingtonexaminer.com/news/campaigns/presidential/3155145/what-we-know-ryan-wesley-routh-suspect-trump-assassination-attempt/.

17   Becker, Kyle (@kylenabecker). ""I have had partners meeting with [Ukraine's Ministry of Defense] every week and still have not been able to get them to agree to issue one single visa." Ryan..." X (formerly Twitter), September 15, 2024. https://x.com/kylenabecker/status/1835463504549327052.

18   Scheck, Justin, and Thomas Gibbons-neff. "Stolen Valor: The U.S. Volunteers in Ukraine Who Lie, Waste and Bicker." The New York Times, March 25, 2023. https://www.nytimes.com/2023/03/25/world/europe/volunteers-us-ukraine-lies.html.

19   TNI Team. "US Mercenary Plans to Recruit Pakistani-Based Afghan Refugees as Fighters for Ukraine." The New Indian, April 1, 2023. https://www.newindian.in/us-mercenary-plans-to-recruit-pakistani-based-afghan-refugees-as-fighters-for-ukraine/.

20   Ibid.

21   Routh, Ryan. Ukraine's Unwinnable War: The Fatal Flaw of Democracy, World Abandonment and the Global Citizen-Taiwan, Afghanistan, North Korea and the end of Humanity. Edited by Kathleen Shaffer. Amazon.Com. Accessed September 16, 2024. https://www.amazon.com/Ukraines-Unwinnable-War-Abandonment-Citizen-Taiwan-ebook/dp/B0BX4W9XKT/ref=cm_cr_arp_d_product_top?ie=UTF8.

22   Starbuck, Robby (@robbystarbuck). "Wow. Attempted Trump Assassin Ryan Routh wrote a book on the Ukraine war. In the book

he tells Iran to assassinate Trump while praising John Kerry for the Iran..." X (formerly Twitter), September 16, 2024. https://x.com /robbystarbuck/status/1835531912787439753/.

23 DeSantis, Ron (@GovRonDeSantis). "The State of Florida will be conducting its own investigation regarding the attempted assassination at Trump International Golf Club. The people deserve the..." X (formerly Twitter), September 15, 2024. https://x.com/GovRonDeSantis/status /1835476568212201744?t=H9f02Tjkow_kCxT91OSJ6Q&s=19.

APPENDIX II

1 Grassley Oversight Summary, "Grassley Oversight Unveils 'Most Detailed Picture Yet' of Trump Assassination Attempt," July 29, 2024, www.grassley.senate.gov/news/news-releases/grassley-oversight -unveils-most-detailed-picture-yet-of-trump-assassination-attempt.

APPENDIX III

1 Grassley Oversight Summary, "Grassley Oversight Unveils 'Most Detailed Picture Yet' of Trump Assassination Attempt," July 29, 2024, www.grassley.senate.gov/news/news-releases/grassley-oversight-unveils -most-detailed-picture-yet-of-trump-assassination-attempt.

ABOUT THE AUTHORS

Jack Posobiec is the *New York Times* and #1 *Publishers Weekly* bestselling coauthor of *Unhumans: The Secret History of Communist Revolutions (and How to Crush Them)*. He is senior editor at Human Events and host of *Human Events Daily*, which has more than 250 million downloads. He is also a veteran US Navy intelligence officer with deployments to Guantanamo Bay and East Asia. Posobiec's final deployment was as intelligence director for Navy Expeditionary Forces Command Pacific—Task Force 75. Posobiec has authored three other books: *Citizens for Trump*, *4D Warfare*, and *The Antifa*. In 2019, Posobiec was awarded a Lincoln Fellowship by the Claremont Institute. A Temple University–Philadelphia, graduate, Posobiec lived in China before settling in Washington, DC, with his wife and two sons.

Joshua Lisec writes books of consequence. He is the *New York Times* and #1 *Publishers Weekly* bestselling coauthor of *Unhumans*. He is also a *New York Times* and *Wall Street Journal* bestselling ghostwriter, with more than ninety books ghostwritten that have been translated into more than one dozen languages. Lisec is best known for his literary collaborations with controversial public figures, capturing their authentic voice and conveying the whole story. Lisec is also the author of the bestselling irreverent guide to entrepreneurship *So Good They Call You a Fake* and creator of *The Best Way to Say It*®writing programs. Joshua has been featured in *Publishers Weekly*, *Newsweek*, *Forbes*, BBC, TEDx, Sky News, and TMZ, among others. Joshua lives with his wife and children near Dayton, Ohio.